MOONLESS
NIGHT

MOONLESS NIGHT

THE WORLD WAR TWO ESCAPE EPIC

B.A. JAMES

PEN & SWORD MILITARY CLASSICS

*'And fear not them which kill the body,
and are not able to kill the soul.'*

St. Matthew, Ch 10, v, 28

First published in Great Britain in 1983 by
William Kimber & Co Limited

Reprinted in 2001, 2002 and 2004 by Leo Cooper

Published in this format in 2006 by
Pen & Sword Military Classics
An imprint of
Pen & Sword Books Ltd
47 Church Street
Barnsley
South Yorkshire
S70 2AS

Printed and bound in England
By CPI UK

Pen & Sword Books Ltd incorporates the Imprints of Pen & Sword Aviation,
Pen & Sword Maritime, Pen & Sword Military, Wharncliffe Local history,
Pen & Sword Select, Pen & Sword Military Classics and Leo Cooper.

For a complete list of Pen & Sword titles please contact
PEN & SWORD BOOKS LIMITED
47 Church Street, Barnsley, South Yorkshire, S70 2AS, England
E-mail: enquiries@pen-and-sword.co.uk
Website: www.pen-and-sword.co.uk

FOR MADGE AND PATRICK

Contents

List of Maps

Preface

I am very glad to have the opportunity of writing the Preface to this new edition of my book published by Leo Cooper/Pen and Sword Books eighteen years after the first edition.

This is the story of a pre-war RAF pilot caught up in the maelstrom of World War II, shot down while flying on a bombing mission from an airfield in East Anglia and trapped behind the barbed wire of German Prisoner of War Camps, as the duel between escapers and Gestapo intensified, culminating in 'The Great Escape' before being flung finally into the holocaust of the Concentration Camps.

It is my story, but I have written too of a number of courageous people I came to know, prisoners of war and others from every walk of life and many nationalities, including German, who opposed the Nazi tyranny. Inevitably, and regrettably, I have not been able to include the names of many others who played a prominent part. I have written of these events as I saw them. To many they may seem long ago and part of history, as indeed they were in 1983 when the first edition was published, and this begs the question, 'Why so long to write it down?'. I can only reply that I wished to forget and for many years did not talk about my long incarceration even to my wife. However, such an experience is forever etched on one's memory. Finally I was compelled to write my story and, for me, the perspective of the years has helped to give it greater clarity and meaning.

Obsessive memories of the horrors of the Nazi Concentration Camps should be avoided, but they should not be forgotten; they were a manifestation of an evil regime such as could arise in any country given the right 'political mix'. We have recent examples world-wide. The safeguarding of freedom must be paramount. For this reason I have given talks to schools on my experiences. On two occasions recently my wife and I have been invited to Berlin by the Oundle History Department to show the history tour group around Sachsenhausen which is now a Memorial site.

I should particularly like to thank Air Commodore Alaistair

Panton CB, OBE, DFC, the late Captain Peter Fanshawe CBE, DSC, RN and the late Lieutenant-Colonel Jack Churchill DSO, MC, for checking facts in my manuscript and making valuable suggestions. I am also indebted to Captain Hugo Bracken CBE, RN, the late Wing Commander K.H.P. Murphy MBE, Wing Commander Bill Stapleton CBE, the late Wally Floody MBE, the late Vic Gammon, Michael Roth and Pat Greenhouse for helping me to make the record as accurate as possible, to the late Paul Brickhill for use of information from his book *The Great Escape*, to Jamie Fitzgerald of Toronto for help and encouragement, and to Colonel Arthur A. Durrand PhD, U.S. Army, Wing Commander Norman Canton MBE, DFC and the late J.A.G. Deans MBE, Mrs June Bowerman, Mark Shore, John Holland, Peter Hurcomb and Earl Moorhouse for contributing material.

I also had great assistance from the Imperial War Museum, the Public Record Office, Air Historical Branch MOD and the Wiener Library who made available material which enabled me to furnish historical background and to corroborate my memoirs of the time.

B.A. James
Ludlow
Shropshire

Prologue

Like moths which in the night
Flutter towards a light,
Drawn to their fiery doom, flying and dying,
So to their death still throng,
Blind, dazzled, borne along
Ceaselessly, all those multitudes, wild flying.

Bhagavad-Gita, Arjuna in Book the Eleventh

The parachute opened with a crack pulling me out of my terminal velocity dive with a jerk which seemed to tear me apart and then I was floating gently two miles up in the night sky over Holland. The stricken Wellington, of which I had lately been the second pilot, had been turned into a flaming hell by the pounding flak shells and was streaking away to the east trailing fire and smoke; held by the dazzling white searchlight beams, the bomber was still on course for a target it would never reach. Seconds later there was a flash as the bombs exploded, and the Wimpy plunged like a fiery comet to the dark earth below.

The swift passage from pandemonium to the utter stillness of the parachute descent left me momentarily floating in space and time, a disembodied spirit wafting gently in the black void above the eerie beauty of the sombre landscape with rivers etched out in silver ribbons by the light of the full moon.

The violent swaying of the parachute shrouds reminded me that I was floating in a physical medium beneath a large silk canopy, and descending steadily towards enemy-occupied territory which I should reach in less than ten minutes. I must try to pinpoint my position. I decided that the two rivers shining in the moonlight must be the Waal and the Maas which both flow into the North Sea south of Dordrecht. Knowing that we had just crossed the coast, I reckoned that I must be about twenty-five miles south of Rotterdam and possibly the same distance from the sea.

It was about eleven o'clock on the night of 5th June 1940, and the last light of sunset was fading in the westering sky. I resolved to walk in that direction, acquire a boat of some sort on the coast, and row or sail back to the Kentish coast.

The ground was now getting close. It is impossible to judge distances accurately at night and it was my first parachute jump; suddenly it seemed to come up and hit me and I found myself in a heap in the middle of a muddy field.

I had tried to go as limp as possible in the last moments of my descent, but nevertheless, sprained an ankle on landing. I picked myself up carefully and tried to accustom my eyes to the gloom of my surroundings. Then, to my horror, I perceived some black shapes looming out of the darkness. A German Army patrol coming to round me up? I hastily buried my parachute in the mud, and was preparing to run in the opposite direction, when there was a 'Moo-oo' followed by several more bovine noises of the same variety. Obviously the local cows didn't like their night's rest being disturbed by this strange apparition just dropped from the skies.

Reassured by these familiar farm noises, I relaxed, found a gate onto a road, and started to limp along it in a westerly direction.

CHAPTER ONE

Through the Looking Glass

'Twas brillig and the slithy toves
Did gyre and gimble in the wabe,
All mimsy were the borogoves
And the mome raths outgrabe.

Alice through the Looking Glass, Lewis Carroll

Bomber Command aircrew had the advantage of operating from a home base with a comfortable Mess and family or friends awaiting their return, but this was outweighed by the disadvantage of a very swift transition in the event of being shot down and landing in enemy territory.

At that time there was very little training given in evasion and escape, it was too early for the establishment of resistance movements and escape lines in recently occupied countries, populations were demoralised, and the evader was on his own in a shadowy and unreal world with every man's hand against him.

I walked westward along the road during the whole of that night, jumping into the ditch at the side of the road whenever a vehicle passed. Once I heard far above me the unmistakable note of a Wellington's Pegasus engines and then the whistle of bombs; again I dived into the ditch. The bombs exploded about 200 yards to the right, quite close to some flak batteries which must have been hit as their firing was much diminished after that. I later met the pilot of that aircraft in a prisoner of war camp; he was Flying Officer James Smalley from my squadron.

I suppose I must have covered about fifteen miles by daylight. I had intended to lie up during the day and go on the following night, but the flat Dutch countryside, intersected by dykes and waterways, seemed to offer no shelter whatsoever. I pushed on, determined to get to the sea as soon as possible; food would be a problem, I had one chocolate bar with me, the other had fallen out of my Sidcot pocket when I was baling out of the aeroplane.

Around 5 a.m. I came to a wide canal with a fast flowing tidal current; it lay right across my path, but I found a rowing boat moored nearby to the bank, and used this to ferry myself across to the other side. A little further on was a village which I tried to skirt

round, but I found this impossible because it was hemmed around
with dykes. As it was still very early, I decided to go through the
village. After a few minutes a man on a bicycle came up behind me;
he slowed down when he was level with me, and said something to
me in Dutch. I wanted to avoid all contact with the population, so
trotted out the only German words I then knew, '*Ja, ja,*' and
adopting an arrogant attitude, marched on, hoping he might mistake
me for a German airman out for an early morning walk, as I was still
wearing my Sidcot flying suit and flying boots over my uniform.

However, he stopped and, staring fixedly at me, said, '*Englisch*'.

I nodded. He looked as though he might be able to help me. He
pointed to his carrier; I sat down on it, and he conveyed me through
the village to a farmhouse at the other end of it. Showing me into a
hay loft, he indicated by signs that he would be back. I lay down in
the hay and the farmer came back shortly with some bread and
cheese and a map of the area. In Dutch, German and a few words of
English he made me understand that I was to rest there and go on the
following night, a plan that greatly appealed to me. He then pointed
to my face and gave me a mirror. I looked into it and saw an
enormous black eye and a lacerated nose with most of the skin off it.
The slipstream must have blown me pretty hard against the side of
the hatch when I baled out of the Wellington. I had not felt anything
at the time and reflected that sudden death must be painless.

Shocked and worn out by the events of the night, and bedded well
down and hidden in a soft bed of hay, I was drifting off into a deep
sleep when I was awakened by someone shaking me. The farmer was
there again with another man.

'*Bruder, Bruder,*' he was saying.

It appeared that the brother owned the farm, and he was drawing
his hand across his throat in a gesture indicating that he did not
much like the idea of harbouring a British airman.

They took me into the living room, where the rest of the family was
gathered, and gave me breakfast while a good deal of 'palaver' went
on. I was considering taking my leave of them, but they kept
repeating '*Bürgermeister*' to me – perhaps he could help me; anyway,
the hour was now well advanced, my ankle was painful, and I could
see German soldiers walking about outside. I felt trapped – perhaps I
had been in too much of a hurry, but told myself I would escape
from a prisoner of war camp later when I was ready, vastly
underestimating the feasibility of this. Then two Dutch policemen,
whom they must have telephoned, arrived, searched me for

weapons, and took me off in a car to the nearest small town.

In the town hall I stood on one side of the room with the policemen while the Burgomaster stood opposite in the centre of a line of local officials. We all drank coffee out of small, dainty cups, but there was hardly a common word of any language between us. It was like a dialogue of the deaf. They made polite noises and deprecatory signs, and it was quite evident that this meeting was intended as an official apology for their inability to help me.

By now my presence in the area was far too well-known for any help to be forthcoming from the locals; a large crowd was watching outside the town hall as the police escorted me back to the car. They then drove me off to the German Kommandantur in Rotterdam.

The Dutch developed one of the bravest resistance movements in Europe later in the war, but I had not been fortunate enough to contact any part of an embryo resistance movement at that time, although if the man on the bicycle had had his way, it might have been different.

'Ah, you too,' said a smart German Luftwaffe officer who met us at the entrance to the Kommandantur. 'Three other members of your crew have also been caught. For you the war is over.'

I was told to sit down in a large general office which seemed to be in use by German Army staff officers, including a very tough and forbidding-looking General who was sitting at a desk writing. A Colonel started to bellow at me,

'So, where are the others of your *Besatzung?*'

'I am told the other three have been caught,' I replied.

'*Du lügst*,[1]' he screamed, 'You lie, you know well there are two more.'

The General's leathery face was set and hard. Without looking up from his papers, he said curtly, '*Genug, Oberst.*'

The Colonel lapsed into silence reluctantly. The General was evidently afraid that he was anticipating my official interrogation which was to follow in another building.

My interrogation was conducted by a Colonel sitting at the head of a large table, around which were seated about six officers, a civilian interpreter and myself.

The Colonel began by barking out the usual questions asking for name, number and rank. Then followed questions based on a technical brief.

---

1   The Gestapo and usually the police used the familiar form of address to prisoners.

'What were you flying?' No reply.

'What height did you fly?'

'I really forget. I'm not much good at judging heights at night.'

'Do not play the fool – you're a pilot and you can read an altimeter.'

'I was only the second pilot, and I was looking out of the window at your flak which was bursting rather close to us.'

'What is your squadron? How many in your crew?

'What is the ceiling of a Wellington?'

So the questions went on. I maintained a uniform silence.

They began to get angry and all started shouting questions at me at once.

'My name is James, my rank is pilot officer, and my number is 42232,' I repeated during a lull. 'This is all the information I am authorised to give you.'

There was more hubbub, then the interpreter, who was undoubtedly Gestapo, seemed to take over.

'Leutnant James,' he said, 'we think there were six in your crew. We have caught four of you, and we have a report of two men crying in a schwamp near where your aeroplane was shot down. Now if you confirm to us the correct number of six, we can send our soldiers to help these men.'

'If these men are in danger in the swamp, why don't your soldiers go to their help, anyway?' I countered.

'Do not make a joke of this,' hissed the interpreter, 'You were flying a Wellington, your captain was Squadron Leader Peacock and you were in 9 Squadron based at Honington in Suffolk. You see we know a lot about you. It will be better for you, I warn you, if you give us correct information.'

This was a good example of the effectiveness of German 'Fifth Column' Intelligence at the beginning of the war.

After these brow-beating tactics had continued for some time, and I had repeated my name, number and rank a few more times, the interrogation ended.

Immediately afterwards, I was driven by car to Amsterdam where I was taken to the Carlton Hotel which was being used as the headquarters of the Luftwaffe. Up on the sixth floor I was put in a room with an armed guard. In one corner was a table on which stood a silver urn filled with ice and bottles of beer, glasses and a box of cheroots.

A suave Luftwaffe Major, immaculately turned out in white

summer uniform, came into the room with affable and friendly mien.

'How do you do, Mr James. What a pity to find you in this situation,' he said in perfect English. 'Shall we have a noggin, and what about a cheroot?'

He poured me a glass of beer and handed it to me.

'I know England well,' he continued, 'I was at Oxford, actually. Lovely country around there – do you know it? There are quite a number of your training airfields in that area, I believe.'

'The country is beautiful around there,' I replied.

'It is a great pity that our two countries should be fighting each other,' said the Major. 'We had no wish to start the war, and there was no need for England to come in against us.'

'Your Leader did not give the Poles much opportunity to reply to his 16 point ultimatum,' I said. 'And we were bound by agreement to help Poland.'

'The Führer had very good reasons for attacking the Poles when he did; he had already been provoked beyond measure by their unreasonable attitude towards Danzig and the Corridor. However,' he went on in lighter tone, 'let's not talk politics, I am sure you did not discuss politics in your Mess – Where was that? At what speed did you say you were flying?'

This 'sweet treatment' interrogation continued for a little while longer; after I'd refused a second beer, the Major took his leave, and the beer and cheroots were hastily removed. I was taken away to a local Army orderly room where I spent the night on a camp bed under armed guard.

The next day I was taken by car into Germany. An officer sat in front beside the driver, and a soldier with a Tommy Gun was beside me in the rear seat. They were all jubilant at the success of the German Blitzkrieg and, not infrequently, kept repeating, all or separately, and in various combinations, the three phrases heard by all prisoners in the early summer of 1940:

'For you the war is over.'

'England in sechs Wochen.'[1]

'England kaputt.'

I asked to stop in a wooded area of the Rhine Valley, planning to make a dash into the forest, but the guard with the Tommy Gun stood close by as I answered the call of nature, and I calculated my chances of survival as nil before getting even half-way to the trees.

---

[1]   England in six weeks.

Our destination was Oberursel near Frankfurt-am-Main where there was a reception camp for RAF prisoners of war called Dulag Luft (Durchgangslager or Transit Camp Air). That evening on my way to the cell I was to occupy for the night, I met Hugh Falkus,[1] also recently shot down, in a Spitfire. He looked as bewildered as I felt. Massive adjustment to this strange new 'Looking Glass' World was necessary in our situation.

After the door had been closed and locked, the reality of my position began to come home to me. Less than 48 hours before I had been a free man on a RAF station set in the English countryside, fighting the war to stop Hitler. Now I was a useless captive sitting in a bare wooden cell in the middle of enemy territory. The standard Red Cross Form was brought in for me to complete; it requested details of service and family background 'so that your next-of-kin can be informed that you are a prisoner of war'. I gave my name, number and rank and handed it back.

The next morning I was taken over to the prisoners' compound and had my first sight of the barbed wire which was to encircle me in various camps for many moons. Here it enclosed three single-storey wooden barrack huts. Walking around were a number of aircrew of all ranks dressed in various combinations of uniform and flying attire, mostly casualties of the German Blitz through the Low Countries and France. They had been thrown into battle against desperate odds in their Blenheims, Fairey Battles (known as flying coffins), Hurricanes and Lysanders; shot out of the sky only a few days before, some not long out of school, their faces wore an expression of disbelief, although they still maintained their youthful exuberance.

The Senior British Officer was Wing Commander H.M.A. Day ('Wings'). I met him standing outside his hut holding his cat which he called 'Ersatz'[2]. Wings had been shot down over Germany in October 1939 while on a reconnaissance flight in a Blenheim. It was his squadron's first operation and, as the squadron commander, he insisted on leading it as his predecessor in the First World War, Major Patterson, had done after he had formed No 57 Squadron, but a cloudless sky and three Messerschmitts had given Wings no chance of returning to base. A former Royal Marines Officer with the erect

---

[1] Now a well known authority on nature study, living in Cumbria.
[2] 'Substitute'. Wings had asked for a kitten, but the Commandant had brought him a cat; he had, therefore, called it Ersatz or substitute kitten.

bearing of that Service, he had been awarded the Albert Medal[1] in 1918 for saving the lives of two men in the torpedoed battleship *Britannia*. He had transferred to the Royal Air Force after the war and had become an ace fighter pilot, leading the aerobatic flight at the Hendon Air Display of 1932. I was to see a good deal of Wings before the end of the war, but I could not foresee that we would be together in the death cells of a concentration camp.

Wings and about fifteen other early prisoners were permanent inmates of Dulag Luft. They had been kept back by the Commandant as being in the older and more responsible age group, and included two Fleet Air Arm Lieutenant-Commanders, Jimmy Buckley and John Casson (son of Sybil Thorndike) and Squadron Leader Roger Bushell who will loom large in the story later.

The Commandant was Major Theo Rumpel who had flown in Göring's squadron in the First World War. He was, nevertheless, not a Nazi Party member and did not sympathise with it, but he was the best Intelligence Officer in the Luftwaffe, and, because of this, he had been persuaded, against his will, to take on his present appointment. He spoke excellent English and was pleasant and courteous.

I was delighted to meet Pilot Officer Bill Webster, our American-born rear gunner, and he gave me news of the rest of the crew. The Germans had told him that Squadron Leader George Peacock,[2] the pilot had gone down with the aircraft. Sergeant Hargreaves, the navigator, had also been killed; his parachute had caught fire on opening too soon. Sergeant Griffiths, the wireless operator/front gunner, and Sergeant Murton, the centre gunner, were both safe, and I was to meet them later.

After three days, Bill Webster and I with thirteen other RAF officers two Fleet Air Arm lieutenants, Wood and Robin Gray, and three French Air Force officers were moved out.

'I wonder what cesspit they're taking us to now?' remarked the bearded Wood, as we rattled off in the bus. His observation was prophetic. At Limburg, about thirty miles to the north, we arrived at a large dreary camp, run by the Wehrmacht, in which most of the prisoners seemed to be French Colonial Troops. We were housed in a dark, dirty, barrack block containing three-tier bunks on which we slept on filthy straw. There was only one tattered book in English

---

[1]   Since upgraded to George Cross.

[2]   A former Cranwell cadet, an experienced pilot; pre-war attached to the Fleet Air Arm, he had recently been awarded the DFC.

called *Cold Comfort Farm* which Paul Royle, a Whitley pilot shot down on his first operation, was gloomily reading. Fed on a diet of Sauerkraut soup and black bread we were glad that this proved to be only a short stay.

We moved on by train to Berlin. We were marched through the streets of the German capital to the Stettiner Bahnhof and were followed, it seemed, by half the population of the city whose first view this must have been of captured enemy airmen. At the station we were herded into a corner to wait for the train, while the people crowded around to gape at us; there was no hostility, merely curiosity. Two young fighter pilots, Pat Greenhous and Nat Fowler both natural comics, put on a miming act, chattering, guffawing and pretending to be mad. The audience looked startled and began to drift away, no doubt confirmed in their opinion that the English were mad after all.

Fifty miles north of Berlin we stopped at Prenzlau where we were taken to a former German Army barracks. As we entered the gate in the barbed wire fencing which surrounded the high brick barrack blocks, we received a tremendous welcome from the inmates. They were Polish officers and we were the first Allied prisoners they had seen for about ten months. There were 3,000 of them, all captured in the autumn of 1939, after the fall of Poland.

The Senior Polish Officer, a Colonel, and some of his officers gave a formal dinner in our honour. There was candlelight, more food and drink on one table than we were to see for a long time, and speeches – a welcoming speech from the Colonel in which he said he knew the war would be won but we must have patience, and a reply from Flying Officer Norman Forbes, the Senior RAF Officer, a tall, enthusiastic Auxiliary Air Force pilot, thanking the Colonel for their splendid hospitality and hoping Poland would soon be free again.

We spent a good deal of time greeting callers in our garage, the only accommodation available; they used to stand politely at the entrance until they had attracted our attention, when they would click their heels and bow in the formal manner of the pre-war Polish Army.

One afternoon the Poles trundled into the garage about eight hand carts piled high with food, clothing and other useful items, all collected from their own meagre stocks – a very generous gesture.

Not long before we arrived one of the Polish prisoners had been literally thrown out of the camp, in one of the most amusing escapes of the war. Wearing a civilian suit converted from a naval uniform, and carrying a small suitcase, he had somehow managed to infiltrate himself into the guard-room, situated within the camp bounds, during a guard change. When the Feldwebel (warrant officer) in charge of the guard returned, he asked what the man wanted.

'I wish to see my brother,' said the Pole.

'No visits allowed,' barked the Feldwebel.

'But he is my brother; surely you will allow me to see him?'

'I repeat, visits are strictly forbidden.'

'But I have travelled 300 hundred miles,' insisted the Pole, 'and I must see my brother.'

'*Du, Schweinhund,*' shouted the Feldwebel. "*Raus*' (Get out).

He grabbed hold of the Polish prisoner and propelled him out onto the street right beside a tram stop. The Pole boarded a tram for the station, caught a train to Stettin, then a ship to Sweden and freedom.

We had heard that a new Luftwaffe Camp was being prepared for us on the Baltic. On 5th July we were taken by train to Barth, Vogelsang and Stalag Luft I which was to be our home for the next twenty-one months.

CHAPTER TWO

Stalag Luft I

Day after day a weary waste of hours.

'Alastor', Shelley

War has been defined as 'long periods of boredom interspersed with short periods of tension and terror.' Prisoner of war life was a minor extension of war. There seemed no end to the boredom which stretched out endlessly into the grey future. We were all young men cut off in our prime from normal life, and forced to live a spartan, closely knit, communal existence, hemmed in by barbed wire, guard boxes, machine-guns, patrolling sentries and dogs. In the early days most of us were regular officers and flying had been the reason for our existence. To be forcibly grounded in such circumstances, with all prospects of promotion and career shattered, worst of all being no further use to the war effort, was a heavy burden to bear.

The war was to be continued in the enemy camp and we were to create our own periods of tension, and often terror, by the establishment of escape organisations, leading to an increasing number of escapes as the war went on, and this caused the Germans to divert ever larger resources towards security measures.

At Stalag Luft I in the high summer of 1940 all this was in the future, and there seemed only a remote possibility of escape from the cramped and dusty little compound in which our small party of twenty were the first to arrive. The two wooden barrack blocks were surrounded by a double row of eight foot barbed wire fencing, six feet apart with dannert wire packed into the space between. A low warning fence about six feet in from the main wire further restricted our freedom of movement. This dreary rectangular area, about 100 yards by 70 yards, was covered at all times by guards with machine guns and searchlights mounted in the watch towers at opposite corners, with perimeter lighting at regular intervals.

There was one gate, on which a sentry was posted, leading into the wire-enclosed Vorlager containing the cell block and a few other buildings, and beyond this was the administrative area. The NCOs' compound with six wooden barrack huts was adjoining. The camp

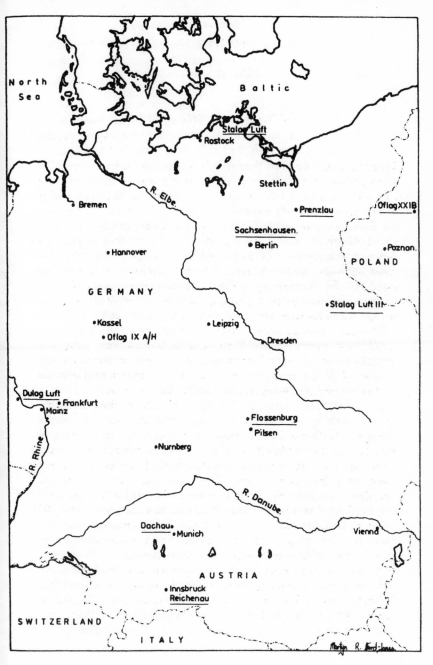

The author's POW and concentration camp itinerary.
(Camps in which author was held underlined thus Prenzlau.)

was situated in Pomerania, near the small town of Barth visible to the south. A dark pine wood restricted our vision on the north side, and beyond this was the Baltic Sea.

As we surveyed this bleak, grey, prison it seemed that we had reached the nadir of misfortune. This could be our home for the duration which, at that time, could have been for a very long time with an uncertain end. In the space of the preceding few weeks the British army had been thrown off the Continent, Paris had fallen, France had capitulated and the German armies were poised, ready to spring onto English soil. Winston Churchill had promised us, 'Blood, toil, tears and sweat.'

I shared a room with Bill Webster and a naval pilot. It was small and bare; it contained two double-tier bunks with straw palliasses resting on wooden bed boards, and there was just room for a small table and three stools. Opposite were the ever cheerful Pat Greenhous and Nat Fowler who, with Peter Cazanove, a suave Old Etonian fighter pilot, hid any feelings of gloom they may have had.

Peter had reason for some bitterness; shot down in France he had managed to reach Calais:

'I tried to get aboard the last ship, a destroyer, leaving for England, but a senior officer stood at the top of the gangway and told me I had to stay and defend Calais. I told him I was a pilot and would be far more use in England: "You will stay and defend Calais," repeated the officer. I tried to impress on him how much it cost to train pilots and that we were short of them, but the old fool wouldn't budge, and having fired a final broadside about the defence of Calais being of the first importance, the gang-plank was hauled up and the destroyer sailed away leaving a perfectly good pilot to be sent straight off to a 'kriegie' camp.'

A field of corn, high and ripe, grew up to the wire outside our window. It would have been an ideal place to break a tunnel, and only a short distance to dig. I had read *The Tunnellers of Holzminden* from the First World War, and I felt that this was an opportunity not to be missed if we wanted to corner the market in tunnels before the next batch of prisoners arrived. The idea was discussed and several of us wanted to push ahead with a tunnel, but as we were a minority and of junior rank we were outvoted. With more resolution, perhaps, we might have carried the day. At any rate the atmosphere of greyness and finality seemed to induce a sense of apathy which deadened the will to action.

The wind of change came very soon in mid-July with the arrival of a further sixty or so RAF prisoners from Spangenberg[1], together with a number of French Air Force officers who occupied the other block. The NCOs' compound was also beginning to fill up.

Squadron Leader Brian Paddon became the Senior British Officer. He had been leading a squadron of Blenheims in France, and most of his squadron had been shot up or shot down.

'I then had the undivided attention of six Messerschmitts,' he concluded. 'And here I am.'

He was somewhat fussy in his manner, and was nicknamed 'Auntie' but he was a volatile and energetic man of thirty-one who lost no time turning his attention to escaping matters. He started to discuss plans with a few senior people, the nucleus of an escape committee which was formed later. Prominent among these was Lieutenant Peter Fanshawe, RN; as navigator of a Skua operating from the old *Ark Royal* he had been shot down, with his pilot John Casson, over Trondheim Fjord in Norway. A regular naval officer, he might have just stepped off the quarter-deck, and he was nicknamed 'Hornblower'. Flight Lieutenant Anthony Ffrench-Mullen was also a member of the 'inner circle'; his Whitley bomber had been hit by flak and he had had to ditch it in the sea. A former Cranwell cadet, his dignified intellectual air disguised a penetrating wit; he became a monk after the war.

'Well, gentlemen,' said Paddon, his rather wild blue eyes sweeping round the meeting, 'We've got to get out of here – a tunnel seems the best plan. Any ideas?'

Ffrench-Mullen was the first to speak, 'We've already made a trap in the floorboards of my room, and I've done a recce underneath. There's bags of room for dispersal of earth from the tunnel and, furthermore, the sides of the hut are boarded up, so the Germans won't be able to see what's going on below.'

After some discussion, it was decided to sink the tunnel shaft at the north end of the hut; it would be about six feet in depth and the tunnel would be pushed out towards the wood with about 150 feet to dig.

The first tunnel at Barth was underway, indeed it was the first RAF tunnel of the war. Security was easy. A watcher posted at the hut entrance had a clear view to the gate and beyond, and could see

[1] Oflag (*Offizierslager* – Officers' Camp) IX A/H Spangenberg Castle near Kassel, used to hold prisoners of war since 1870.

any Germans approaching in plenty of time to give the alarm. Only Fowler, Greenhous and Bill Stapleton of the first arrivals were included. I decided to watch and wait; it would be a long war. There seemed no other way out. An assault on the wire would have been suicide and, indeed, was never tried under normal conditions during my twenty-one months at Barth, although three daring schemes succeeded in exceptional circumstances and these receive honourable mention later in the story. There was another secret tunnel with only six workers. No doubt Michael Roth the magician with his knowledge of magic, illusions and secret compartments helped to conceal its whereabouts. Among the others were Wright, a South African, who designed the first air pump from German jam tins, and Peach who had travelled from Hong Kong on the trans Siberian Railway to join the RAF.

Appelle, or roll calls, were held morning and evening by Leutnant Hans Pieber, accompanied by the watchful Feldwebel Glemnitz and a small squad of armed guards, when we were lined up in two ranks to be counted. Pieber had been an engineer in civilian life and had spent some time in South America. He used to boast that he held Nazi Party card No 49, although his early allegiance to Hitler was belied by his demeanour. He was a mild-mannered little man, studiously polite, and spoke good English which, with Teutonic thoroughness, he was always trying to improve. He was often the butt of our discontent and suffered much abuse at our hands over the years.

The guards were conscripts from all walks of life and they seemed ill at ease in their helmets and new military uniforms. They were an obvious target for our youthful exuberance. We called them 'goons' and often whistled a popular ditty like the 'Wizard of Oz' in time to their marching when they went off after *Appell*. This caused so much irritation that the SBO soon put a stop to it. But the popular sport of 'goon baiting' was often irresistible to the younger prisoners and continued in one form or another for most of the war.

The first year at Barth seemed to us the longest of the war. Not many new prisoners arrived, and the old 'line shoots' about the last air battles we had fought began to grow cobwebs. The supply of Red Cross parcels to Germany had been disrupted by the Nazi Blitzkrieg across the Low Countries and France. We subsisted on the German ration for a non-working civilian: a cup of Ersatz coffee, made from acorns, in the morning, a bowl of soup, usually Sauerkraut, with a

few potatoes at mid-day, and one fifth of a loaf of black bread[1] with a
pat of margarine and a small piece of sausage or cheese in the
evening, supplied on a room basis and divided up by the room
'stooge' for the day – very accurately as he always had to wait until
the others had chosen their portions! These rations amounted to
barely 800 calories per day, less than half the optimum required for
an adult human being. The pangs of hunger were ever present.

The Germans supplied, for two or three months, a few rather
nondescript items purchasable with *Lagergeld* or camp money for
which one third of our pay was deducted monthly at source. Among
these were some cigarettes and 'Red Biddy' wine. Some nicotine
addicts elected to swap their mid-day bowl of soup for cigarettes, in
some cases for cigarette butts which were shaken out and the
contents rolled up into nasty-looking and worse-smelling 'weeds'.
Cigarette rollings and 'Red Biddy' on an empty stomach did not mix
well, and, in the case of one officer, led to his death from throat
cancer about a year later in another camp.

One evening, after the wooden shutters outside had been closed
over the windows by the guards, the normal routine of reading,
talking, card playing or just 'bunk bashing' was interrupted by the
noise of heavy objects rolling down the corridor. The cause of the
disturbance was a previously sober, solemn and bearded former
Imperial Airways pilot whooping it up after a surfeit of 'Red Biddy'.
He was dancing about completely naked, singing, shouting and
throwing objects down the corridor. Soon the whole block joined in
the action, the concentric rings were removed from the stoves in the
kitchen and joined the hardware which was flying to and fro at
alarming speed. Pandemonium reigned. Then there was a cry of
'Goon in the Block'. A squad of guards had burst in. They arrested
the dancing dervish and hauled him off to the 'cooler'[2] for the night.
We were all very young and it was such noisy and inconsequential
incidents that sometimes relieved the boredom.

The camp staff were all members of the Luftwaffe who behaved,
for the most part, in a civilized manner towards the prisoners. In
these early days, particularly, our relations with the Germans were
good, provided that Higher Authority and the Nazi Party were kept
at a distance.

[1] It was a heavy, soggy mixture of rather questionable ingredients. The sour
taste at first offended the palate, but there was little else to eat, and it could be
improved by toasting when there was fuel.
[2] Prisoner of war slang for solitary confinement in cells.

Major von Stacheleski, the second Commandant at Barth, was a humane and thoughtful man. He was imbibing one evening in the Mess bar, as was his custom, when he fell to thinking about the poor British locked up in their compound with nothing to drink but tap water and Ersatz coffee, and the more he drank the more he dwelt on their sad state. Then he could stand it no longer. He gave orders that some boxes were to be filled with a good quantity of bottled beer, and he went with them himself when they were delivered to the compound where they were received with due gratitude and joy by the inmates.

Unfortunately this incident[1] was reported to Higher Authority and the Commandant was relieved of his post immediately.

For the first few weeks there were no books. Among the first books to come into the compound were some German grammars of the Method Gaspey Otto Sauer and I started to learn German with a view to using the language outside the wire when opportunity arose. Some German lessons were given by Hauptmann Buchvig, the smooth Austrian Security Officer, probably to find out who the German speakers were. I also found a Russian grammar of the same Method and became interested in the Cyrillic Alphabet; here was a challenge and a means of passing the time. With the help of Flight Lieutenant Wally Valenta, who had been the navigator of a Czech Wellington crew, I found the alphabet to be the least of my difficulties; mastery of the complicated grammar was the main task. This was the beginning of a lasting interest in languages.

Parole as a word of honour in the military sense is normally inflexible. Yet even the strictest rules can be bent and still remain within the law, where the ethical implications become blurred. In the hot months of that summer the Germans used to take us down to the creek for a swim and once a week for a walk. On these occasions a parole book had to be signed on the way out, usually under the observant eyes of Glemnitz. Flight Lieutenant Charlie Crewes and Flying Officer Tony Hudson managed to slip out one day without signing the book, with the aid of a little diversion from fellow prisoners. With only two guards escorting us, it was easy for them to get away as we straggled through the woods during the walk. Their

---

[1] Captain Simoleit, Head of the *Lagerführung* at Barth, formerly a professor of History, Geography and Ethnology, described this incident in his book written after the war.

disappearance was covered up on two *Appelle* by the simple expedient of the two squadron leaders, who always lined up separately, joining the ranks which made the numbers correct – but the Germans forgot about the squadron leaders!

Crewes and Hudson were caught the following day when the small yacht which they had commandeered and in which they were hoping to sail to Sweden ran aground in a creek on their way out to sea. It was the first escape from Barth, and they got only three days in the cooler. After that all walks and swimming parties ceased; a predictable result which would have happened sooner or later. So-called privileges were nearly always curtailed after escapes.

Two more officers escaped a week or two later. With the co-operation of the NCOs they managed to get into the NCOs compound and went out on a working party disguised as sergeants. They slipped away from the working party but were caught several days later. Time in the cooler was increased to a week.

One day that summer Ffrench-Mullen made a close inspection of the electrical wiring in the roof of our hut and uncovered the suspected microphones. The mains circuit was then connected to the microphone circuit, an electrical tour de force which undoubtedly caused considerable confusion at the listening post in the Vorlager. In a very short time the compound gates were flung open to allow the entry of a swiftly moving posse of guards headed by the stocky figure of the outraged Commandant, Major Oertel, who proceeded straight to the SBO's room and arrested Squadron Leader Paddon without formality, amid much angry shouting about sabotage.

Pilot Officer Joe Hill, one of the interested onlookers, observed an irrepressible goon baiter slipping a potato onto the muzzle of a rifle slung over the back of one of the guards, and expressed his amusement with a loud guffaw. Major Oertel turned angrily towards him.

'You cannot laugh at me,' he shouted. 'I am ze Commandant. Arrest this man.'

'Auntie' Paddon and Joe Hill were taken off to the cooler; this time for two weeks, now to become the standard stretch in cells.

By late autumn a new hut had been built in the field to the west of our hut. Ken Doran, an Irish squadron leader with the first double DFC of the war, saw the opportunity of an escape. The watch tower had already been moved down to what was to become the new corner of the compound, leaving a blind spot in the wire between the new block and our hut. Doran, with two others, cut their way through the

wire one evening after *Appell* and hid in the empty hut. After dark
they crept out. Shots were fired and two were caught as they were
trying to get through the narrow opening in the new wire fence.
Doran got away, but was caught about three days later by a farmer
with a pitchfork and arrived back in camp with a lacerated face.

I remember returning with a party from a football game in the
field outside the main wire and seeing Peter Tunstall quietly slip off
an army great-coat revealing home-made Luftwaffe working overalls
and jack boots. Putting on a smart Luftwaffe cap he stepped out of
the column and marched confidently back in the opposite direction,
past the guard at the end, and away into the Pomeranian
countryside. He was not away for long, but he had begun a notable
career walking out of camps dressed in German uniform, a career
which led to and continued in Colditz.

Our fighter pilots were heavily engaged at this time over southwest England and not many came down over enemy territory. From
the few who arrived at Barth, usually as a result of chasing German
aircraft across the French coast, we learnt something of the epic air
battle being fought in the skies between Fighter Command and the
massed might of the Luftwaffe. We felt that our pilots flying Spitfires
and Hurricanes, guided by the new radar, must win the battle; yet,
there was, perhaps, a lurking doubt. One day in October, somebody
received a clothes parcel in which some garments were wrapped in
newspaper; it was the front page of the *Daily Express* of 15th
September 1940 with banner headlines '184 German Aircraft Shot
Down', the highest number of enemy aircraft destroyed in one day to
date. We knew that the Battle of Britain had been won.

It would be specious to pretend that all gloom vanished, but, at
least, the underlying feeling of uncertainty was replaced by a mood of
youthful optimism. This was somewhat untempered by logic,
reflected in a sweep we held on the date of the end of the war. Most
people forecast 1941; only two predicted 1945. The winner got his
money. Bob Stark, the efficient New Zealand 'Acker Basher', made
sure of that. It was, perhaps, just as well that we did not suspect the
weary years ahead of us.

The grey autumn days came upon us, shortening the daylight
hours. Doors were locked and outside shutters swung over the
windows by the guards as darkness fell. Sealed up in our wooden box
the dull monotony of our unnatural existence was brought home to
us and thoughts of food, never far away, turned uppermost in our
minds. In the kitchen there were always those who were spinning out

the meagre ration by toasting or baking on the stove very thin slivers of bread; there was little else to cook, and this process eliminated the sour taste. One or two of these burnt waferlike offerings could always be saved for breakfast, to avoid going too hungry in the morning.

Theatricals helped to cheer us up. They were held in the dining room with tables placed together to form a stage, and were organised mainly by Hugh Falkus, Ffrench-Mullen and Greenhous who wrote, produced and acted in comic skits, sometimes with a small 'Greek Chorus' as supporting cast for the rowdier acts. Once we were allowed over to the NCOs' compound to see one of their shows. Michael Roth was entertaining us with some very professional conjuring shows.

The tunnel, started from the centre block in July, was found in November when it was under the wire. The whole compound was immediately evacuated to the Vorlager where we spent three weeks in very cramped conditions in a small hut, allowed out for a walk for an hour a day only. Even here Ffrench-Mullen already had a tunnel well under way, with dispersal in the roof, by the time we left and returned to the main compound.

One of the first things we noticed was that the boards around the sides of the huts had been removed. There was a new type of guard wandering about the compound dressed in overalls and carrying a long metal rod for prodding into the ground to find tunnels. We called them ferrets.

Christmas 1940 came. Nat Fowler and Milner, both excellent artists, brightened the dull walls of the hut with their festive drawings and paintings. Christmas dinner was held in the dining room, a little more meat in the soup, a few more potatoes and a piece of rather soggy dark-coloured dough which was called Christmas pudding. But there was some beer and 'Red Biddy' and there was a recitation of all forty verses of 'Eskimo Nell' by Ffrench-Mullen standing on a table. An impressive performance which I had not seen equalled even during the five years I spent in Canada.

CHAPTER THREE

Hope Deferred

Hope deferred maketh the heart sick.

Proverbs Ch 13, v 12

Pomerania, an ancient Baltic province of Germany, was once inhabited by Slavonic tribes and derives its name from the Slav words, '*po*' meaning 'by', and '*more*' meaning 'sea'. Between the sea and the flat, agricultural hinterland lies an area of lonely salt marshes, sandy dunes and creeks, interspersed with dark pinewoods, not unlike the Norfolk coast. A pleasant enough place in summer for free holiday makers, but in winter reduced to an icy desolation by the Baltic winds.

On a freezing February morning in 1941 I stumbled out on *Appell* with the other ill-nourished and thinly-clad prisoners; most of us wore only the uniforms and shirts, now threadbare, in which we had been shot down, and the north winds were biting.

This was not to be quite the usual *Appell*. After the count Leutnant Pieber drew himself up and tried to assume a military and commanding attitude.

'Shentlemens,' he intoned, 'I haf something to tell you – and I am sorry, but maybe you vill not like it.'

'We'll tell you if we don't,' came a muffled shout from the ranks.

'Because of actions against our prisoners,' Pieber raised his voice. 'Because of actions against our prisoners in Canada, I haf to tell you that some of you are being moved from here to another camp.'

There were rumbles and shouts of dissent: 'What actions? . . . explain yourself. . . . Why are you taking it out on us? . . . bastards.'

'Quiet, all of you,' ordered Squadron Leader Paddon.

'Herr Pieber, please explain this. What has happened to your prisoners in Canada?'

'Our prisoners have been badly treated. They have been shut up in barracks and not allowed out.'

'Do the buggers good,' somebody called out.

'As a consequence,' continued Pieber, in measured Teutonic

phrases, 'it has been ordered that fifty of you are to be sent to a camp in Poland.'

After the shouts of protest and general hubbub had died down, Paddon told Pieber that he wished to make a formal protest to the Commandant. 'If you wish, Squadron Leader,' replied Pieber.

The Commandant told Paddon that the German prisoners in Canada had been chained up and that this was quite inexcusable and entitled the Germans to take similar measures against a few British prisoners. Paddon also learnt that he was to be included in the 'purge'. This was not surprising since the Germans held him responsible for the Centre Block tunnel, and he had recently walked through the gate with Milner, who spoke excellent German, both dressed as German workmen with papers appropriated from workmen who had been in the compound. Unfortunately they had been recognized by one of the camp staff as they were walking through Barth. Now Paddon[1] was being sent off with the others to live, as we heard later, a semi-subterranean existence in an underground fortress at Thorn.

From new arrivals we heard that the German prisoners had been accommodated in former private houses in Ontario. The area was unfenced and lightly guarded, so they had no difficulty in wandering away, some not to return until caught. Not surprisingly the defences were strengthened to keep the prisoners in bounds. It was this which led to the Thorn reprisal. It was completely untrue that they were chained up.

Later that winter the Germans issued us with British Army battle dresses and Polish Army greatcoats from captured stocks, and this helped to keep us a little warmer.

Flight Lieutenant 'Pappy' Plant, a Whitley pilot shot down in early summer 1940, was a tall, bearded Canadian from Alberta and looked like an Old Testament prophet; he was, in fact, a lay reader in the Episcopal Church and used to conduct religious services until the arrival of a padre. Plant was also a dedicated tunneller who planned and organised the first tunnel of 1941 from the East Block. The

---

[1] Squadron Leader Brian Paddon was eventually sent to Colditz where he had an altercation with a German NCO. He was charged with insulting a Feldwebel by calling him a *Schweinhund*. His defence was that he did not call the Feldwebel a *Schweinhund*, but rebuked him for treating him (Paddon) as though he were a *Schweinhund*. Paddon escaped, on the way to his court martial in Leipzig, from Stalag XXA Thorn, and reached England via Sweden, in June 1942. He was awarded the DSO.

French officers had departed at the end of the previous year.

I joined Pappy's tunnelling project. The winter snows were piled up around the side of the hut and we hoped it would deter the ferrets from looking underneath. 'Muckle' Muir, a Scottish Hampden pilot with a splendid P/O Prune[1] moustache, made a trap in the wooden floor of a room at the north end of the hut. Although these traps were hard to detect with dust swept into the crevices, more sophisticated traps had to be made later. The tunnel was to be dug out towards the trees beyond the wire, but we found that there was so little clearance between the floor of the hut and the ground that a great deal of time had to be spent making trenches for dispersal of the earth that was to come out of the tunnel.

In those early digging days our lack of experience was counter-balanced by an impatient eagerness. It was an excess of zeal untempered by elementary attention to security which led to the discovery of this tunnel scheme. The nightly noise of 'tin bashing'[2] and carpentry for tunnel accessories must have attracted the attention of the patrolling guards. The block was cleared one morning after *Appell* and a search soon revealed the trench works underneath the hut. We had to return for a spell to our tedious 'kriegie' existence, but spring was coming and the leaden hours were relieved by further plans for escape. We hoped for better luck next time.

By spring the Red Cross had established communications through Switzerland via the former Thomas Cook Organisation. A regular flow of food parcels started to arrive, and were issued by the parcels officer on the basis of one parcel per man per week. I well remember the meal in our room after the first parcels issue. We ate solidly for some hours, it seemed, as goodies from various tins appeared: cheese, corned beef, stew, biscuits (hard tack), prunes, even cocoa, but best of all, delectable tea. We were careful to eat slowly; a man in another camp died after bolting the entire contents of his first Red Cross parcel too quickly.

Our daily calorie intake was now up to about 2,000, still below the minimum for good health, but the parcels made a tremendous difference to our well-being, the difference between near starvation

---

[1] So called after the wartime RAF training cartoon character.

[2] POW terms used in reference, mainly, to the construction of air lines by joining empty food tins together. (A few food parcels arrived at infrequent intervals from autumn 1940)

and an adequate diet. Increased energy led to a proliferation of escape schemes.

The walrus-moustached Len Hockey was a forthright Bristol business man who had recently occupied the rear gun turret of a Wellington. We often pounded round the circuit together and in the early summer of 1941 got ourselves moved over to the newly opened West Block, the object being to look for fresh fields for escaping. We were not disappointed.

Squadron Leader McColm, the Australian Block Commander, soon started a tunnel which was to run out into the field to the west. Flight Lieutenant Alastair Panton DFC was to be in charge of digging operations; he was a former Cranwell cadet with great drive and energy, and had already managed to evade twice in France, after being shot down in his Blenheim – but, it seems, he was fated to go into 'the bag'. The standard trap was made in the floor of one of the rooms. As ferrets now crawled about underneath the huts, we had to camouflage the tunnel entrance, this was done by placing a strong wooden lid over the shaft about two feet below the surface of the ground, and when the tunnel was closed up earth was spread over it to match the surroundings.

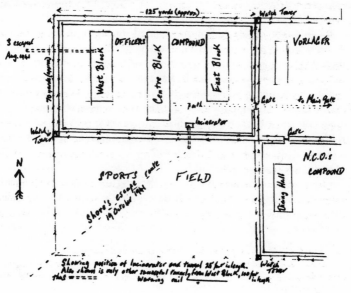

Stalag Luft I

Around this time there arrived in the compound a cheerful and lively flight lieutenant called John Shore, recently the pilot of a Wellington from my old squadron, No 9 at Honington. While returning from a raid on Cologne both his engines had failed, and he and his crew had had to bale out. His enthusiasm for escaping was boundless. His numerous and persistent death-defying schemes for getting outside the wire, one of which, I believe, included disguising himself as a dog, were all turned down by the escape committee. He was nicknamed 'Death'. Finally his energies were steered into safer channels, and he and I were put in charge of dispersal for the West Block tunnel.

To draw suspicion away from the West Block the earth from the tunnel was to be dispersed underneath the East Block. Death Shore and I at first arranged for the earth to be carried over in the large food containers used for bringing rations from the cook house in the NCOs' compound. When it seemed that the continual passage of these containers between the blocks, under the noses of the guards, could arouse suspicion, we got people to carry the earth across in bags concealed beneath army greatcoats and similar voluminous clothing – they were early penguins.[1] The soil was emptied through a trap in the floor and dispersed in trenches dug by Plant's men the previous winter.

The diggers were steadily pushing the tunnel out towards the wire. About five feet in depth, it was planned for a length of about one hundred feet to break out thirty feet beyond the wire. There was an air pump, and an airline made from wallpaper. No shoring was necessary; it was found at Barth that the soil was sufficiently firm to be able to dispense with wooden props, as had been used in the Centre Block tunnel, provided that the tunnel roof was kept in the shape of an arch, from earliest times one of the strongest architectural forms known. Security was tight and there was no night work.

One of my room-mates had been Flight Lieutenant Harry Burton who had been an instructor at my Wellington OTU. His slightly casual air belied a dour Scottish determination which was to find him a one-way ticket to Sweden. In May he made a daring and ingenious escape. He managed to get himself sentenced to two weeks in the cooler, smuggling in a hacksaw concealed in his clothing.

---

[1] The name given later to those who carried soil or sand for dispersal, and particularly those involved in the Great Escape.

Cutting through the bars of the cell window, he scrambled out one night to be caught immediately in probing searchlight beams. He froze against the wall of the cell block. The searchlight moved on and Burton crept to the Vorlager gate. There was a sentry on the gate but, every now and again, he went off on a regular beat, and while he was away Harry scraped hard, making a trench under the gate. It was a nerve-racking job and he had to edge back into the shadows whenever he heard the sentry returning. At last the trench was big enough. He squeezed underneath the gate and walked quickly out of the camp.

Burton walked to Stralsund and then across the island of Rugen to Sassnitz, a distance of about fifty miles. At Sassnitz the ferries ran to Trelleborg in Sweden. When Burton arrived it was daytime and he was only able to make an inconclusive reconnaissance of the dock area, so he went off to a beach overlooking the docks and did some sun-bathing. He observed a ship flying the Swedish flag. That night he smuggled himself aboard and arrived safely in Sweden. It was the first RAF 'Home Run'.[1] It was a great encouragement to all of us when we heard the news.

Plant, Wing Commander 'Hetty' Hyde and others had tunnels underway in various places, but the West Block tunnel was ready first at the beginning of August.

The lingering Baltic summer twilight was fading into the night as the guards closed the West Block shutters. McColm and Tim Newman, a rugged young New Zealander, were already down the tunnel preparing to break out. In the darkened corridor shadowy forms with home-made packs containing hard rations and some extra clothing were silently taking up position.

Hockey and I took our places, numbers 12 and 13, in the queue of about thirty would-be escapers, all of whom had worked on the tunnel. Sitting on the passage floor, backs to the wall, we quietly discussed our plan to walk along the coast to Denmark and then try to get across to Sweden. We had modified our uniforms to try to make them look like civilian clothing of some sort. Few escape aids were then available, we had neither papers nor money and only a rudimentary map.

We were on the verge of breaking what was to be the first

---

[1] Burton was awarded the DSO and eventually retired from the RAF as Air Marshal Sir Harry Burton.

successful tunnel at Barth. The atmosphere was charged with excitement and expectancy, and, as we edged up the wall towards the trap room, we somewhat naively anticipated a fairly easy passage home once we were out of the tunnel. Bitter experience was to teach us that the hardest part of any escape began outside the wire.

Suddenly the crack of a rifle shot rent the silence. It was followed immediately by the sound of several more shots.

'Hell! What's happened?' shouted somebody.

'All right, back to your rooms quick,' ordered the exit co-ordinator, '"Lucy" Lockett's been seen going down the flare path without his trousers. The rest of you have had it this time.'

There was turmoil as people rushed about in all directions trying to disperse themselves and their escape equipment as fast as they could. The Germans soon pounded in and searched the block for half the night.

The guard in the watch tower must have heard the sound of somebody scrambling out of the tunnel exit in the field; at any rate he swung his searchlight around to reveal Squadron Leader Lockett emerging from the hole minus his trousers which had slipped off on his way down the tunnel. He sprinted off into the darkness carrying his trousers over one arm, followed by a hail of bullets.

McColm and Newman were already out; the latter was caught about three days later, but McColm and Lockett reached Rostock on foot. Lockett was caught trying to board a Swedish ship in the docks, hut McColm managed to get aboard; he hid in the coal locker and went to sleep. Unfortunately he had a very loud snore and he was discovered before the ship was out of German waters. The Captain refused to keep him on board and handed him over to the German pilot. McColm was sent to Colditz.

The West Block was cleared for a thorough search and the installation of extra security measures such as the digging of inspection trenches which were dug underneath the other blocks as well, leading to the discovery of the other tunnels. I found myself back in the East Block.

For some of us escaping became a way of life. It was not only a way of passing the time, but, more important, it obliged the Germans to divert increasingly bigger resources towards security measures. As the war went on the odds became more heavily weighted against us; the stakes were high, but we learnt to live with failure – and sometimes to die. The chances of making a 'Home Run' were small. Certainly only a tiny percentage of those who escaped from prisoner of war camps in Germany actually got home.

For every new anti-escape measure introduced by the Germans we nearly always had an answer. After the discovery of air lines made by joining food tins together, the Germans brought in a rule that all parcels were to be opened in the dining room under the supervision of a German, usually Glemnitz, with all tins to be opened and emptied onto plates. The empty tins were then thrown into a high-sided wooden container which was carried outside the camp by our orderlies, emptied at a dump in the wood and then returned to the dining room.

At one parcels day that summer there was a good deal of cursing and grumbling about the nuisance and inconvenience of this laborious procedure. Glemnitz's leathery face creased into a wolfish smile.

'Ah, Jentlemen,' he said, 'But you see we have to stop you from escaping.'

Two feet away in the container, concealed beneath a false bottom, was Lieutenant Filmer, a South African Fleet Air Arm pilot, waiting to escape. Slowly the container filled up with empty tins, as Filmer lay, tense and perspiring, in the confined space below.

At last it was full. Glemnitz turned to the waiting orderlies.

'All right, boys.' He had worked in England for a few years and spoke excellent English. 'You can take it away now.'

The four soldiers grasped a handle at each corner. They lifted it up, and the empty food tins and Filmer were carried through the compound and Vorlager gates and out to the dump beside the wood. They diverted the guard's attention and on a pre-arranged signal Filmer pushed open the specially-made hinged flap at one end of the box and crawled out, quickly disappearing into the trees.

Filmer got hold of a bicycle on which he rode to Denmark, crossed the border and promptly went to sleep under a tree. He awoke to find a Danish soldier standing over him with a rifle. He had no alternative but to accompany him to the nearby frontier post.

'I am an escaped British pilot,' said Filmer to the guard commander who spoke good English. 'Can you help me?'

'I should like to help you,' the officer replied, 'but I am strictly controlled by the Germans, and if they heard that I had let you go, I would be shot.' He thought for a minute. 'I tell you what I suggest. Danish workers go regularly into Germany.' He pointed down the road towards the German frontier post. 'You go back down there, and I think you will pass into Germany without trouble. You can

then come back over another part of the frontier, but make sure you
are well inside our country before you stop next time.'

Filmer thanked the Danish officer and walked down the road to
the German frontier post.

'*Was ist das?*' asked the German official, pointing at Filmer's
haversack.

'*Essen,*' replied Filmer.

'*Gut, weitergehen,*'[1] said the man, and Filmer was back in Germany.

He made his next attempt to enter Denmark that night. He was
swinging himself hand over hand beneath a foot bridge which
spanned a small river running along the frontier, when a food tin
worked loose through a hole in his haversack and clattered onto the
stones below. The German guard above was alerted and Filmer was
finally recaptured.

One day that summer a tall, lean wing commander with taut upper
lip and narrowed eyes strode through the gate, followed by about
eighteen assorted British prisoners, to the accompaniment of some
boos, snide remarks and hostile looks from a number of onlookers.
Wings Day and the permanent inmates of Dulag Luft had been
recognized and identified with soft living: regular walks and skiing
on parole, plentiful 'booze and baccy' and so on. Such were the
rumours circulated by prisoners who had passed through the camp
in transit, arousing resentment fuelled by paranoid fantasies so
easily induced in prisoner of war life.

When it was learned that they had been sent to Barth for escaping
from a tunnel they had been digging for over a year, hostility soon
evaporated. Their life of ease was seen as a blind to lull the Germans
while they dug the first successful RAF tunnel of the war.

In the group were personalities like Major John Dodge, who had
been a lieutenant-colonel in the First World War at the age of
twenty-three, American-born, he was related to the Prime Minister
by marriage; Lieutenant-Commander James Buckley of the Fleet
Air Arm who had been in charge of the tunnel at Dulag Luft, and
Squadron Leader Roger Bushell, South African-born barrister who
had been commanding No 92 Squadron, Spitfires, when he was shot
down in France in 1940 at the age of thirty. Bushell had been caught
on the Swiss Frontier. 'I could have taken a girls' school across if I'd
chosen a spot a few hundred yards to the west,' he declared with

---

[1] 'What is that?' 'Food.' 'Good, go on.'

some bitterness. A man of forceful personality, his penetrating gaze was given an almost sinister twist by the permanent droop in his left eye caused by a skiing accident – he had been a skier of Olympic standard. He was destined posthumously for enduring fame in the annals of RAF escaping.

Wings took over as Senior British Officer and gave impetus, if any were needed, to escaping activities with his own style of leadership, combining Royal Marines discipline with a swashbuckling pre-war RAF 'Flying Club' approach. He appointed James Buckley to head the escape committee. An intelligence section was set up. The wind of change is never popular, and the changes were made with little ceremony – Wings had been annoyed at the hostile reception. However Buckley proved to be exceptionally capable and impartial. With the Commandant's agreement, Wings also established a communal fund financed by a compulsory levy on a percentage of officers' pay; this was used mainly for the purpose of giving the NCOs some money, as they received no pay in the camp although they were able to earn a little on working parties. The money was to be refunded to us after the war. The Germans also debited the communal fund with charges for barrack damages and with hefty fines for escaping!

In the meantime our comrades in the NCOs' compound had not been idle on the other side of the wire. They now numbered about 750 and came from all walks of life. By general agreement they elected a committee to run the compound with James 'Dixie' Deans[1] as chairman or, as the Germans called it, 'Man of Confidence', a young sergeant pilot with a very wise head on his shoulders. Deans, through force of personality, carried on in this capacity in various camps until the end of the war.

The will to escape was no less evident than in our compound, and a number of tunnels had been dug. Under Deans' leadership the escape organisation was put on a firm footing with George Grimson as the central figure. Grimson, a rather aloof character, was one of those coldly determined people thrown up in the holocaust of war, dedicated to hitting the enemy where it hurt most, in this case by escaping as much as possible. He was Roger Bushell's counterpart in

---

[1] 'Dixie' Deans, although in poor health for some time, has been President of the Royal Air Forces ex-POW Association for many years, and is remembered and honoured by 'ex-Kriegies' all over the world.

the NCOs' compound and, like Bushell, he made the supreme sacrifice. More will be said about him later.

John Bristow was the wireless 'Whizz Kid' who designed and made the first radio receiving set at Barth from parts scrounged by himself on working parties, tin, odd metal scraps, tinfoil, wire etc. The valves were obtained by devious means from the German radio in the Vorlager. From this the first BBC News Bulletins were received and read out by a team of news readers under the supervision of Peter Thomas, then a sergeant pilot, subsequently an MP and Secretary of State for Wales.

The Gestapo had already raised their ugly head. In September 1940 Sergeant Lascelles, following a request from Squadron Leader Paddon, volunteered to go out on working parties to collect any information that might be useful for escaping. When Paddon left he requested Lieutenant Fanshawe to maintain contact with Lascelles who continued to send messages over to the officers' compound, now under the code-name 'Hornblower'.

The Germans found the messages during a search, hidden behind panelling, in April 1941. When they discovered the identity of 'Hornblower', Fanshawe was arrested, together with Lascelles, put in the camp cooler and interrogated by the Gestapo. They were both in great danger, as they could have been charged with espionage, and we were very worried about them. Fanshawe at first denied being Hornblower but admitted it later in the hope it might help to clear the matter up. He was sent back to the compound and later taken to a prison in Stettin for a week for more questioning with Lascelles. Fanshawe was then sent back to Barth, and we thought that was the end of the matter but, on 20th November, they came for him again and he was taken off to the Wehrmacht-untersuchungsgefängnis (Military Interrogation Unit) at Tegel near Berlin for further grilling with Lascelles, who had been in solitary confinement at Stettin for some months. We were relieved when they were both returned to Barth on 20th March 1942.

CHAPTER FOUR

The Incinerator

So every bondman in his own hand bears
The power to cancel his captivity.

Julius Caesar, Shakespeare

In September 1943 a new Security Officer arrived to investigate escaping activities at Barth. Hauptmann Ippisch, although an Austrian, was a disagreeable man who set about his task by marching us every day to the NCOs' compound where we were confined all day in the dining hall, thus separated from the NCOs who were locked in their barrack huts. This continued for about three weeks while anti-escape measures were being installed in our compound.

It was during these weary hours that Death Shore came and asked me if I would join him in a project which entailed tunnelling from a small brick-built rubbish receptacle standing near the wire in the officers' compound. It was called the incinerator, although, as far as I remember, rubbish was never burnt there. A shaft had already been dug by previous operators but the scheme had been abandoned as being non-viable – in other words, in RAF parlance, 'too dicey'. Shore had obtained the permission of the escape committee to take over the enterprise.

Tedium fell away in the face of this challenge. It appeared to be a very good opportunity for a 'blitz' tunnel into the football field which was enclosed by only a single strand of wire and, although covered by machine-guns and searchlights from two watch towers, should be reasonably easy to cross on a moonless night. The main difficulty would be entering and leaving the incinerator during the day time under the noses of the guards while building the tunnel. A means had to be devised for this when we returned to the compound after the searches.

In the low roof of the incinerator which sloped gently towards the wire was a small square opening through which rubbish was thrown. Spectators always stood on the roof to watch football games just the other side of the wire. Alastair Panton, a leading member of the escape committee, was detailed by Jimmy Buckley to organise football games morning and late afternoon until the tunnel was finished. Shore and I were to stand with the spectators before entering the incinerator and join them again when we came up in the evening.

On the first day Shore and I were standing on top of the incinerator waiting to go down. The watch tower seemed to overshadow us and the guard on the gate was uncomfortably close. We felt very vulnerable but we were standing in the middle of a tight group of spectators and they were well padded out in army greatcoats and other bulky forms of clothing.

'OK, men,' said Panton. 'The goons are watching the football – go.'

Quickly Shore and I dropped through the opening, the cover of which was immediately pushed back by the shuffling feet of the football supporters, leaving a small chink for air. The dim light revealed a small compartment about six feet square and about three feet in height. There was a brick wall separating it from the other compartment of the incinerator. On the compound side there was a door which was normally used for emptying rubbish, but arrangements had been made to keep our compartment clear and all rubbish had been thrown into the adjoining compartment.

We found the trap in the concrete floor concealing the shaft which had already been dug to a depth of about five feet. We had about twenty-five feet to dig under the wire into the football field. Dispersal would be a problem. We decided we should have to make a hole in the brick wall dividing us from the other compartment and throw the earth in there.

It took us an hour or so to scrape the mortar away and loosen enough bricks to make a small hole in the wall.

Then we took turns to dig the tunnel out from the base of the shaft. Hacking away with a knife the digger loosened the earth at the face and pushed it back to the disperser who threw it out of the shaft with a tin bowl and through the hole into the next compartment. All that day, stripped to the waist, and sweating, we worked silently and almost mechanically.

After seven hours we had dug about six feet of tunnel just big enough to crawl in. By the time the spectators arrived for the football game at five o'clock we were quite ready to join them. With overcoats covering our dirty bodies we waited until, towards the end of the game, the cover was pushed aside. A short while later, amidst the cheering and shouting, came a muffled, 'OK, men – come up.' We scrambled out into the light and fresh air.

Every day until the tunnel was finished the same procedure was followed. On the odd occasion when it was not possible to arrange a football game, in the evening, Panton coopted some orderlies to come and empty some rubbish. We slid out through the door backing onto the compound and merging with the orderlies who were wearing exactly the same overcoats walked back with them to the centre block, unnoticed by the Germans.

We worked feverishly. It was a blitz tunnel as football games on this frequency could not be maintained indefinitely. As the tunnel lengthened our rate of progress slowed a little and we had to employ a small sledge, a length of rope at each end, to bring the earth back from the face. However we found ourselves ahead of schedule and, after four days, calculated that we had dug far enough. Shore pushed a stick up through the ground on the evening football game and Panton pinpointed it at some five feet beyond the wire. It remained only to dig upwards to within about six inches of the surface, in preparation for the breakout, and we were ready to go when the lights went out on Bomber Command's next operation in the area.

The next morning John Shore and I were pacing round the compound going over our escape plans once more. We planned to walk the fifty miles or so to Sassnitz on the island of Rügen where we would try to board a ferry for Sweden.

'Muckle Muir, Tim Newman, John Wilson and Bush Parker, the Aussie, wanted to use the tunnel after us,' Shore was saying, 'but I told them we wanted four hours' start.'

'Assuming the air raid lasts that long,' I replied. 'Well, it is our tunnel, and it's going to be tricky enough getting in, almost like a wire crawl. Anyhow we've got our exit traps made – mine in my room and yours in the dining room, I believe.' Unfortunately, we happened to room in different blocks.

'That's right,' said Shore. 'They treble the guards in the compound during an air raid, so we'll have to look slippy getting out. . .'

'Good God,' I exclaimed, 'look at that.'

A horse and wagon had drawn up beside the incinerator. The German driver had got two of our orderlies onto the job of clearing out the rubbish.

'Hell's bells,' muttered Death. 'No – it couldn't happen, not after all that work.'

Moonless Night

We watched spellbound as shovelfuls of earth, with a little rubbish mixed in, arced into the wagon. It continued for a full half hour. The German smoked his pipe and watched impassively. When the incinerator was empty and the wagon full, he climbed up onto his seat, urged his thin and sad-looking horse into motion, and went off with our earth. It must have been the only time in the whole war when the Germans obliged by dispersing soil from a tunnel to a point outside a POW camp. We thanked God for the literal Teutonic mind instructed to watch only for escaping 'kriegies'.

Two nights later, on 19th October, all perimeter lights went out – but there was no air raid siren. This was unprecedented. Was it an air raid or only a temporary fault? I hesitated, probably for only about the length of time it took me to get my kit together. Reflecting on it now, it was probably a factor which cost me my freedom. Then I decided to go. I grabbed my home-made haversack containing hard rations. My room-mates opened the trap for me. As I was about to go down, a stage whisper came up from below.

'You OK, Jimmy?'

'OK, John,' I answered. 'I'm coming.'

Swiftly, I dropped down into the black void below, found one of the inspection trenches and groped my way out to the side of the hut. I was just in time to see the shadowy form of Shore disappearing into the incinerator. It was a moonless night but light enough to discern objects at fairly close range.

As I was starting out towards the incinerator, two guards suddenly came round the corner of the Centre Block and I dodged back into the shadows. The guards went into the block, and I launched out again towards my goal. More guards came pounding down the path leading from the gate to the Centre Block cutting off my line of approach. All at once, the compound seemed to be alive with Germans. Suddenly, there was a lull in the activity. This was my chance. I crawled quickly out to the path on my way to the incinerator which, by now, had become a chimera, a hazy milestone on the way to freedom.

At the moment I reached the path, a dark shape suddenly loomed above me. A torch flashed onto me; in that instant I instinctively recognized Buchvig, the Security Officer, and I knew I would never get out of the camp that night. He gave the alarm as I scrambled back under the hut.

I tried, in vain, to find the trap leading up into my room. If I could get back into the hut, I could, perhaps, try again when things were quieter. I was defeated by the inky blackness underneath the hut. Then I heard the growling and barking of the dogs. Torchlight illuminated the darkness and gutteral German voices came nearer as the dogs followed my scent. Soon they were on me; the Alsatians were held back as the guards grabbed me. I was led out into the floodlit compound where I was surrounded by gesticulating Germans screaming with rage, and all seemed to be pointing some sort of firearm at me. I could distinguish the words, '*Hände hoch!*' I raised my arms; it seemed appropriate anyway in the circumstances.

In the hard glare of the searchlights I reflected briefly that I was causing an excellent, if unwitting, diversion for John Shore's final exit from the camp area, since I appeared to have the undivided attention of most of the camp staff.

Hauptmann Buchvig, in his smooth Austrian manner, finally broke up the party, and I was marched off to the cell block. Alone in my cell, I thought back rather bitterly on the events of the night. Shore was obviously on his way to Sassnitz and I could have been with him if, perhaps, I had waited a little longer . . . got out a bit sooner . . . exercised a little more caution . . . but unsuccessful escapes are always loaded with bitter regrets which it is best to forget as speedily as possible. I dropped off to sleep on my hard bed. There was nothing else to do.

In the morning, after my mug of ersatz coffee and some black bread, the cell door opened and the Commandant, Major Burchardt, entered with his adjutant. He spoke very good English.

'Good morning, Herr James,' he said. 'That was very bad luck. It was a good try and a very good tunnel. Better luck next time.'

He was a German officer of the old school. He knew, also, what it was like to be a prisoner. He had escaped from a civil internment camp in South Africa in the First World War.

After he got out of the tunnel, Shore crossed the football field and went to the wood beside the Flak School where we had arranged to meet. When I did not appear, he set off down the road, walked through the silent streets of Barth – it was then about midnight – and on to Stralsund. He was wearing a home-made German workman's cap and had civilian buttons sewn onto a modified tunic, but possessed no papers. He reached Stralsund at about 8.30 a.m. and lay up in a wood. His rest was somewhat disturbed by a Flak unit who marched into the wood and spent the day singing and firing guns.

That evening he made an attempt to commandeer a bicycle just outside Stralsund, but a man came out of a nearby hut and called out. Shore dodged behind a tree and waited; the man went back into the hut and returned almost immediately with another man who had a lantern. Shore decided that the bicycle was not for him and continued the journey on foot across the bridge to the island of Rügen and along the road to Bergen where he spent the day in another wood. He was now about halfway across the island. The next night he went on along the railway line. Towards morning he heard the sound of breakers on the coast and shortly after came to the little summer resort of Binz. He left the railway line and walking into Binz, now deserted and desolate, he saw a signpost for Sassnitz.

As he walked down the coast he noticed some fishermen's boats and thought that one of these could be useful in the event of his not getting aboard a ship. By this time his feet were getting painful. As he was now very near Sassnitz and it was nearly daylight, he hid up for the day in a plantation of firs.

When night fell, Shore walked through Sassnitz Railway Station; beyond, two big gantries stood out like monumental signposts and led him down a path to the harbour. Standing at the edge of the water he saw the twin arches at the entrance to the ferry terminal. This was the final hurdle. How was he to get in and board a neutral vessel that would take him to Sweden? The best way seemed to be to get onto a train which was to be taken aboard the ferry. Nearby he saw a truck standing on one of the lines leading up to the ferry entrance; he climbed underneath the tarpaulin cover and went to sleep. The next afternoon the truck started to move – back to the station. Shore jumped out quickly.

By now, dirty and dishevelled, he made another reconnaissance of the harbour. He saw a Pullman car on a siding near the ferry and climbed underneath. Once more he found himself being shunted towards the station, and again he jumped off. This time he ran up a bank covered in blackberry bushes where he hid and watched. He soon spotted a Swedish three-master, but he knew he must wait till night came before making an attempt to board her. In the meantime a raging thirst was his main preoccupation. He found some elderberries which helped. In a quest to assuage the rest of his thirst he climbed up to some houses at the top of a bank and then went down a narrow track passing an old woman who said something to him about the station. He did not reply, but went quickly back to his hiding place. Here he was suddenly very sick, probably as the result of his having eaten what he thought were elderberries.

When it was dark again Shore went down to the harbour and walked onto the Swedish ship without hindrance, but when on board he noticed an obvious Gestapo man watching him. He asked a sailor if he could see the Captain. On being told that the Captain was not on board, he walked off the ship and went towards another Swedish ship followed by the Gestapo.

Suddenly another Gestapo man appeared, '*Wohin gehst Du?*' he asked.

'*Ich bin Schweder,*' replied Shore. '*Hans Kultur,*' swiftly inventing the name of a ship, and continuing towards the vessel followed by the German. When he got there he shrugged his shoulders muttered, '*Nicht hier,*' and slouched off. The Gestapo man caught up with him near some Danish ships towards which Shore had decided to direct his footsteps.

'*Deine Papiere,*' he barked.

'*Nicht verstehen,*' answered Shore.

The German called to two Danish sailors, ordering them to come and show what he meant by papers.

Then came salvation in the form of a drunken Danish sailor who appeared reeling along the quayside.

'*Ole, ole, guten Abend.*' He put his arms around the Gestapo man and Shore, '*Un' wie geht's, meine Freunde?*'

'*Ach, Quatsch,*'[1] shouted the German, shaking off the drunken man's embrace. As he turned to the other two Danes demanding their papers, Shore walked off and merged quickly into the shadows of the dockyard. He decided to wait for the skippers of the two Danish vessels to come back. Soon after, two men walked past, but to his question, 'Danish?' They replied, '*Nein, gute Deutsche.*'

Still tortured by thirst, Shore walked to the station and had a drink from the hydrant he had noticed earlier.

On his way back to the harbour, he saw two Pullman coaches on a siding. He got into one of them, and had another drink and a wash in the toilet. Feeling despondent and, by this time, almost past the point of caring whether he was discovered or not, he fell into a fitful sleep in one of the carriages.

Some instinct awoke him in the early hours of the morning. All apathy and gloom dispelled, he left his Pullman coach and walked quickly to a point where he could see the ferry terminal. There,

[1] 'Well, well, good evening, and how are you my friends?' 'Oh, rubbish.'

standing out in the muted lighting of the docks, were the funnels of a ferry boat. At this moment a line of trucks was being shunted towards the ferry terminal. The mercurial Shore dashed across the intervening fifty yards and managed to scramble onto a low truck on which rested a military lorry bound for Norway. He rolled underneath the lorry. The line of trucks rumbled on through the arches onto the quayside beside the ferry. Surely there would be a search here? But the trucks edged slowly up the ramp onto the ship and into the dark cavern beneath the superstructure.

Tense and expectant, Shore lay under the lorry waiting. He felt the gentle vibration when the engines started, then the shuddering and creaking of the ship's gear as the propellers churned up the water pushing the vessel away from the dockside. When the ferry was underway and he felt it heaving on the Baltic swell, he climbed into the cab of the lorry in which he sailed exultantly into Trelleborg some hours later.

The Swedish authorities contacted the British Consul in Stockholm and John Shore was soon on his way back to England where he arrived on 29th October 1941. He was awarded the Military Cross.

CHAPTER FIVE

Baltic Winter

The wind was a torrent of darkness among the gusty trees,
The moon was a ghostly galleon tossed upon cloudy seas.

'The Highwayman', Alfred Noyes

At the beginning of December 1941 I spent another two weeks in solitary confinement in the cell block, after being discovered under a hut on a fresh tunnel scheme.

A short period in cells was sometimes a relief from the unchanging daily round and the close communal existence forced upon one in a prisoner of war camp. A normal friendly chap with whom one would have been quite happy to converse daily at a lunch-time session in the Mess bar at home, after a few months at close quarters in a small room, would irritate unbearably with eccentricities of habit or speech, either real or imagined. It was a great exercise in tolerance.

My time in the cooler on this occasion was quite eventful. Pearl Harbour was bombed by the Japanese on 7th December, and the Americans came into the war. The first Russians I had seen came into the camp for a rest. Through the bars of my cell window I saw two of them pulling a cart heaped with clothing; some of this slid off onto the ground, and the German guard ordered them to put it back. Slowly and painfully the starved and emaciated men stumbled back and with quivering hands replaced the fallen garments. In German eyes they were *Untermensch* (subhuman) with no right to existence. In many other camps their lives were swiftly extinguished. On the East Front Heydrich's *Einsatz Gruppen* (Action Groups) shot tens of thousands of Russians, both military and civilian, Jews and other 'undesirables'.[1]

I think it was then that I thought I might be able to tunnel my way out of the cell. I noticed some loose concrete on the floor in a corner; probably a previous occupant had had the same idea. With my knife and fork I started to loosen it still further in an effort to make a trap. The small amount of soil I could have hidden under my bed. In the event it would have taken too long, and I couldn't think of a way

---

[1] The Soviet Union had refused to sign the Geneva Convention.

of extending my time in detention except by assaulting a guard.

If continual lack of privacy had irked in the compound, after two weeks in the cooler I sincerely desired the company of my fellow prisoners once more. The usual banal banter and rather aimless chatter about goons, wire fever and the probable end of the war seemed almost amusing. The inconclusive philosophical and political discussions on anything from Mediaeval Monasticism to Marx and Metaphysics, God and the Universe, even cast a mantle of erudition on the expounders. These discussions were sometimes enlivened when the 'Dodger', Major John Dodge, dropped in to give some fatherly advice, more often to provoke a political argument.

The Major had been Conservative Parliamentary Candidate for Gillingham in the immediate pre-war election. He had had a colourful and eventful life. In the First World War he won the DSC at Gallipoli with the Royal Naval Division and the DSO in France as a lieutenant-colonel. After the war he had professed to being a socialist and had gone off to the Soviet Union to see the 'New Jerusalem' for himself. He was arrested in the Caucasus by the OGPU, accused of spying and locked up for two months, narrowly avoiding liquidation. Since then he had been a staunch conservative. In 1939 he joined up again as a major and was captured at St Valéry with the 51st Highland Division. He tried to escape by swimming out to some British ships anchored far out at sea, but they sailed away before he could reach them, and he had to swim seven miles back to shore where he was recaptured. Another escape had resulted in his being handed over to a Luftwaffe officer by a frightened civilian; hence his presence in Luftwaffe camps – nearly always better run and with better conditions than other camps in Germany – and his relationship to Winston Churchill had helped to keep him there. I was to see a good deal of the Dodger in the last year of the war.

Pursuing his favourite theme on the merits of capitalism, the Dodger would launch into some pseudo-Marxist who had been discoursing on the dialectical process in history.

'My dear fellow,' he would exclaim, jabbing his finger at the man to emphasise each point, 'I used to think like you when I was your age. When I went to the Soviet Union in 1921 I was a firm socialist and I thought it was the promised land, but I was very soon disillusioned.'

'That was because they put you in jug.' 'Not at all,' continued the Dodger, 'I became convinced that collective socialism was inefficient as an economic system, and it has been enforced in Russia by a totalitarianism which has put twenty million into concentration camps. Competitive free enterprise means freedom for all.'

Sometimes Tony Trench, the mathematician, would pause from his equations to give us a lecture on karma and reincarnation, his legacy from a childhood spent in the Far East.

Besides talking, our main diversions were bridge, chess, reading and 'getting educated' in any subject offered under the Education Programme run by Harvey Vivian, a former Clifton College Schoolmaster. The theatre people were busy organising shows both in our compound and in the NCOs' compound, and we exchanged visits. A New Zealand padre called Walton arrived and took the Anglican services in the camp. The Roman Catholics were being taken into Barth for Mass, but in 1941 the priest refused to officiate for prisoners of war.

A new intake of prisoners came into the compound just before Christmas. I immediately recognized two members of 9 Squadron whom I had known in 1940, as they came through the gate, Tom Kirby-Green, now a squadron leader, and 'Conk' Canton who had been my regular companion around the inns of Bury St Edmunds. Conk had had a bad time. The Merlin engines of his Wellington II had caught fire, as was often their habit in this aircraft, over Crete, and he had given the order to bale out. He landed in the sea just off the coast and was badly lacerated by coral while wading ashore. He was then severely beaten up by the Gestapo and his crew, shot.

Escaping continued. Nat Fowler, who was in charge of parcels distribution, walked out of the parcels store in the Vorlager in German uniform he had made himself. When he was well away from the camp he slipped off the uniform and continued in a civilian suit also home-made. He was caught at Sassnitz trying to board a ferry for Sweden, and sent to Colditz. Fowler subsequently escaped from Colditz and got into Switzerland whence he returned to the UK. Unfortunately he was killed in a flying accident soon afterwards.

'Tommy' Thompson, a tall, lanky, Scot who had worked for the Johnny Walker whisky firm before the war, taught us to distil 'hooch' from dried prunes using food cans in which the raw wine from the fermented prunes was heated up to 98°C, the steam was then led off the top and condensed in a crude apparatus consisting of a rubber tube laid down a wooden trough over which ran cold water from a tap. The drops from the end of the tube were guaranteed to blow the top of your head off. It was just in time for Christmas.

Christmas 1941 seemed to be dominated by Wings' friendly and extrovert personality. He was in his element on a festive occasion. In between visits to numerous bars set up for the occasion, we pulled him round the compound standing on the parcels cart. Every time we passed a 'goon box' or the guard on the gate, Wings ordered a halt; he would then make a speech, the main content of which was *'Deutschland kaput'*, but the Germans were rather confused when Wings then led us in song with a rendering of 'Deutschland über Alles'; other songs in his repertoire on this occasion were 'A Life on the Ocean Wave', 'When I die', a dirge in support of alcohol, and 'Tipperary'.

Shortly after, we were gripped in the ice and snow of a particularly severe Baltic winter. The north-east wind howled and screamed over the camp; it gusted through the trees and blew snow off the creaking boughs in great swirling clouds. A good deal of it found its way through cracks in the walls of our huts. We plastered newspaper over the walls; this helped, but mostly the paper just ballooned out.

This ill wind from the Arctic gave us a good ice rink which was made by flooding the area between two blocks. Skating and ice hockey were enjoyed throughout the winter. We made the sticks, the skates were sent out by the YMCA, and we were coached by the Canadians. Barry Davidson from Calgary was a leading ice hockey player, and was to be commended by the YMCA for encouraging ice hockey and sport generally. The winter snows were the opportunity and the occasion for some daring escapes.

Tommy Thompson decided to take a holiday from hooch-making and infiltrated himself into the NCOs' compound. Then he and two sergeants, Johnny Shaw and Evans, crawled across the football field draped in white sheets. Shaw was seen and shot dead by the guard in the watch tower. The other two were caught later.

One prisoner attempted a novel, if rather chilly, escape from the football field. During a rugby game he got himself buried in the snow, with his escape rations and warm clothing, in the midst of a scrum down. He had a cold wait under the snow until the evening, and then the searchlight revealed a cloud of steam rising up from the snow where he was buried; it was observed by the guard and his attempt was over.

Three men went over the wire in daylight during the winter blizzards, one in January and two more in March. On both occasions the guard had retreated into his box, the windows of which were covered with frozen snow. Choosing a spot just below the platform of the watch tower, they walked over on top of the snow, which had drifted to the height of the fence, and were soon swallowed up in the white wilderness, but they did not last long in the arctic conditions and were soon back in the 'cooler' warming up.

Pat Leeson, an excellent German speaker, also went out in the March blizzard dressed as a chimney sweep in home-made top hat and tall coat, as worn by sweeps in Germany, carrying imitation wires, weighting ball and brush. The real sweep was in the compound sweeping chimneys. Leeson's blackened face served as a good disguise and with a forged pass, copied from the pass 'borrowed' from the sweep on a previous occasion, he had no difficulty in walking past the guards on both gates, the first merely remarked on the depth of the snow and the second made no comment whatever as he waved Leeson on after glancing at the pass. It was unfortunate that the weather happened to be so cold, and he was caught again after a few days.

I also had an idea for getting out through the gate. I thought it might be possible to walk or run out at night during a 'flap' in the uniform of a Gefreiter (Corporal) shouting loudly, '*Los! Los!*' on the principle that loud noise and bold action, particularly from a corporal, would induce the guard to open the gate at once. I had suitably modified an RAF airman's greatcoat (indistinguishable in colour from the Luftwaffe, at night) and made a Luftwaffe roundel which I had sewn onto the front of a RAF forage cap. The block escape representative came and told me one night that the lights had gone out and there was some sort of disturbance in the compound. I put on my uniform but just as I neared the gate the lights came on again.

Ker-Ramsay, the block escape representative, conceived the idea of making a trap in the wall of the end room nearest the wire to lead into a deep snow drift piled up against the side of the hut. I joined him in this project, we made the trap and started to dig a 'blitz' tunnel, but the thaw came sooner than expected and put an end to it.

News that we were to move to a new camp sometime in April led to another escape by Leeson only six weeks after his previous attempt. This time he dressed as a Luftwaffe Gefreiter and took two men, one of whom was Peter Cazanove, out through the gate with the story that he was taking them to the new camp. Such initiative deserved success, but they were all caught again.

At the beginning of April, leaving the camp honeycombed with numerous tunnels, forty-five in the officers' compound, we were all moved by train down to Stalag Luft III at Sagan in Silesia.

CHAPTER SIX

Göring's Model Camp

They dug and heard nothing more
they did not grow wise, invented no song,
thought up for themselves no language.
They dug. . .

'There was earth inside them.' Paul Celan

The Silesian pine forest marched darkly around the barbed wire defences, guard boxes and perimeter lighting enclosing the bare sandy compounds on which stood the austere wooden barrack huts built to house 800 officer aircrew and double that number of NCOs.

This was Stalag Luft III near the small town of Sagan. The camp had been built on Göring's[1] orders, with special emphasis on security, to accommodate the increasing number of airmen shot down in the mounting bomber offensive. 'Call me Meyer and let daisies grow out of the palm of my hand, if one bomber gets to Berlin,' he had boasted in 1940. He had not been able to stop the bombers getting through, but Göring could build camps to imprison enemies of the Third Reich.

Half-way between Berlin and Breslau, we were a long way from neutral territory. The huts were a long way from the wire, and the camp was built on sand – soft yellow sand which went down to unimaginable depths below the thin layer of top soil. Nevertheless, the camp probably had better conditions than most others in Germany. Göring had a chivalrous feeling for his 'fellow flyers' and was able to get the best for the prisoner of war camps run by the Luftwaffe. At Sagan Colonel von Lindeiner, a former cavalry officer, now sixty-two years old, headed a hand-picked staff. Political considerations may have influenced Göring in that most of the German prisoners in Allied hands at this time were aircrew.

---

[1] In 1933 Göring had formed the Gestapo, at first his private terror squad, and had built the first concentration camps at Dachau and Sachsenhausen. In the same year he declared, 'Every bullet which leaves the barrel of a police pistol is my bullet. If one calls this murder, then I have murdered. I ordered all this . . . my mission is only to destroy and exterminate.'

In spite of the dubious prospects below ground, I did not have the same sense of finality as when I had entered Stalag Luft I nearly two years before. Although German armies were thundering across the Russian steppes towards Stalingrad, Rommel was rolling our army back in the Western Desert and the Japanese were thrusting up through Burma, there was a feeling, now that the Americans were in the war, the Germans and Japs would be stopped in their tank tracks before long and that this could be the beginning of the end.

It was the beginning of a new phase of POW life. Any change from the confines of the small compound at Barth would have been welcome. Here we had a larger cage in which to exercise, slightly bigger rooms, new surroundings, and withal a new spirit seemed to be abroad, not least among the escaping fraternity.

A new compound always presented opportunities of escape to the vigilant. Almost at once I queued up for a wire crawl. Somebody had noticed a blind spot in the wire; he was to cut through at night with a pair of home made cutters and about a dozen others, including me, were to go through after him. However, the Germans, apparently, also spotted the flaw in the defences and put an extra guard on before we could put the plan into operation. Crawling across one hundred yards of bare compound swept by searchlights required not only luck and the diligent use of any cover available, shadows thrown by tree stumps and folds in the ground, but also a minimum number of guards on duty.

In the meantime we learnt that a team from the first party to arrive from Barth was happily driving a tunnel through the soft sand. Under Panton's energetic leadership they were 'hell bent' on achieving maximum footage per day on their way to the wire.

'Nothing to it, old boy – six feet a day – no trouble at all.'

But trouble soon came. There was no shoring and there were plenty of falls. The big Canadian fighter pilot Wally Floody, among others, got buried. The tunnel was not far below ground level and it was easy to push air holes up to the surface, but it was through these that the tunnel was discovered by the ferrets a short while later.

Soon after our arrival a number of new faces appeared in the compound; they belonged to members of a RAF draft from the Army Camp at Warburg, Westphalia. They were seasoned prisoners who brought with them a number of new skills developed in collaboration with their army officer comrades; these included the art of forging false documents, map making, finesse in tailoring, and dyeing.

Blended with the expertise from Barth, the compound now

contained a plethora of rugged individualists who possessed an unrivalled knowledge of the art of escaping. These were welded into an escape organisation by Wings Day and Jimmy Buckley, who continued to head the escape committee. There were now three operational sections dealing with the three main methods of escaping from a prison camp – tunnelling, wire projects and walk-outs through the gate. Of these escape through a tunnel was the most satisfactory; it usually ensured a head start of at least eight hours, maximum rations and escape kit could be taken, and it made the most trouble for the Germans. This was why hundreds of prisoners were willing to work long and laborious hours on tunnel schemes, many of which had small chance of success.

There were special sections for duplicating maps, using gelatine from food parcels, and for the production of forged identity papers and travel documents, the latter known as the 'Dean & Dawson' Travel Bureau under the artist Flight Lieutenant Tim Walenn.

This was the basis of the organisation which, expanding steadily, engineered a number of successful escapes leading to one of the greatest escapes in history nearly two years later in the North Compound, yet to be built.

'Foodacco' was another idea brought from Warburg. This was a form of Exchange and Mart, the unit of which was the cigarette. Items of food and tobacco were exchanged on a system of points. It was run by two Canadians and soon showed good profits which were channelled by the SBO into the communal fund, with an allotment set aside for bribery of the Germans.

Charles Bonington was a parachute captain captured in the Western Desert when his aircraft was shot down while on a Special Air Service operation. A former Australian journalist, in his early thirties, he was the father of Chris Bonington, the future mountaineer. At Sagan he was one of my five room-mates. Among the others were Len Hockey and Joe Cullen, the latter an amusing and extrovert character, although his tales of sexual prowess grew a bit tiresome until they drew the comment from a Polish officer of mature years:

'Vel, ven you get to my age you'd sooner have a hot dinner.' After that Joe seemed to think more about food. In a prisoner of war camp the sexual urge, in any case, soon disappeared, but one never forgot about food.

In the room opposite lived Captain Griffiths, a flying Marine, who had been taken prisoner very early in the war. Flying a Skua, he had bombed a German U-boat from a very low level, so low that he had been blown up by his own bombs, and subsequently taken on board the submarine he had attempted to destroy.

'I've got a plan, Jimmy,' said Bonington one day soon after our arrival.

'You always look as though you are planning, Charles,' I replied. Bonington, behind his polished Ampleforth and Oxford manner, was a tough little man with wary and watchful blue eyes, and a journalist's nose for opportunities.

'Yes, but this plan has the blessing of the escape committee. We dig a tunnel out from the corner of the next block to the Wash House – first leg – then the tunnel goes out across the sports area.'

'And out under the wire,' I continued. 'Nearly as long as Sydney Harbour Bridge.'

'It would be about three hundred feet altogether, I should think,' said Bonington. 'And I thought you would be just the chap to run the tunnelling side of it. As you know, my back got crocked when the aeroplane pranged.'

'OK, I'll do it,' I agreed, 'if you look after everything above ground, including reliable stooges.'

We got Griffiths, an experienced tunneller who had been in the Dulag Luft breakout, to run one of the shifts while I ran the other and we recruited about thirty more.

We made a trap in the floor of the room nearest the Wash House, then sunk the shaft to a depth of about six feet concealing it with the standard wooden trap covered with about two feet of soil when not in use. At the base of the shaft I had a large chamber made for storing sand from the tunnel. Unwisely it was constructed with a flat roof and was unshored.

Working one shift in the morning after *Appell* and one in the afternoon, with fat lamps for lighting and holes pushed up through the ground for air, we dug the tunnel out towards the Wash House. The sand from the face was pushed back down the tunnel by a human chain to the storage chamber whence it was dispersed under the block.

It was easy digging, but the flat roof of the storage chamber bothered me; so I collected some wood and went down one day to shore it up. I was just starting the job when there was a terrifying soughing noise, followed almost immediately by a 'Whoompf' and all was darkness. I was pinned down beneath an unquantifiable weight of sand. It seemed that the whole roof of the chamber had collapsed on top of me. I was unable to move my limbs, then I found that my head was free, and I called for help. Luckily, one of my team was nearby and he managed to dig me out after a while.

Two other ambitious tunnels were under way. One of them was run by Peter Fanshawe, now promoted to lieutenant-commander, with Ffrench-Mullen among the chief diggers, and the other by Muckle Muir. A feature of these tunnels was the enormous depth, fifteen feet below ground to defeat the seismographs, with no shoring and relying for air on holes pushed up to the surface with long sticks. There were some alarming and dangerous falls when these holes were made; the sand would come thundering down, building up to a great pyramid as the fall reached up to the top soil, often burying the digger below. The ferrets eventually noticed the air holes and the tunnels were discovered. Another fruitless effort; we were disappointed but not discouraged.

Tunnels continued to proliferate. A novel idea was introduced by Floody. In order to throw the ferrets off the scent, a crooked tunnel was devised so that the air holes were placed irregularly. No shoring was used and the right angled turns proved such an inherently unstable design in soft sand that the results were highly dangerous. After several diggers had been pulled out almost asphyxiated the project was abandoned.

One day that summer a parade was arranged at short notice for typhus injections in the sick quarters in the Vorlager. Charles Bonington and I decided that this would be an opportunity to break away while in the Vorlager and hide ourselves in the coal shed with a pair of wire-cutters; we thought it would then be fairly easy to cut through the Vorlager wire when darkness fell.

The wire-cutters were not available. Somebody else, it seemed, had booked them for another scheme. We should have to dig a tunnel – well, we were getting used to digging and the shed was close to the wire.

In sick quarters we avoided the injections, positioned ourselves in the middle of the long column of prisoners and as we passed the coal shed on the way back slipped inside.

The sound of the passing column faded as it headed back to the compound leaving us alone with several tons of coal in the silent shed. We scrabbled the coal out with our hands at the side of the shed nearest the wire, heaping up a wall of coal around us, until we got down to ground level. Then in a timeless vacuum of sand, sweat and coal dust we dug the shaft and over twenty feet of tunnel; we were about halfway to the wire, and it was the afternoon of the following day, when into the shed without warning stepped a German guard – it was raining and he came in to shelter. Although we crouched down behind our wall of coal, he must have seen the tops of our heads. He came over to investigate and another dream faded. We spent the next two weeks in the cooler.

The watch tower guard was aiming his rifle at two figures retreating into the pine forest; it seemed for a moment that a brilliant escape would end in tragedy. Wings Day, standing next to Jimmy Buckley, was about to shout at the guard, but Buckley restrained him. The two escapers, Flight Lieutenant Ken Toft, an Irishman, and Flying Officer Nicholls, an American of the Eagle Squadron, had nipped over the warning fence and gained the cover of the blind spot[1] beside the barbed wire fencing, from there they had quickly cut their way out and were away into the trees.

The operation had been organised by Buckley, and was a masterpiece of split-second timing between the diversion teams, watchers and escapers. Spellbound, those concerned watched the last phase in this unlikely phantasmagoria of which the two escapers were unaware. Slowly the guard lowered his rifle – if they were escaping prisoners, let them go, he was not going to be blamed for not having seen them sooner. Buckley's gamble had paid off.

Toft and Nicholls were caught soon afterwards. They deserved better luck; but, at least, they received a bottle of whisky from the Commandant in recognition of their daring feat.

Such magnanimity did not extend to Wing Commander Douglas Bader, the legless fighter ace, a very forceful personality who carried on his own private war against the Germans behind the wire. When it was suggested to Bader that he go to Lamsdorf Medical Compound so as to have better care and attention, he naturally refused. He was forcibly removed by the Commandant who appeared in the compound at the head of a large contingent of guards. He escaped from Lamsdorf and finished the war in Colditz.

New intakes of prisoners arrived from time to time and kept us in touch with the home front, and gave their opinions as to when there

---

[1] The watch tower was set back behind the double barbed wire fencing and the guard was unable to see the area immediately in front of it on the compound side due to the fence poles appearing as a solid wall to his line of vision. After this escape the watch towers were extended over the wire so that the guard could see between the poles.

would be a 'Second Front' – there was still two years to wait for that. Among the new arrivals were Squadron Leader Sherwood and other survivors of the low level daylight raid on Augsburg on 17 April 1942.

A notable new arrival was Group Captain H.M. Massey, DSO, MC who had been an RFC pilot in the first World War. He was flying with a Lancaster crew for experience, just before promotion to Air Commodore, when they were shot down – it also happened to be the crew's last operation before being put on rest. He told Wings, with whom he had served between the wars, to carry on as usual – he wished to be Senior British Officer in name only.

That summer the first US Army Air Force pilot entered the camp. He was Lieutenant Colonel Albert P. Clark, a tall red-headed young man of twenty-eight, later to become a General. He came at the height of a plague of flies and wasps which were making life unbearable in the compound. This stemmed from conditions in the outside latrines which were indescribable due to the insanitary method of construction and infrequent emptying. Clark, the son of a doctor who was a Health Inspector, knew how pit latrines should be constructed, and he led a campaign, with the SBO's approval, to improve conditions, with so much success that the Germans adopted his methods in other camps.

These sanitary operations led to a notable success by the escape organisation. A drainage ditch had been dug from the latrines to a point near the wire. Henry Lamond, a New Zealander, saw the opportunity for a 'mole' tunnel which he had invented at Barth. He got Jack Best and Goldfinch to join him. They hid in the drain one evening, and from there burrowed through the ground towards the wire in the fashion of the insectivorous animal after which the tunnel was named. Kept alive by air holes pushed up to the surface, they scrabbled the sand from the tunnel face pushing it back and filling in behind them. All that night and the next day they sweated underground in this moving tomb. They broke out the following night about midnight and were free for five days before being caught in a boat in which they were sailing up the River Oder. Best and Goldfinch were sent to Colditz from which they escaped again.

Some thirty to forty tunnels were dug from under blocks in the East Compound that summer, but none was successful; there was at least sixty yards to dig to the wire. Our tunnel ran into seepage from the wash house and had to be abandoned. The 'mole' tunnel was the only one to succeed.

Late that summer Roger Bushell, of whom no news had been heard since he sawed his way out of a cattle truck six months previously, came back to us from a Gestapo jail in Berlin. He had reached Czechoslovakia but was caught in Prague in the mass arrests following the assassination of Heydrich. The Gestapo had burst into a flat where he was in hiding and had taken him to Gestapo HQ in Berlin. Von Lindeiner's intervention had saved his life, and he was released with a warning that he would be shot if he attempted to escape again.

Bonington and I put our names down to go on a draft which was being sent off to a camp in Poland. A change of scenery was always welcome to a prisoner; the unknown beckoned and opportunities for escape could unfold in unexpected places.

In September 1942 we were on our way to Poland by train with Wings Day and about four hundred others.

CHAPTER SEVEN

Polish Interlude

Oflag XXI B sprawled over a gentle slope near the small town of Szubin in north-western Poland. Gloomy, brick-built barrack blocks stood at the highest point and brooded over the compound which contained a large white house, formerly a girls' school, a chapel and other buildings, and was interspersed with paths, an earth recreation area and even some sad-looking gardens which grew a few vegetables. The barbed wire perimeter and watch towers were familiar enough, but it was a change from the flat, sandy wire cages of Barth and Sagan.

Some Army and RAF NCOs were housed separately in the converted school stables.

Our living accommodation was primitive. The barracks were divided into two halves, with about 80 prisoners in each half. We positioned steel lockers and two-tier bunks to make small messes each containing about eight people, leaving a corridor down the middle. The bunks and palliasses were bug-infested and the outside communal lavatories stinking and festering. The camp was administered by German Army personnel whom Wing Commander 'Hetty' Hyde summed up as a 'bunch of bastards' when he handed over as SBO to Wings. Hyde was shot down in a Manchester bomber (the forerunner of the Lancaster) in 1941 and had been at Warburg with 400 RAF prisoners with whom he had come to Szubin.

Charles Bonington and I were in a mess which was furthest from the block entrance. This we were to appreciate before long. The night 'loo' was situated at the entrance and we were, therefore, spared to some extent the clattering noise of the nightly procession of clogged feet whose owners, under pressure of soup, ersatz coffee and cold, were induced to make frequent nocturnal journeys down the centre corridor.

Feldwebel Glemnitz, who had accompanied us from Sagan, had been rudely rebuffed by the German Army personnel in the Guard Room on arrival, after he had proffered advice on the handling of escape-conscious RAF prisoners of war. He had stormed back in a great rage shouting, 'These Army *Dummköpfe* – they know nothing, so I tell you escape!'

A speech greeted with a roar of approval, and shouts of: '*Befehl ist Befehl.*'

Wings had a stormy first meeting with the Commandant. Accustomed to civilized behaviour from Lindeiner and previous Luftwaffe Commandants, Wings had remained standing at ease while the Colonel barked out his instructions. The Commandant with his cold blue eyes, flushed face and mien of a Prussian bully, bellowed at Wings to stand to attention. Wings reminded him that he was a Wing Commander and, therefore, of equal rank to the Colonel, and that he was also the Senior British Officer. The Commandant thumped the table and bawled that he was not to be spoken to by any prisoner without permission. Wings, mustering his Royal Marines parade ground voice, his six foot four inches towering over the German officer, loosed off a broadside which finally silenced the enemy. Saluting smartly, Wings turned on his heel and marched out. Subsequent interviews were conducted coldly and politely, but the answer to any request was always in the negative.

The stage was set under harsh Teutonic management, with a backdrop of grey autumnal Polish skies, for another act in this endless and weary saga of POW existence; but a change of scene put fresh heart into flagging spirits already jaded by up to three years incarceration. The turn of the tide on the world stage was a further reason for encouragement. The Battle of Alamein had been won and Montgomery's Eighth Army 'was hitting Rommel for six' in the Western Desert. On the Russian front von Paulus' Army Group had been surrounded and decimated, except for the remnant which surrendered at Stalingrad.

I cannot recall a POW camp in which morale was so high. Activity seemed to burgeon in every corner; tunnels were being built under every stone, behind buildings and under latrines. Communal living made activity more pronounced – you could not fail to notice in a barrack room of eighty assorted 'kriegies' if somebody was busy assembling fabric (perhaps for a hot air balloon) making a German uniform, or just carrying earth from a tunnel to some dispersal point.

An early activity was the construction of scaling ladders for an assault on the wire, and the hammering and sawing by amateur carpenters rose above and added to the general cacophony for several weeks.

The proposed assault on the wire stemmed from a brilliant idea put to good effect at the Army Camp at Warburg where four teams each of ten persons with a ladder apiece stormed the wire one night after the perimeter lights had been fused – each having an extension which was pushed up and tilted over to bridge the two perimeter fences. Nearly all got clear of the camp; there was a lot of shooting but the only casualty was one officer slightly wounded in the foot. Two Army officers got home. It was called Operation Olympia.

A similar operation was now to be mounted at Szubin. It was to be called Operation Forlorn Hope – an unfortunate name. A Fleet Air Arm Officer, Lieutenant Commander Norman Quill, trained two teams with naval precision. On the night the boundary lights were fused by throwing a wire cable over the lighting cables. The teams dashed forward like naval gun teams and threw their ladders against the wire; almost simultaneously the lights came on again, and the operation went into reverse at great speed. The Germans had brought their emergency lighting system into operation.

The night was made hideous by the stamping of boots and the shouting of guards and the security staff. They were convinced that an escape had been made and milled around the barrack rooms for hours counting and recounting the uncooperative prisoners.

The escape committee, headed by the breezy and efficient Jimmy Buckley, had instigated and encouraged a good deal of this activity to take full advantage of the opportunities arising in a new camp when German security could often be caught off guard. The distance to the wire from the blocks was short and several blitz tunnels had been started.

Bonington and I had already staked our claim in the hard earth of Szubin. We worked first on an outside tunnel run by Panton which ran into a patch of rock, and was abandoned in favour of a tunnel from an outside latrine. Access to the new tunnel was through one of the lavatory seats above the stinking cess pit, thence a noisome and rather hazardous transit through a trap in the brick wall behind and into the chamber being constructed for storage of earth. Here it was necessary to operate with picks as the ground was so hard – a real contrast to Sagan sand.

Flight Lieutenant Edwards, a Fairey Battle pilot – pre-war he had flown Hawker Harts on the North-West Frontier – rose to his feet one morning after breakfast: 'I'm browned off with this place,' he announced casually, 'I'm going over the wire.'

His comrades had heard it before. 'Have a good circuit,' somebody said, as he ambled out; but this time it was to be a short circuit.

When he was half-way around, Edwards stepped over the warning fence, made for the wire and started to climb up.

'*Halt – oder ich schiesse,*' shouted the guard as he levelled his rifle at the lone figure climbing up the inside fence. Edwards continued, undeterred, and as he placed his hand on the top strand of wire the guard fired – his body shuddered, the hand relaxed its grip, and he dropped like a stricken bird to earth.

There was a near riot when the Germans refused to allow us to approach the dying man. I remember seeing him carried off on a stretcher, ashen-faced and badly wounded in the groin, to die in the camp hospital shortly afterwards.

Another tragedy struck soon after. A young flying officer called Lovegrove fell off the top of the big white house, used as a hospital, to crash to his death three storeys below on the concrete path at the entrance. He was a member of the mapping intelligence department, and a desire to get a good view for his survey had toppled him to his death.

Under bleak November skies we watched a party of Polish Jews working in the swampy area below the camp. They were being employed to do some work on one of the drainage canals; under pitiless Nazi overseers, they were beaten to the ground for the smallest peccadillo, the women forced to urinate in full view in the open.

In the shadow of these tragic events, life continued at a high pitch. Half a dozen tunnels were edging out towards the wire, and I still worked my rather smelly sessions in the latrine tunnel. Football matches were played regularly. I played at right back for my block which finished, I remember, near the top of the league. Although hardly First Division standard it was good 'kriegie' football which induced frenzied inter-block rivalry. A pantomime was in preparation for Christmas. A programme of lectures on various subjects was underway. I continued my Russian studies under George Parker, whose mother was Russian. As he presided gloomily over his class, huddled in his greatcoat, his long saturnine face and disdainful expression gave credence to his claim to be descended from the Kings of Georgia. However, his Royal mien belied a dry sense of humour. He was a good teacher, and I even reached the stage where I was able to teach an elementary class the Cyrillic alphabet and the rudiments of grammar. I rounded off my studies with a scientific subject-celestial navigation, by which the old, slow bombers could be navigated. This was quite a popular class taken by the Naval expert, Peter Fanshawe.

Spiritual needs were attended to by the resident padre in the camp chapel for Anglicans. The Roman Catholics at first had no opportunity to attend Mass, but the SBO made a request to the Commandant for a priest to visit. This was one request that was granted and thereafter a priest visited regularly.

The Poles were extremely cooperative, in spite of the death penalty if they were caught helping prisoners of war. Polish workmen came into the camp nearly every day and regularly lent us their passes and other documents for copying; through them we were in contact with families in the neighbourhood and also with the Polish Underground. As an example, a Polish girl used to send in a camera. Photographs for passes were taken under strict security, then camera and film were smuggled out again. The Polish girl developed the film overnight and the photographs were usually in the hands of the escape organisation in the morning. Documents and forged passes were often buried in tins in the garden or sewn into a medicine ball.

The 'blitz' tunnels had been discovered. There were now three long-term tunnels underway for use in the spring; Panton's latrine tunnel running north, and two running west, one from a barrack and the other from a latrine near the wire. Earth was dispersed either in the latrines or spread over the gardens, a relatively easy matter as the buildings could be used for cover. Two men cut their way through the wire using wire-cutters made from stove bars, and somebody else went out hidden on a lorry, but they were all caught again.

A batch of American aircrew officers arrived, full of enthusiasm and exuberance. This grated on the older prisoners, particularly when their escape plans ran foul of RAF initiatives. One young American, still in his flying boots, was found entangled in the wire with a pair of home-made wire-cutters, in defiance of the escape committee. He was lucky not to have been shot by the guard.

The Senior American Officer was Colonel 'Rojo' Goodrich, a West Point graduate and Southerner with wiry red hair and complexion to match, from which his nickname was derived. Wings gained his confidence, and together they tamed the young American frontier spirit and channelled it into more productive efforts – within the guidelines born of the hard experience of the older prisoners.

The only Home Run during this period was scored by the NCOs. On 16th December a RAF Sergeant, P.T. Wareing, walked away when collecting bread from Szubin station. Travelling on foot and by bicycle he reached Danzig and hid aboard a coal ship. He reached

Halmstad, Sweden, just in time for Christmas 1942.

That Christmas at Szubin, my third in captivity, is memorable for a pantomime written by Alastair Panton, and for a liberal, by 'kriegie' standards, supply of home-made hooch. Unforgettable was the Royal Christmas Card addressed to the RAF prisoners of war at Szubin, bearing the Royal Arms with a photograph of the King and Queen and the two Princesses. The Germans were impressed by this thoughtful gesture.

On New Year's Day there was a repeat performance of the pantomime. At the end of the show Wings strode onto the stage and called for attention.

'I've asked you to stay,' he began in his booming voice, 'because I have a New Year's message for you. I'll make it short. You are aware that it is everybody's duty to escape if possible. I have been accustomed to polite and correct treatment by Luftwaffe Commandants. Here I have not received this courtesy, in fact this Wehrmacht Commandant has been damned rude to me. He hopes to retire as a General. He won't.' His voice rose to a crescendo. 'I intend to get people out in large numbers. So get busy. Happy escaping and a Happy New Year.'

This verbal blast, starkly martial in its simplicity and directness had a powerful impact on weary prisoners, instilling fresh enthusiasm into dedicated escapers, lifting flagging spirits and impressing even the sceptics.

Almost simultaneously the chilling blast of an East European winter enveloped the camp in a blanket of ice and snow. Temperatures dropped to about 20° below zero Fahrenheit at night. In the cold, draughty barrack rooms we tried to keep warm by piling all our clothes on top of the threadbare army blankets, made even more necessary by the old British propensity for fresh air; all windows were flung open after lights out regardless of outside temperature. We were sometimes lulled to sleep by a selection of gramophone records played by Flight Lieutenant Churchill – a sort of 'kriegie' Hundred Best Tunes.

Food was in short supply with only half a Red Cross parcel each a week in addition to the usual German ration of soup and potatoes at mid-day and sausage, marge and bread in the evening. To add to the winter of our discontent the Germans continually carried out searches, and inhabitants of blocks were moved, in turn, down to the old wooden bug infested huts at the bottom of the compound.

Regular processions of prisoners trudged through the snow carrying or dragging their assorted possessions. George Parker solved the problem by piling his belongings onto an old pram which he called 'Speriamo'. There was always hope, but George had to wait two years before he pushed 'Speriamo' to liberation on the winter march of 1945 from Sagan.

Flight Lieutenant 'Spud' Murphy was the hard-working compound adjutant. Spud had been shot down in a Whitley over Norway in April 1940. He also had a long wait for the winter march on which he was to have his own form of transport.

A radio had been made from parts smuggled in from Sagan. Variable condensers were made from old biscuit tins, cut to shape and insulated by melted-down gramophone records, paper formers held coils wound to match condensers, while a piece of paper with a pencil line acted as resistor. The valve was the only component not home-made, and this had been appropriated from a radio store by a sergeant on a working party.

The radio was kept well hidden in the daytime; it was brought out at night to tune in to the BBC News. The following day the barrack room news announcers, of whom I was one, gathered to be briefed on the previous night's broadcast by Sydney Smith[1] who was news editor. We had to memorize it. Then back in our blocks, standing up on a chair, like town criers we assembled the inmates and relayed news of the latest Allied advances in North Africa on the East Front and in Burma, and now there was nearly always a report of a heavy bombing raid, usually in the Ruhr. At last the tide seemed to be turning, and these were heartening interludes carried out, of course, under strict security.

I continued to work regular shifts on Panton's latrine tunnel. One of the stooges had the undignified and rather odorous task of sitting on the throne above the trap, so that he could pass pre-arranged signals quickly in the event of 'goons in the abort'. He would have been assured a high place in the breakout, but in the event the tunnel had to be abandoned because of excessive moisture.

The west latrine tunnel, run by an enthusiastic and capable Canadian, Flight Lieutenant Eddie Asselin, was nearing completion. The entrance was through one of the lavatory seats, then a trap in the brick wall behind led into a large chamber from which

---

[1] Squadron Leader Sydney Smith DFC; after the war Foreign Correspondent of the *Daily Express*, and author of *Wings Day*. He had already made one escape.

the tunnel went out beyond the wire to a length of 150 feet, diving at one point to a depth of 17 feet to avoid the seismographs.

On the day planned for the breakout the escapers would have to be battened down inside the tunnel between *Appell* at 5 p.m. and lock up at 9 p.m. It was estimated that thirty-three people could be accommodated in the tunnel for some six hours without suffocating. Additionally there were to be ten 'ghosts' who would go into hiding as soon as the break out had been made. This would have the dual purpose of misleading the Germans as to the actual number who had gone through the tunnel, and would be useful cover for later escapers up to a total of ten.

On the afternoon of 5th March just before the night of the tunnel break, Flight Lieutenant Joe Bryks and Squadron Leader Morris departed inside the sewage disposal wagon. Joe was a Czech, known to us as Ricks to protect his family in Czechoslovakia; he spoke both Polish and German and was the main contact with the resistance outside. He had arranged for the Polish driver to leave his wagon, duly rinsed out, inside the camp for an hour or so. The Pole had then returned to drive it through the gate with its human contents; a brave act, as he would certainly have been shot if caught. As it was, the two men would be presumed to have escaped through the tunnel.

'Your turn to be put down, sir.' Wings could have wished for a more encouraging turn of phrase as he received this message shortly after five o'clock from one of the 'undertakers', as members of the despatching party were called.

The air in the tunnel was foul as the escapers lay head to foot in the damp, black void waiting interminably for the breakout. The air pump supplied sewage tainted air to bursting lungs. Asselin, Buckley and those who had worked on the project were near the head of the tunnel. They were followed by officials of the escape organisation, administration and entertainments selected by the SBO, and lastly the SBO, Wings Day.

When it seemed that this nightmare of black, airless claustrophobia would be their lot for ever there was a whiff of fresh air. It was just after 9 p.m. and Asselin had broken out. Slowly like a human centipede the line of escapers started to wriggle forward, gasping and lunging through the narrow tunnel. There were unaccountable stops when the black silence closed in once more. Were they going to die in this rat hole after all? Then the feet in front would start slithering forward, accompanied by heavy breathing and low cursing, and the awkward wriggle would begin again. At last the exit shaft was reached and the escaper, after ascertaining the position of the guard on the wire, staggered out into the potato patch and began his journey.

Buckley and Thompson, a Dane whose real name was Jorge Thalbitzer, were heading for Denmark whence they hoped to cross to Sweden. Aidan Crawley[1], with a forged letter from Krupps identifying him as a travelling executive, was heading west by train. Peter Stevens, Jewish-born in Germany whose first language was German, was going in the same direction. Danny Krol and Otto Cerney, a Pole and a Czech, were making for their respective countries. Most of the others were on foot heading for the Baltic ports.

In the camp early the next morning the first prisoners up and about were walking round the circuit doing a discreet inspection of 'Asselin' and found it undiscovered. A fast thinking Wing Commander, 'Happy' Hull, nipped back to his block, collected his escape kit, and was through the tunnel and away across the fields without detection.

The Commandant was now 45 men short, including the 'ghosts' and the two who went out on the disposal wagon, and he was not long to remain at his post. He was replaced by a courteous and correct Austrian. Wings' New Year speech had not been an idle boast.

After the escape 300,000 German troops were diverted to search the area surrounding the camp and all frontier areas, in addition to thousands of police and Home Guard, backed by a vast network of telephone lines.

All the escapers, with the exception of Buckley and Thompson[2], were recaptured within two weeks and returned to the camp for two weeks cooler. Some of the train travellers put a good distance between themselves and the camp. Crawley was caught on the Austrian border between Munich and Innsbruck. Tommy Calnan and Robert Kee[3], disguised as Italian and French workers respectively, after spending one of the nights out in a dog kennel, were caught in Cologne on 9th March. Tony Barber[4], although he

[1] Parliamentary Under Secretary of State for Air in the post-war Labour Government

[2] Thompson's body was washed ashore near Copenhagen, but no trace of Buckley was ever found. It is thought that the small boat in which they were attempting to cross to Sweden had been run down by a ship on a foggy night.

[3] The well known broadcaster.

[4] Chancellor of the Exchequer in the Tory Government 1970-74.

spoke Danish and had papers as a Danish worker, was picked up by the Gestapo after a few days. The 'ghosts' were discovered after a month in hiding during which time the Germans had been looking for them all over Europe.

This escape attracted the attention of the SD (Sicherheitsdienst, the Intelligence Arm of the Gestapo). For a month they took over the administration of the camp; all camp staff were interrogated and all the Wehrmacht officers were court-martialled. The compound was full of SD men, the barracks were searched and turned upside down. But they could display curiously flat-footed incompetence. In one barrack there was a barrel of beer, and Lieutenant Commander 'Bungie' Bracken, a whimsical naval pilot, did a good trade selling them glasses of beer for Reichsmarks which went straight into the escape fund. One SD Officer sat on the barrel which had a false bottom concealing most of the forged papers and maps in the compound. Their biggest error was one of omission.

Beneath the night latrine at the end of the block near the west wire lurked another large tunnel. Run by Squadron Leader David Strong and Dickie Edge, it had electric light tapped from the mains and was shored, but it was undetected by the SD. It was discovered not long after the SD had left, through carelessness; a guard spotted what was almost the last box of earth being passed out of the window. The barrack was searched and the tunnel was found; by this time it was 110 feet in length and 60 feet beyond the wire.

This marked the end of a long hard winter in Poland. Early in April the camp, which now contained nearly 800 prisoners, was evacuated to Sagan.

There was a false start. On the proposed day of departure we were loaded into cattle trucks at the station – giving the escape-minded, particularly those with saws, cause for rejoicing. The wily Glemnitz knew quite well that he could expect to lose a few prisoners along the line. He protested to the Army authorities that he would not be responsible for escorting such an escape-conscious gang of 'kriegies' in this form of transport. After about half an hour we were told that cattle trucks were not good enough for officers, and we were marched back to the camp.

The next day we set off in Third Class carriages. The train stopped for the night in a siding in Poznan surrounded, it seemed, by all the police in town. Late the next evening we were back in Sagan.

CHAPTER EIGHT

North Compound, Stalag Luft III

The tang of freshly cut timber pervaded the desiccated spring air of Sagan. The stumps of hewn trees jutted sadly from what had recently been the forest floor, but was rapidly being transformed into a desert encircled by nearly a mile of barbed wire fencing and guard boxes – a fresh cage containing numerous newly built barrack huts, kitchens and latrines for the incarceration of up to 1,500 aircrew who continued to arrive in ever increasing numbers.

When I arrived in mid-April 1943 with most of the Szubin contingent, including Wings Day, Goodrich and Fanshawe, a few trees were still standing giving the semblance and dim hope of environmental preservation.

In the previous fortnight since the arrival of a large party from the East Compound, in which a number of prisoners remained, the number of trees leaving the compound had almost been equalled by the number of 'kriegies' accompanying them; but most of the would be escapers had not gone further than the gate. 'Scharnhorst' Cross[1] had climbed underneath one of the vehicles which had then proceeded on a zig-zag course over the roughest ground, coming to a stop at the gate where the ubiquitous Glemnitz jumped down from the front seat and called, 'Herr Cross, you can come out from under now – the rest of the journey will be on foot to the cooler.'

We lost the trees. In spite of the SBO's protest to the Commandant, they were chopped down on security grounds.

I found my old friend Len Hockey installed in a room with two South Africans, Flekser and Bergh and a Rhodesian, Tapson, all casualties of the North African campaign, and McDonald, a chummy New Zealand Bank man who had been navigator on a Lancaster. I joined them in the sixth and last bunk available.

'Well, young Jim,' said Hockey, an old man of thirty, 'this big Boer farmer from the Cape,' indicating Bergh, 'has volunteered to do all the cooking for us.'

---

[1] Squadron Leader Ian Cross was awarded the DFC for bombing the German battle-cruiser *Scharnhorst*.

'I suppose that means the rest of us do room stooge once every five days,' I replied.

'That suits me,' said Flekser, a scientist from Johannesburg. 'I'll have time to get on with my studies in between washing up for you lot.'

'No time for tunnels this year, Flekser?' I asked. He had worked on my tunnel the previous year in the East Compound.

'No fear, I've had enough of sand – here and in the desert. If the other boys want to become generals they are welcome to work on as many tunnels as they like.'

He was referring to the group of South Africans who were persistent tunnellers. They didn't become generals. Some of them were shot by the Gestapo a year later.

The opportunistic sallies among the departing trees had served to cloak the big plans afoot for mass escape underground. From Conk Canton, who had become Roger Bushell's adjutant and who was always ready with news of any sort, I learnt that the X or Escape Organisation had literally got themselves dug in.

Under the direction of Roger Bushell, who was 'Big X', three tunnels were to be built on a massive scale; 'Tom' from Block 123 near the west wire, 'Dick' from the adjoining block further from the wire, and the fateful 'Harry' from Block 104 to go out under the wire on the north side and then under the Vorlager. Wally Floody, the Canadian who had done such sterling work in the East Compound, would be the engineering expert in charge of tunnelling. They would be like small mines – vertical shafts sunk to 25 feet, the tunnels were planned to thrust out for hundreds of feet at this depth to avoid the seismographs, complete with air pumps, air lines, electric lighting tapped from the mains and railways.

'Isn't dispersal going to be a problem with tons of sand coming out of these mines?' I asked.

'That's all taken care of,' replied Conk confidently, 'Hornblower who is i/c dispersal has just come up with a brilliant idea. Trouser bags hanging down inside trouser legs, the ends secured by pins operated by strings leading up to each pocket, and the penguins just amble round the compound with their hands in their pockets trickling sand out when the goons aren't looking.'

Vast quantities of wood were going to be needed for shoring the tunnels in the treacherous yellow sand at such depths. Squadron Leader John Williams, an Australian, in charge of carpentry, sent his men to all corners of the compound to levy bed boards, remove boards from the double flooring under huts, strip battens off walls or commandeer any suitable timber available. Johnny Travis, who had been a mining engineer in Rhodesia, was a key man in the engineering section, together with the Australian, Digger McIntosh, shot down on the suicide Maastricht raid in May 1940, and Muckle Muir. Tin bashing was one of their specialities, which included making air lines from Klim Milk tins out of Red Cross parcels.

Tim Walenn expanded his 'Dean & Dawson' Travel Bureau for forging documents; the red-moustachioed Plunkett ran the mapping section; clothing, both civil and German military tailoring, was under Tommy Guest.

This complex organisation could not have functioned without strict and efficient security, with watchers or stooges placed at strategic points covering every part of the compound when work was in progress. This was the responsibility of George Harsh, an American in the RAF; past his mid-thirties with greying temples, tall and sardonic, he had an air of rugged distinction and controlled security tightly, ably assisted by Tom Kirby-Green. I joined his organisation.

From now on no private tunnelling was to be allowed. All resources and experience were to be pooled in 'Tom', 'Dick' and 'Harry'. The traps concealing their entrances were the most sophisticated yet devised and were constructed by Polish officers who were expert engineers. 'Tom's' trap was in the concrete floor of a small passage beside the kitchen. 'Dick's' trap was in the sump in the centre of a wash room – the sump was normally half full of water, but could be drained quite easily to operate the trap which was in the concrete wall at the side. 'Harry's' trap was probably the most elaborate. In every living room there was an iron stove which rested on a tiled base. These tiles were taken up in one room and fixed onto a wooden platform which was made to hinge up and down. The shaft was sunk immediately below it. The stove was equipped with detachable wooden handles so that it could be quickly moved whether alight or not. With three such tunnels being constructed simultaneously it was possible that one might succeed.

The excitement and activity of escape planning could not erase the dull monotony of prison camp existence. You noticed it, of course, more particularly in a period when there was a lull in escaping activity, after tunnels had been found, or there was a dearth of ideas which was not very often. Indeed, however you occupied your time, and most people kept busy doing something, there was always the consciousness of captivity – dense and impenetrable barbed wire, guards, guns and dogs, pressing in on the harshly symmetrical lines of the bare wooden barrack blocks, each with a dark central corridor flanked by a dozen identical rooms with uniform two-tiered bunks, tables and stools.

Freedom was a dim memory and it was hard to conceive of life other than as a prisoner of war; the early morning call to *Appell*, often exhorted by shouts of *'Raus, 'raus, schnell'*, from the guards, the sleepy shuffle out to the parade ground where, lined up in blocks, we would be called to attention by the stentorian voice of Bill Jennens, the adjutant, the equally powerful bellow of Wings Day would tell somebody to 'Put that bloody cigarette out', the routine count by Pieber and his staff.

Then the daily chores, if you were room stooge, washing up dishes, sweeping the room out, queuing for dhobie water, or queuing for soup at the kitchen, walking round the compound (circuit bashing), reading the notices on the camp notice board, just reading or playing cards, 'bunk bashing' until evening *Appell*, then supper, usually the main meal, doors locked and shutters closed at 22.00 hours, followed by more talking or 'line shooting' by new 'kriegies' – soon cured after everybody in the room had been more than well acquainted with how the chap baled out over 'Happy Valley' (The Ruhr) or ditched in the North Sea – and lights out at 23.59 precisely. Such an existence is epitomised in the famous words of Winston Churchill who was a prisoner in the Boer War:

> . . . a melancholy state. You are in the power of your enemy. You owe your life to his humanity, your daily bread to his compassion. You must obey his orders, await his pleasure, possess your soul in patience. The days are very long. Hours crawl like paralytic centipedes. Moreover the whole atmosphere of prison is odious. You feel a constant humiliation in being fenced in by railings and wire, watched by armed men. . . .

If you let it get in on you too much, you could go mad – and some did, barbed wire psychosis in its ultimate form.

The will to survive is strong, and we kept sane by keeping active in various pursuits. Besides, new prisoners were frequently appearing with news of the outside world. The old regulars mostly turned up as much decorated Senior Officers and as likely as not had been pilot officers with you somewhere at the beginning of the war. There was time promotion to flight lieutenant for POW's. There was a large admixture of aircrew who came from all walks of life, in fact, by this time, the regulars were far outnumbered by the war-time volunteers. The compound now contained about 1,200 prisoners. People pursued many and diverse activities; they lived in worlds of their own which interpenetrated and met in the communal life we were forced to share.

The stage exercised the talents of many. The Germans had surprised us by putting a site at our disposal and allowing us to build our own theatre; a project in which most people took part, helping to move tons of sand, and humping bricks and materials for the experts to assemble. The result was an auditorium which held 350 seats, made from Canadian Red Cross plywood crates, stage and indirect lighting and other refinements.

Wing Commander Larkin, a versatile man who played the guitar, among other accomplishments, became entertainments officer and under his direction, with the talents of Kenneth McIntosh, producer, actor and director, Rupert Davies, of *Maigret* fame, Peter Butterworth, well known in the *Carry on* series, Tolly Rothwell who wrote the *Carry On* series, John Casson, son of Sybil Thorndike, Pat Greenhous, Anthony Ffrench-Mullen and many others, a series of West End plays were produced, eventually at the rate of one a fortnight – *Rookery Nook, Design for Living, Pygmalion, Macbeth, Blithe Spirit*. These and many others helped us to forget the barbed wire for a little while and were a big factor in helping to keep up morale. One man arrived in the camp with a ticket for *Arsenic and Old Lace* which he had hoped to see in London, but heavy flak over Germany obliged him to change his plans and he saw it instead at Sagan!

The theatre was also the home of an excellent symphony orchestra of some forty musicians covering a full range of instruments conducted by Arthur Creighton, and of the Jazz Band, a leading member of which was the bearded Canadian, Hardy de Forest.

Another enterprise undertaken by the prisoners was the creation of a sports area. This entailed much back-breaking work removing the numerous tree stumps and levelling the ground for soccer, rugger, cricket or any other sport for which individuals had the strength in which to compete. I ran in the mile in the camp sports that summer; I just managed to stagger across the finishing line and felt ill and weak for several days afterwards. The Red Cross parcels with the German rations were just sufficient to sustain normal life, but allowed for little extra physical effort. The diet for escapers was supplemented by a concentrated escape ration according to a formula worked out by Lieutenant Eric Lubbock of the Fleet Air Arm who was a dietetic expert of international repute.

Academic endeavour played a big part in the life of the camp and was directed by Harvey Vivian as at Barth. There was a large reference and lending library, the books sent by both the Red Cross and the YMCA. We had qualified lecturers for most subjects, examination papers issued by professional bodies through the Red Cross, the examinations properly invigilated by 'education types'. It was a profitable way of passing the time, but there were drawbacks.

Continual study within the close confines of the compound was like wearing blinkers. When there was no more need to study the blinkers were removed and the barbed wire and 'goon boxes' once more crowded in on the senses. In a few cases this led to temporary insanity.

Lice carried typhus and were always viewed with alarm by the Germans. A typhus epidemic could spread well beyond barbed wire. At Sagan, any de-lousing necessary was always done in the East Compound. Here was a splendid opportunity to find some lice, alert the Germans and then put to good use the de-lousing programme they would surely introduce.

On a warm day in June, the 'louse alarm' having been duly triggered off, and after several de-lousing parties had gone through the gate, another party formed up escorted by two *Unteroffiziere* outfitted by the clothing department, two Belgian officers speaking fluent German. A forged pass took the party through both gates, and they set off down the road towards the other compound.

Following immediately after them was a party of six Senior Officers, including Colonel Goodrich, the Senior American Officer, and Wing Commander Bob Tuck, the fighter ace, also escorted by an *Unteroffizier*, Bob van der Stok a German-speaking Dutch officer. They passed through the first gate with a forged pass and the story that they were going for a special conference with the Commandant. At the second gate the guard became suspicious and telephoned the Security Officer. It was bad luck, but they had created the required diversion for the first party who, seeing the attention of the guards, who overlooked the road, fixed on the scene at the gate, melted into the woods and went their different ways, mainly to the railway station.

Major Broili, the Security Officer, was soon on the spot. He was delighted that the Senior Officers had been caught red-handed.

'You cannot fool our guards, you know,' he chuckled. One of the Senior Officers heartily agreed with him. Just then one of the guard-room personnel, who had become suspicious, ascertained on the phone that the first party had not arrived in the other compound, and told Broili.

Broili's face went pale, 'How many did you say were on that party?'

'Twenty-nine, Herr Major,' replied the guard.

'*Was? Neunundzwanzig,*' shrieked Broili, and rushed off to phone the Commandant.

After that we stood on the parade ground for several hours while the Germans counted and re-counted, checked and re-checked with individual photographs. All the escapers were caught, most of them at the station and in the woods around Sagan, but one of them managed to get within a few yards of freedom; he got into Czechoslovakia where the Czech underground bought him a new suit and sent him on his way by train to Switzerland. He was caught crossing the frontier.

Disappointment and frustration were sometimes dispelled by Red Cross dried prunes and raisins distilled by the camp brew masters in the production of hooch as at Barth, only the process was taken a stage further by double, or even treble, distillation resulting in genuine Sagan spirits. I remember one party for which a few gallons of this brew must have been saved.

From dawn on 4th July, 1943, the camp began to resound to the beating of drums and the blare of bugles as a bunch of 'Red Indians' followed by an army of American 'Colonists' emerged howling from their blocks to re-enact the Boston Tea Party with 'kriegie brew'. On this occasion the Americans were joined by the British, and together we marched round the compound and through the barracks singing and whooping as we celebrated American Independence – to the astonishment of the Germans who could not understand why the British, or for that matter, any nation, should want to celebrate the loss of colonies. The party culminated in Colonel Goodrich, Wings Day, Peter Fanshawe and a few more being thrown into the fire pool.

Underground, 'Tom', 'Dick' and 'Harry' were pushing ahead steadily and a considerable footage of tunnel, about sixty feet, had been completed on each. In August, it was decided to cease work on 'Dick' and 'Harry' and to concentrate on finishing 'Tom' as quickly as possible. There were two reasons for this. A rumour was abroad that a new compound was to be built to the west just where 'Tom' and 'Dick' were to come out; this gained some credence when a number of trees were cut down in this area. The other reason was that the new compound to the south was nearing completion, and Group Captain Massey had been told by the Commandant that the Americans, of whom there were now 500, would soon be moved into it. Many of the Americans had worked on the tunnels and we wanted them to have a chance of going out.

I was working shifts in the security organisation. One key position was at a window of a room overlooking the gate. The man who sat here was known as the 'Duty Pilot' whose job it was to check all traffic in and out of the gate, so that an exact record of ferrets and other Germans in the compound was always to hand.

One day Glemnitz strode up to the window and said, 'Mark me out, will you,' and was out of the gate before the startled Duty Pilot had recovered himself. The incident was reported to the escape committee who decided that the Duty Pilot should remain in situ since this was the only position from which an exact tally of 'goons' could be kept, and Glemnitz would soon spot any new position.

About a week later Glemnitz again walked up to the Duty Pilot's window, and asked, 'Has Rudi been in today?' The D.P. consulted his list and replied in the negative. 'Oh, hasn't he,' exclaimed Glemnitz, 'Rudi is for the cooler.'

Rudi, one of the ferrets, got four days in the cooler. Better still, 'Rubberneck', the chief ferret, received two weeks extra duty and confinement to barracks for failing on supervision.

About six hundred worked in the escape organisation in various capacities. This was nearly half the total number of prisoners in the compound. The remainder were not opposed to escaping and were always ready to help when required, even when brought to the limits of discomfort by frequent levies on bed boards for tunnel shoring. A number of the older 'kriegies' had grown weary of the grinding labour and frequent frustrations of tunnelling; although still willing to have a go if the opportunity occurred, they had mainly retired to follow other pursuits – entertainment, music, administration or just 'doing their own thing.'

There was a small group which did not fit into any normal category. They were known as the 'irreconcilables' – individualists who held extreme views, nurtured, mainly, on Engels, Jung and Freud, on all forms of human activity from politics to bird-watching.

These pseudo-philosophers found it hard to integrate in ordinary activities and their room-mates harder still to countenance them. Some rooms were found for them where they could be together and were free to drive one another 'round the bend'. In the modern climate of psychology and 'do gooding' they might have had a more difficult time, or perhaps some of them could have been protagonists of enforced psychiatry!

In September 'Tom' was pushing out fast and had reached the wire. There had been some bad falls, dangerous at such a depth, but diggers had luckily escaped injury. Fanshawe's Penguin organisation, which employed over 200 people, was getting rid of the sand as fast as it appeared. Then Glemnitz started a campaign in the area of block 123. A ferret had been seen watching in the woods opposite and had perhaps spotted some unusual activity in this area. At any rate, the block was searched several times, and others nearby; on a final search of 123, a ferret probing around the concrete floor in the passage outside the wash room with a pick axe, by pure chance, hit on the trap.

'Tom' went out in a blaze of glory. The tunnel was about three hundred feet in length, and the Commandant seemed to take great pride in showing it off to journalists and photographers from Berlin and boasting about what a wonderful tunnel his prisoners had made. A sapper from an engineer unit was brought in to blow it up. He placed an excessive charge, and half the roof of the hut was blown off. In addition one of the main drains of the camp was broken just beyond the perimeter wire, and the Germans had to dig down twenty feet to repair it. In the process a watch tower, with the guard in it, slowly subsided and came to rest at a crazy angle. 'Tom' had completed his bit for the war effort. (Appendix 'C')

Our American friends were taken off to their new compound a week later. We were sorry to see them go, but we soon established semaphore communication with them across the wire. The Germans liked to divide and rule. They offered the Canadians a 'nice new compound of their own'. The Senior Canadian said, 'Sure, if our British pals can come along too,' and the matter was dropped.

To lull the Germans all tunnelling was temporarily suspended. 'Dick,' and 'Harry' were sealed down. Passes, maps and compasses would be needed again, and work on these continued.

Under close security, Tim Walenn's team of artists produced to a high degree of accuracy the whole gamut of passes necessary in the Third Reich. Most of these were copied from originals obtained by the contacts of Wally Valenta, through a combination of bribery, blackmail or just picking pockets. Working three to four hours[1] a day for a year they produced 400 documents, many of which later carried escapers past stringent checks, and some back to England. Plunkett and his staff, who were dispersed throughout the compound, worked just as hard tracing and manufacturing, with a home-made mimeograph, maps showing escape routes to neutral and occupied countries. Al Hake, an Australian, produced a compass a day from melted down gramophone records and magnetised needles. Tommy Guest and his tailors worked industriously turning out business suits, German uniforms and any other sartorial gear required. Hockey produced imitation leather work in the form of belts and pistol holsters.

Roger Bushell ensured that all these escaping aids were immediately concealed in various hiding places – behind false walls of rooms or cupboards, down 'Dick' or in the outside earth latrines. Not a single item was lost in any of the frequent searches made by the Germans.

The man walking nonchalantly up to the wire in the NCOs' compound with a ladder over his shoulder was dressed in overalls, leather belt and German field service cap, and he carried an ammeter with leads dangling. He went to a spot near the guard tower, shouted to the sentry and passed over into the warning area. Placing his ladder against the inner fence he climbed up, spanned the two fences with a short plank onto which he scrambled, and proceeded to unscrew one of the perimeter lights which he tested with his ammeter.

He repeated the operation at the next light, but here he dropped his pliers into the dannert wire just inside the outer fence.

'Darf ich aussen den Stacheldraht niedersteigen um meine Zange zu holen?' he called to the guard.

'Jawohl,' came the reply.

The man climbed down and retrieved his tool.

[1] It was not possible to work longer for security reasons, as it was, some forgers suffered permanent injury to their eyes due to poor lighting and inadequate diet. The equipment used was generally primitive, pencils, ink, poor nibs, box of paint and brushes, some uneven rulers and set squares. 'Official' stamps were usually made from linoleum or the rubber heels of boots. Typewritten documents, surprisely, were the easiest things to forge, but for a mass escape a German was sometimes bribed to get a stencil done on a typewriter some distance from the camp.

'*Diese blutige Engländer,*' he exclaimed, as he walked away down the wire, '*Immer kummer.*'[1]

The guard chuckled and cursed.

Outside the line of vision of the guard boxes the man disappeared into the dark pine woods. George Grimson was on his way again after his third escape in German uniform. Unfortunately, he was recaptured five days later at Stettin trying to board a Swedish ship. His finest hour was still to come.

At the same time the NCOs were preparing to move to Heydekrug on the Baltic. They had arrived at Sagan with the officers, and had since been joined by a group from Camp IIe at Kitchain near Finsterwalde where the first mass escape of the war had taken place, fifty-two men through a tunnel 230 feet in length.

'Eyes right,' ordered James Deans, as the column of smartly marching men started to swing past the main gate of the officers' compound where Group Captains Massey and MacDonald with Wings Day came to the salute and held it until the long column had passed.

'*Verdammt,*' Hauptmann Pieber was heard to mutter, 'These men are soldiers. Why can't they do this when I take the parade?'

Let us follow the fortunes of the NCOs for a short while at their new camp on the Memel Peninsula, in Lithuania.

Within two days of arrival at Heydekrug, Bristow's radio was operational and the news readers were busy. In a very short time their 'Tally Ho' Escape Organisation run by Jock Alexander with Grimson and Morris, was planning and supervising a number of escape schemes which included several tunnels. One tunnel built from an outside 'abort' was successful; fifty men packed into the tunnel ready to go out, nine escaped, but the tenth was seen and the Germans started firing down the exit hole – luckily no one was hit.

The next day there was complete turmoil in the camp while the Germans attempted to make an accurate count of prisoners who kept disappearing and then reappearing again in greater numbers. Finally, the Germans placed three ladders together in the form of a sheep pen.

'Ve are going to have a sheep count,' announced the Lageroffizier.

There was a chorus of 'baas' as the prisoners were checked through the pen by an officer and several guards. But they had

---

[1] 'May I climb down outside the wire and get my pliers?' 'Yes, certainly.' 'These bloody English, always causing trouble.'

forgotten to guard the flanks and the prisoners just ran round the side and got counted again.

The Commandant came on the scene and asked Dixie Deans, 'Vy is this?'

Deans expressed suitable disbelief of the situation. But an Australian, Godfrey Loder, noted for his dry sense of humour, had his answer, 'You bastards treat us like flaming animals, so we're breedin'.'

The theatre, music and education flourished. Frank Hunt, now a Professor of Music, and Larry Slattery, who played for the London Philharmonic, ran a splendid classical orchestra and Eddie Alderton, who became a professor at an American university, organised a comprehensive educational programme, which became known as the barbed wire university.

The 'Tally Ho' organisation completed plans to get George Grimson out for a daring and complicated operation – the establishment of an escape route. One day in January 1944, Grimson walked out of the camp in German uniform complete with rifle. In the course of the following weeks he established along that part of the Baltic coast a chain of safe houses supplied with rations and equipment. In February he met Paddy Flockhart in Danzig and got him aboard a Swedish ship; ten days later he was back home. In April Grimson met Warrant Officer R.B.H. Townsend-Coles and Sergeant John Gilbert in Danzig following a message from the escape committee through a German contact, Munkert, an interpreter in the camp. Grimson managed to get Gilbert aboard a Swedish ship, and he also got home, but Townsend-Coles was caught and executed by the Gestapo. Munkert was arrested later and also executed.

Grimsom himself disappeared shortly afterwards in '*Nacht und Nebel*[1]' a very courageous and self-sacrificing man.[2]

A very remarkable Home Run was scored by a young warrant officer navigator called Cyril Rofe. In August 1944 he slipped away from a working party near Thorn in Poland with a companion, Karl Hillebrand a corporal in the British Army. The risks were high because they were both Jewish. The first part of the journey was by train. When the woman ticket collector had looked at their travel documents, she took them and showed them to some people sitting

[1] 'Night and Fog' Hitler's decree of 1941 empowering Secret Police to seize anyone endangering German security and make them vanish without trace.

[2] *The Sergeant Escapers* by John Dominy.

opposite, 'Look, you should have travel permits like these,' she said, handing the forged documents back to the startled escapers. After five weeks on foot through Poland and Czechoslovakia, during which time they became separated somehow, Cyril met a party of Cossacks in the Carpathians. They supplied him with a horse and, although he had never ridden before, he rode with them in a cavalry charge through the German lines. Led by the Colonel with drawn sabre, about 100 Cossacks in their red-topped fur hats burst out of a wood into a bare valley covered by German fire. They galloped on, men and horses fell all around but they gained the Soviet lines – and Cyril Rofe was free at last, after over three years in captivity. His companion, Karl, also managed to cross the lines in a different place.[1]

The shadow of the Gestapo was beginning to fall over prisoner of war camps. By 1942 Dulag Luft which had been a small transit camp for RAF, had become a big Interrogation Centre for Allied aircrew, incorporating some dubious methods of interrogation including overheated cells. The Commandant, Colonel Killinger, and his staff were not in favour of these methods. They were put on trial after the war but cleared of guilt. Their struggle against Nazi brutality is illustrated in the incident of the captured British airman who was walking between two guards when they met an SS officer who ordered them to shoot the prisoner. When they refused he drew a revolver and shot the airman himself. Colonel Killinger immediately travelled to Berlin to protest at this outrage.

In April 1943 an Order of the German High Command expressed concern at the increasing number of prisoners escaping in German uniforms and in civilian clothing.

The order went on to state: 'Each POW has to be informed that by escaping in civilian clothing or German uniform he is not only liable to disciplinary punishment but runs the risk of being court martialled and committed for trial on suspicion of espionage and partisanship, in the affirmative he may even be sentenced to death.'

There was no doubt that the Nazi High Command was now taking a serious view of the increasing number of escapes from POW Camps and was alarmed at the ever growing resources required to counter these escapes with the consequent detrimental effect on the German war effort.

The import of the above order was underlined and spelt out in a

[1] *Against the Wind* by Cyril Rofe

letter dated 6th October, 1943, from the Commandant to Group Captain Kellett, the SBO of the East Compound at Sagan:

> In order to remove all doubts and as a warning to POW's the action of POW's which may lead to an examination by a Court Martial and possibly to a sentence by the Court are set out below,
> 1 All assaults on any person or any actions damaging to the German war effort.
> 2 The following are to be regarded as damaging to the German war effort:
> [There followed sub paras (a) to (e) which listed destruction or damage to buildings and equipment, theft of bed boards for tunnel building, alteration of uniforms, the theft of tools or materials, unjustified use of electric power in tunnel building, forgery or theft of papers, maps, etc.]
> 3 It is again emphasised that any person found in the uniform of a German soldier or official or in civilian clothes must expect to be examined by a court martial on suspicion of espionage, sabotage or banditry.
> You are required to bring the above to the notice of all POW's.
>
> von Lindeiner,
> Colonel and Commandant.

This letter was circulated to the Senior Officers in the other compounds and all prisoners were made aware of its contents.

It had undoubtedly followed on the large number of escapes at Sagan, culminating in the brilliant 'Wooden Horse' Escape from the East Compound.

All was quiet in the North Compound as autumn faded into winter. Two men managed to cut their way through the wire and get down to the Czech border before being recaptured. Two more tried to get over the wire after a guard in one of the watch towers had been 'squared', but they were seen by the other guard, shot at and recaptured.

Valenta's intelligence contact organisation was functioning very effectively. In one case a German *Gefreiter* who had been 'tamed' was asked to go to Paris to contact French Resistance and obtain from them certain passes used by French workers in Germany. He agreed, his fare was paid by the 'X' organisation and he brought back the passes. One of the most remarkable pieces of information was obtained by Sydney Dowse; his contact Hesse, who was in the censorship department, reported that his girlfriend, an Austrian Baroness with influential connections, had been in the vicinity of Peenemünde and had noted a large number of scientists engaged on war work involving rocket-propelled missiles. As usual we got this important information back to England, and there is good reason to suppose that it helped to shorten the war by many months.

I continued my German and Russian studies, the latter with a cheerful Polish officer called Hubicki who was a very good teacher. I sat and passed my Royal Society of Arts examinations in both languages. I still hoped for the opportunity of using these languages outside the wire. I was not to be disappointed.

In November 1943, Major C.R. Diamond, a past member of the philharmonics, brought his Glenn Miller band from the South Compound and played to enthusiastic audiences on four successive days. On the last day, while walking back to their compound they played 'America' to the annoyance of the Germans who forthwith banned them from practising for four weeks.

It was a White Christmas, as always in these parts. Frank Bergh, our 'Cape Cook' excelled himself by making an enormous cake and producing two large meals for our room. He must have been saving rations for months. Six pairs of representative 'trotters' – two South African, one Rhodesian, one New Zealand, one English and one Anglo-Canadian (myself) – were well dug in for much of the day. Len Hockey arranged the 'brew' which was more potent than usual.

One syndicate managed to produce a brew which was 87% proof on the doctor's analysis. On this festive season some bottles of the stuff were given to Germans as presents. One of the guards was given a bottle on one freezing night; he drank it all in a minute or two and collapsed. The two dogs with him dragged their master one hundred yards across the snow to the gate. He was then given twenty-one days in the cooler. Another guard in a watch tower was thrown up a bottle; he also drank it at one sitting after which he fell out of his box. His fate is not recorded.

CHAPTER NINE

The Odds Lengthen

Early in January 1944 I was pacing round the snow-blanketed compound on my daily circuits when I met Peter Fanshawe, the Dispersal Chief, pacing the 'quarter deck' in the opposite direction.

'Ah, Jimmy,' he hailed, 'I've been looking for you. How would you like a job?'

'Well, I am unemployed at the moment as most of us are,' I admitted, 'and if I have to stick around this place much longer, I'll be permanently unemployable. What's cooking?'

'"Harry" is being opened up and I want you to run a dispersal team under the theatre.'

'Well, it will be a change from digging,' I replied. 'But under the theatre – that sounds like a bright idea.'

'Yes,' said 'Hornblower'. 'As you know we built it ourselves and the "below decks" part of the auditorium floor is completely enclosed. Sand will be brought from the tunnel in kit bags after dark and emptied down the trap which Travis has been making underneath one of the seats. As far as I can see, we shall need two dispersal teams with about six chaps on each – you'll be in charge of one and Cross will be in charge of the other. I've done a recce underneath and there is plenty of room. I'd like you both to come and have a look at it this afternoon.'

I noticed that the number of the seat was 13. I am not normally superstitious – except for lucky omens, like black cats – but weeks later I had very good reason to give some credence to the ill omen engendered by this number. Swinging the seat back on the specially constructed Travis hinges, Ian Cross and I clambered down through the trap into the dark space below the auditorium. With the aid of a fat lamp we soon confirmed there would be ample room for all 'Harry's' sand, provided some preparatory trenches were dug to facilitate ease of movement and rapid dispersal.

We decided that it would be necessary to construct one main trench up the middle and about eight smaller trenches leading off. It was a bigger task than we had expected. Before we could complete all the work on the trenches, digging on the tunnel had started and the yellow sand began to cascade down through the trap under seat 13, so that one team of six men had to disperse while the other continued to hack out trenches.

Deep down below block 104 the disused workings of the great tunnel were stirring. Wally Floody and Ker-Ramsay led the digging teams who began to forge ahead at an average of about four or five feet a day, although well in excess of this later. The operator in the air pump compartment at the base of the twenty-eight foot shaft worked the handles of his kit bag bellows back and forth drawing clean air down from the surface and pushing it out along the Klim milk tin pipe line to the workers at the face. The carpenters and tin bashers worked in another compartment preparing wood for shoring and fashioning tools and airlines for the lengthening tunnel. The sand was hauled back on a trolley running on rails made from beading battens, stripped from room walls, and was stored in a third compartment ready to be hauled up in kit bags for the penguins to carry to the theatre after dark. The trap at the top of the shaft was kept closed during working hours, the stove sitting on top of it burning red hot, but Pat Langford, who was in charge of the trap, could open or close it in twenty seconds in case of emergency.

George Harsh sat in a room opposite 'Harry's' trap. He had a constant stream of information fed to him by messengers of his security organisation and he knew the position of every 'goon' in the compound.

Every night under the theatre Cross and I worked with our teams dispersing the sand as it poured down through the trap from the penguins' kit bags. We hauled it along the channels in aluminium wash basins attached to ropes, packing it down hard as the loads from the rapidly shuttling basins were dumped. The tunnellers also worked during this period when they could take advantage of the electric light tapped from the mains, as power was switched off in the day time when fat lamps had to be used. All work had to stop by ten o'clock when the barrack doors were closed and locked.

The 'inner cabinet', Bushell, Fanshawe, Floody and Harsh met daily to discuss progress and make decisions.

The tunnel was nearly two hundred feet long, the first 'half-way' house called Piccadilly Circus at one hundred feet, when in early February, the full moon came and lit up the snowy compound with a brittle radiance. Fanshawe insisted to an impatient Roger that all work would have to stop until the moon had waned; the penguins, he said, would be spotted in no time by the guards on the wire, not to mention any prowling ferrets.

When work started again on 10th February mishaps came about. Floody was buried under two hundred pounds of sand which slipped from the roof of the tunnel, and was pulled out half unconscious. Long was badly injured by a bed-board which fell nearly thirty feet from the top of the shaft and caught him on the head.

The tunnel was under the *Vorlager*, the second 'half-way' house – Leicester Square – completed, and less than 150 feet to go to the wood on the north side of the camp, when rubberneck and his ferrets became very active. Block 104 and other blocks were searched, and there was a snap *Appell* but the diggers were able to get out in time. The Germans even engaged a water diviner; they imagined he might be able to locate tunnels. An old man with a drooping moustache, he wandered along outside the wire, his hazel rod waving vaguely in front of him, followed respectfully by Rubberneck and Broili, the Security Officer. Shadowed by a derisive crowd of prisoners, he stopped opposite every block except 104.

Roger Bushell, to help allay suspicion from himself, started rehearsing the part of Professor Higgins in the forthcoming theatre production of *Pygmalion*.

Heinrich Himmler, through Kaltenbrunner, controlled RSHA[1] a vast and fearful apparatus for the exercise of the ruthless suppression and terror which kept the Nazis in power. Its seven *Ämter* included departments which ran the concentration camps, the Special Action Groups (*Einsatzgruppen*) who specialized in extermination – about two million people in the occupied territories during the war years – the Gestapo headed by Gruppenführer Heinrich Muller, and the Kripo (Criminal Police) headed by General Nebe. In addition there was a special security department for the prevention of escapes by prisoners of war. The man who was talking to the Commandant of Stalag Luft III one day in February was the Breslau representative of this special department, Kriminal Direktor Brunner, who called at the Commandant's request because von Lindeiner strongly sensed that a big escape was brewing.

One can only speculate on the conversation in the Commandant's office. What is known is that it lasted for less than an hour after which Brunner departed having made no inspection of the camp defences, nor did he order that the seismographs, which had been removed for

---

[1]   Reichssicherheitshauptamt: Central Security Headquarters.

maintenance work, be reinstalled for the emergency which the Commandant feared. It is possible that it was higher Nazi policy to allow the escape to take place so that an opportunity would be presented for harsh deterrent action. This was suspected after the war by the Judge Advocate General's department when the evidence was being sifted in the Sagan murders case.

Brunner may or may not have told the Commandant of the recently issued 'Stufe Romisch III' Order that any recaptured escapee officer prisoner of war was not to be returned to the military authorities but handed over to the Gestapo, and this was not to be revealed to other POW's, the German military authorities, the Protecting Power or to the International Red Cross. They would simply disappear without trace.

In early March this order was amplified by *Aktion Kugel* (Operation Bullet) issued in a secret circular by the Berlin Gestapo Chief, Muller. This decreed that all recaptured escapee officers, other than the British and Americans, were to be taken in chains to Mauthausen Concentration Camp and there executed by any convenient means.

Von Lindeiner was also visited about this time by the Gestapo who told him that very harsh measures would be taken against any escaped prisoners in future. It was even suggested to the Commandant that he might have to shoot prisoners in the compound. He remarked to a subordinate afterwards that he would sooner shoot himself than carry out such an order.

Well aware of the ominous cloud that was gathering, von Lindeiner called a meeting of the senior officers, doctors and chaplains from all compounds and tried to impress on them the serious consequences that would follow a mass escape.

Von Lindeiner was a humane man who sincerely wished to dissuade his charges from any action which could result in severe reprisals being taken by the Gestapo. However, his words of warning went unheeded, and it is doubtful if knowledge of the contents of the two Gestapo Orders would have made any difference – because 'Harry' was nearly ready to break.

Rubberneck went on leave at the beginning of March, but not without a Parthian shot. He and Major Broili appeared on *Appell* one morning with about thirty extra guards. Nineteen names were called out, including Floody, Fanshawe, Harsh and Bob Tuck; they were searched and marched off to Belaria, a new compound about five miles from the main camp.

Some of the most important key workers had gone, but they obviously did not suspect Roger whose low key profile had paid a good dividend. Ker-Ramsay took over as chief tunnel engineer after Floody's departure. Momentum did not slacken, indeed it had to be speeded up if 'Harry' was to be finished before the chief ferret came back from leave. The tunnel advanced inexorably, almost frantically – in nine days 112 feet were dug and shored, the record was 14 feet in one day – carried forward by the skill and determination, not only of the diggers, but of all the 600 dedicated members of an organisation built up from the experience of over four years of pitting our wits against our captors.

It was a race against time, but hair-trigger security enabled the smooth working machine to drive the tunnel out to its final length of 365 feet. Then the exit shaft was pushed up 25 feet to within a few feet of the surface, planned by the amateur surveyors, to break out just inside the wood.

By this time 80 tons of sand had been moved in the two months since the 'blitz' on 'Harry' had started, so the members of our two teams under the theatre must have handled about 40 tons of sand each during this period, including the 12 tons dispersed down 'Dick', the disused tunnel. (Appendix 'C')

Although it was 14th March, the weather was arctic. Rubberneck was back from leave; his first move was to clear everybody out of block 104 and search it with a gang of ferrets. They spent four hours in there but found nothing.

Roger Bushell was now convinced that the tunnel must be operated as soon as possible and, in the face of some opposition, decided that it should be in the next moonless period; the 24th March was selected as the most suitable.

The task of selecting the men to go out on the tunnel was difficult and delicate. It was estimated that two hundred could be got out in the time available to first light. The first hundred names were specially selected. Of these, the first thirty places were reserved for those who, in the opinion of the escape committee, had the best chance of getting home, and they were nearly all fluent German speakers. I was delighted to find that I was number 39 out and was to travel by train for the first part of the journey as one of a party of twelve with papers as foreign workers on leave from a local wood mill. The last one hundred names were drawn from about 500 names which were put in a hat.

As I prepared for this mass breakout I was gripped by the mounting tension and excitement pervading the compound. I sewed civilian buttons onto the old tunic I was wearing when I was shot down; it had long since been stripped of flying badge and rank braid. I acquired a pair of Middle East khaki trousers and a workman's hat from the tailors. I placed the trousers on the floor at our room entrance to make them suitably grubby, and made a small haversack to carry my escape rations and a change of socks.

Marshals were allocated on the basis of one to about ten escapers. Their job was to brief and supply escape kit to every man in their group. Our party of twelve was to catch a train in the early morning at Tschiebsdorf, a country station near Sagan, travel about 100 kilometres to the south and get off at Boberöhrsdorf near Hirschberg not far from the Czech frontier. Jerzy Mondschein, a big bluff Polish flying officer, who spoke fluent German, was to present the Woodmill Leave pass, an excellent production from the forgery department, and buy the tickets at the station. I had planned to go alone after leaving the train party but it was suggested to me that I might like to team up with Sortiras Skanziklas; I had no objection, he was a cheerful Greek fighter pilot and I had planned my escape route down the Danube valley to Greece, so Skanziklas could help us cross over into Turkey.

The other members of the party were Major John Dodge (the Dodger), Flight Lieutenant 'Pop' Green then 57, shot down as an air gunner in a Whitley, a First World War MC, and a very fit man for his age, Squadron Leader John Williams, an Australian, who was to lead us out of the camp area as he was one of the few who had been taken out on walks by the Germans, Flight Lieutenant 'Rusty' Kierath another Australian, Flight Lieutenant Jimmy Wernham, a Canadian, Lieutenant Doug Poynter of the Fleet Air Arm, Flight Lieutenant Johnny Bull who had been one of the chief tunnellers, and two Polish officers, Kiewnarski and Pawluk.

The first thirty were all travelling by train from Sagan station in smart business suits. Marcinkus, the omniscient Lithuanian, had worked out timetables and produced a mass of information on most of the routes to the Reich borders from material supplied by Valenta's contacts. Some people had elaborate identities with supporting papers. Roger Bushell, who spoke fluent French as well as German, was travelling as a French business man accompanied by Lieutenant Scheidauer of the French Air Force; they were heading for Paris and the French underground. Wings Day was assuming the identity of 'Colonel Brown', an Irishman who had been converted to National Socialism, out on parole from his POW camp. He was to be escorted by Peter Tobolski, a Polish officer who spoke perfect German, in the uniform of a German corporal with a genuine Luftwaffe airman's paybook and a forged travel document.

All departments, except clothing which worked to the last, had now closed down. Passes, maps, money, ration cards, compasses and clothing kept hidden till now, mostly down 'Dick' were being distributed as men were briefed. Stooges worked overtime and the whole camp was in a fever of excitement as final preparations were made. Nobody thought seriously, if indeed they thought at all, of the possible, or probable, consequences of a mass escape on this scale. If we had taken time to reflect, the reaction of the majority could probably have been summed up in Roger's words when Sydney Dowse passed on to him Hesse's warning that he would be shot on recapture after an escape, 'I am not going to be caught.' How many of us had said, 'I am not going to be shot down'? In war it is always the other fellow who is going to 'buy it'.

The people going on foot or the 'hardarsers', most with papers as foreign workers, maps, compasses and some money, had a larger issue of Lubbock rations than the train people. In the coldest March for thirty years, with freezing temperatures, the prospects were bleak in the snowy countryside.

Roger was worried about the foot sloggers as he walked round the compound with Wings on the evening of 23rd March. He said, 'We've got to go tomorrow, but I hate having to make the decision, because very few of the "hardarsers" will make it.'

'They wouldn't have much chance anyway,' replied Wings grimly. 'About a hundred to one, even in good conditions.'

'You think I'm right then?'

If Roger wanted support for his decision, he was speaking to the right man.

'This is an operational war, Roger. It isn't just a question of getting a few people home, because very few will make it. It's just as important to make trouble for the Germans, and if we only get half the planned number out it will certainly do that.'

'Right, we'll go,' said Roger, 'Thank you, Wings.'

CHAPTER TEN

The Great Escape

'I wouldn't put a dog out on a night like this,' said one of my room-mates gloomily, as we were sitting having supper on 24th March. It was to be my last meal at Sagan. The others had not drawn a place on the tunnel, but the cook had laid on a large farewell spread to prepare me for a long cold walk. We ate in silence. It was as though impending doom had thrown a dark shadow to chill the tense excitement in the air.

At nine o'clock it was time to go. I checked my escape kit again: papers, money, compass, maps, and gathered up my home made pack containing rations and a few oddments of spare clothing. As I was leaving, I remembered the store of cigarettes under my bed.

'So long, you bastards,' I said, 'You can have my fags. I'll be able to buy plenty in the Mess when I get home.'

'We'll save them for you,' rejoined Hockey. 'You'll need them when you come out of the cooler. Good luck, anyway.'

On exact timings, shadowy figures were converging on Block 104. I reported first to Wing Commander Norman in Block 109; he was being kept informed of all Germans in the compound, and routed escapers accordingly.

'OK,' he said, ticking my name off on a list, 'Get the all clear from the stooge at the door.'

I walked into Block 104 where Squadron Leader David Torrens was standing at the end of the corridor.

'OK,' said Torrens, checking his list. 'Room eight.'

I found other members of our party in the room, and we were joined a few minutes later by Nick Skanziklas, looking very much like a Greek worker in his cut-down, dyed overcoat and cloth cap.

All regular inmates of Block 104 not involved with the escape had been evacuated to other huts for the night. The block was fast filling up with odd-looking characters in an assortment of clothing ranging from smart business suits and trilby hats to plus fours, workers' trousers, old coats, berets and cloth caps, carrying suitcases, bundles and packs. Group Captain Massey came in and wished us luck, at the same time, with von Lindeiner's warning in mind, he enjoined people to avoid provocation if caught.

A German *Gefreiter* suddenly appeared in the doorway of the hut and started to clump down the corridor. Torrens turned to stone; at the last minute success might be snatched away from us – 600 men working for a year on probably the biggest escape tunnel in history, now, perhaps, all in vain – Torrens, a tall dark, powerfully built man, set off down the passage at a fast stride, preparing to tower over the little corporal and head him off, annihilate him, anything to get rid of him. As they came face to face Torrens with relief recognized Tobolski, the Pole who was to escort Wings. A controller had forgotten to warn him.

At ten o'clock the guards locked up the huts, as usual. There had still been no movement down the tunnel in which seventeen men were already positioned waiting to go out. Ker-Ramsay, in overall charge of the exit, had been down for hours making preparations, but had left the final breakthrough to Johnny Bull and John Marshall, the volatile former Halton apprentice who had been one of the leading diggers. They were having difficulty, we heard, loosening the tightly packed roof boards at the top of the shaft.

The minutes dragged on. Excitement was at fever pitch as two hundred escapers, crammed into a hut normally holding only one hundred, tried to talk and behave as usual; the atmosphere became stifling, we began to sweat and shed our outer garments.

At last there was a stir. News filtered through that they had broken out, but an unfortunate mistake had been made by the surveyors; the exit hole had come up ten feet short of the wood, worse it was only forty-five feet from the brightly lit perimeter fence with the watch tower looming very close.

A consultation with Roger waiting to go out at Number 4 resolved the difficulty. A controller was to be placed behind a 'ferret fence' on the edge of the wood, a rope leading off to the top of the shaft, one tug on it would indicate to the man emerging that the coast was clear. It would be much slower but it was the only way now. Johnny Bull took up position as the first controller, and the mass breakout started.

There was more delay when the air raid siren sounded and all lights were turned out plunging the tunnel into total darkness until the fat lamps were lit, then followed a bad fall which blocked the tunnel until it was cleared by Birkland, the Canadian hauler in Leicester Square; he, too, was going out later.

The lights had come on again when my turn came well past midnight. Henry Lamond, the Controller at the top of the shaft, inspected me for bulky objects, and I was on my way down the long ladder to the base of the shaft where Muckle Muir was crouching controlling the traffic on the railway; beside him in the pump chamber a man worked the air pump back and forth pushing fresh air down the tunnel. I lay down flat on the trolley, my pack in front of me, gave the rope a tug and started to move towards the lights of Piccadilly Circus. I felt that I was really on my way now and the hundred foot haul up the tunnel with my nose only a few inches from the rails added to my sense of exhilaration. At the Halfway House, the enlarged section of the tunnel, I crawled past the sweating hauler, pulled the trolley back from Leicester Square, gave the rope a tug and I was on my way again, another change at Leicester Square, and then the final 130 foot haul to the end of the line. This was a very painless departure from a prisoner of war camp.

I edged past the blanket hung to deaden noise and screen light, and stood up at the bottom of the exit shaft. I looked up and saw stars framed in the rough outline of the exit hole twenty feet above me. At last a view of the sky outside the wire. '*Per Ardua ad Astra*'. It was hard to imagine a more appropriate context for the motto of the Royal Air Force than at that moment. There had been much toil for all concerned, but worth every moment, I thought, as I climbed silently up the ladder towards the stars.

I gave a tug on the rope hanging down over the top of the shaft, after a few seconds there was an answering tug, the all clear – I clambered out onto the frozen snow, its whiteness enhanced by the reflected glare of the arc lamps on the wire. The 'goon box' towered overhead and I could see the sentry away to the right on his beat. My every movement sounded to me like a pistol shot as I crawled the ten feet to the 'ferret fence'. Behind the brushwood hideout crouched the Controller, George McGill a Canadian, he gave me the 'thumbs up' and I slithered on along the rope leading to the rendezvous in the wood. Dim shapes materialized into members of my woodmill leave party. Nick Skanziklas arrived just after me and we were all present.

It was about 1.30 a.m. when we started off in single file led by John Williams. Moving through the trees like a procession of ghosts we skirted round the French and Russian compounds to the west, then headed south-east on a compass course through the forest for Tschiebsdorf where we were to catch our train at 5 a.m. We marched forward at a fast pace, with none too much time in hand, due to the delay in leaving the tunnel; occasionally on roads, sometimes on trails, but mainly through the trees which was heavy going. Once we came to a clearing across which the north wind cut like a knife. Several voices were raised in anguish,

'Bloody cold', and 'Where the hell are we, anyway?'

'Shut up, you silly bastards,' came a sharp admonition. 'Somebody will hear us.'

'OK, fellows, relax,' came the Australian drawl of John Williams. 'There's only kriegies damn silly enough to be around on a night like this. If we press on on this course we'll hit the line somewhere near Tschiebsdorf.'

We plunged into the forest again and plodded on for another hour; four o'clock and there was still no sign of the railway. We held a short conference and decided to head due east; this way we were bound to come to the railway and at the same time ensure that we did not miss the station. Presently we emerged from the forest onto the railway line, turned south and soon arrived at the station.

Mondschein presented the leave pass and requested twelve tickets to Boberöhrsdorf.

'*Zwölf?*' repeated the booking clerk incredulously, then he retreated and appeared to be busying himself getting the tickets, but within a minute was at the window again,

'*Zwölf Fahrkarten?*' he asked once more.

'*Ja, zwölf,*' Mondschein answered aggressively.

The German disappeared again, while we sat around the small waiting room-cum-booking office pretending to look a lot more unconcerned than we were feeling. At last the man appeared again, and this time with our tickets. An elderly farmer and his wife came in and, looking with some alarm at the pirate crew draped around the walls, went out again without delay.

The train steamed in on time. We piled into one of the old six wheeled coaches. There was a gangway down the centre with compartments on each side to seat four. We conveniently filled up three of these, leaving no room for anyone to sit beside us. There appeared to be nobody else on the train except ourselves and the two we had seen at the station.

We rattled slowly southwards across the snow-covered Silesian countryside, stopping at every station and halt. Gradually the train filled up, later with school children, but no one paid any attention to us. There was only one alarming incident when a formidable conductress started to admonish one of our group in a loud voice, and then we realized she was ticking him off for smoking in a 'non smoker'. As we got further south, the country became hilly and it began to snow. It was a poor prospect for foot slogging which was going to be our role in a short time.

When we got off the train at Boberöhrsdorf around nine o'clock there wasn't even a ticket check. We just walked through a gap in the fence out onto the road where we separated and went our different ways.

Nick and I walked to the other side of the village where we joined a road which ran along the side of a wooded hill, an outcrop of the Riesengebirge (Giant Mountains), a formidable obstacle on our route to the Czech border. We turned off the road and began our ascent into the mountains – there was no alternative if we wished to avoid meeting Germans. All that day we toiled across the mountainous snow laden terrain. Straining upwards on the lower slopes, every step an effort in the soft, clinging snow. On the higher slopes floundering through deep snow up to our waists, now and again hitting a trail which led southwards. We plunged into the deep valley of the Bober, crossed a bridge and scrambled up the precipitous slope the other side. Hauling ourselves up by the bare roots of trees clinging tenuously to the steep eroded hillside, we at last came to level ground, a small plateau, the trees thinned and we dragged on and on across a white waste of snow.

A deer stall provided us with some rest but it was hardly shelter. While one lay in the straw filled trough, the other tried to keep warm in front of a small fire of dried sticks we had managed to light. It was so cold that sleep was out of the question and the small heat from the fire merely caused steam to rise up from soaked footwear. Towards evening we had had enough, besides we wanted to pinpoint our position before dark. We moved on.

The ground started to slope gently downwards; soon we came to the edge of the forest and found ourselves looking over a broad valley beyond which lay rugged, mountainous country, deep in snow. To the east was a fair-sized town which we knew to be Hirschberg.

The temperature was dropping and Nick gazed disconsolately across the valley to the mountains beyond. He was shivering and I could see he was blue with cold.

'We've got about forty miles of that to cross before we reach the Czech border,' he said.

I had been used to Canadian winters of 30°F and more below zero, but I began to see that survival might be in question for both of us, with our limited rations and thin clothing, if we went on over mountains in these conditions.

We took the valley road to Hirschberg. Nobody seemed to take any notice of us. A farmer passing on a horse drawn cart called out that it was very cold for the time of the year. I agreed heartily with him. We were gaining confidence. Passing Hirschberg West Station on the road leading out to Polaun near the frontier, and mindful of our recent successful train journey, we decided that it would be quite safe to go in and buy tickets to a point nearer the Czech border; after all, the forgers had supplied us with excellent passes.

As we approached the ticket office in the crowded booking hall I saw, out of the corner of my eye, two figures start to move out from the wall towards us; we converged at the wicket. A policeman in teapot helmet and a civilian were standing in front of us.

'*Papiere*,' demanded the policeman gruffly.

We produced our passes confidently, but he merely glanced at them, put them in his pocket, inspected the contents of our packs, and said peremptorily, '*Komm mit.*'

I protested that we were foreign workers on perfectly legitimate leave of absence, and that our old mothers were waiting to see us. He replied that it would only be necessary to come to the station to answer a few questions and then we could go on. He grasped me firmly by the arm, the other man took hold of Nick, and, watched by an interested crowd of spectators, we were marched off in the gathering dusk.

Back at the tunnel mouth beside the wood at Sagan, on the early morning of 25th March, in the dull grey light of a wintry dawn, a patrolling German sentry, cold and morose, almost fell down the hole. Len Trent[1] had just emerged as the 79th man out and was lying doggo in the snow, hoping that the guard would not see him. Reavell-Carter was in the wood waiting to lead the next group out. Mick Shand, a New Zealand Spitfire pilot, lay prone in the snow on his way to the trees.

The guard just missed stepping on Trent, and then stopped. He must have noticed the track in the snow leading into the wood. Then he saw Shand. Swinging his rifle off his shoulder, he took aim. Suddenly there came a cry from the wood,

'*Nicht schiessen, Posten – nicht schiessen.*'[2]

---

[1] Squadron Leader Trent, vc, DFC.

[2] 'Don't shoot, sentry – don't shoot.'

Reavell-Carter had seen the drama silhouetted against the perimeter lighting of the camp. The shot went wild. Shand sprang up and zig zagged into the shelter of the wood.

The guard then became conscious of three things in quick succession. Trent rose up like a ghost beside him. Roy Langlois appeared wraithlike from behind the ferret fence, and the tunnel exit swam into his vision. Stupefied, he looked down the long tunnel shaft and saw Bob McBride clinging to the top of the ladder. By this time the man was almost unhinged, he was muttering incoherently to himself and shaking his head. Then he fumbled for his whistle, put it to his lips with trembling hand, and gave a long blast on it. It was 5 a.m.

When the full extent of the escape became known, the order for a *Grossfahndung* (National Alert) was given on the highest authority (see Appendix A).

Police and security services went onto full alert all over Germany, also an SS Panzer division which happened to be in the Sagan area. There was little chance for the 76 escapers to slip through the net, even those with watertight papers and several cover stories, like Roger Bushell and Scheidauer who were caught near Saarbrucken; having passed an exhaustive Gestapo check, one of the officials shot out a question in English, an old trick, but Scheidauer who was French and had been speaking English for months, answered in English.

When Hitler was informed of the Mass Escape he flew into one of his increasingly frequent rages. Calling a conference with Göring, Himmler and Keitel, he ordered that all the recaptured officers were to be shot. Göring objected on the grounds that it would look too much like mass murder to shoot all and, anyway, reprisals could be taken against German prisoners in Allied hands.

'Then more than half are to be shot,' shouted Hitler.

Himmler fixed the number at fifty and set up the machinery for their execution (Appendix A).

Bushell and Scheidauer were among those shot. After interrogation at Gestapo Headquarters at Saarbrucken, they were taken along the Autobahn at dawn on 29th March, towards Kaiserslautern, accompanied by Dr Spann, the Gestapo Chief at Saarbrucken, and Kriminal Sekretär Emil Schulz. The vehicle was stopped and Bushell and Scheidauer were told that they could get out to relieve themselves. When their backs were turned, Spann, carrying out his orders to the letter, gave a sign to Schulz and they both fired their revolvers simultaneously into the necks of the two officers. Their bodies slumped to the ground. Death must have been instantaneous and one hopes that they did not know that they were to be executed.

This was not so in some other cases, notably in the Kiel killings, also on 29th March. Squadron Leader Catanach, an Australian captured at Flensburg, was told casually by SS Sturmbannführer Johannes Post that he would be shot; Post was collecting a theatre ticket for his mistress at the time, the while watching Catanach's face for his reaction to the announcement of the *Himmelfahrt*.[1]

Catanach merely asked, 'Why?'

The execution site was chosen and Catanach was shot in the back. Christensen, a New Zealander, Espelid and Fugelsang, two Norwegians were taken shortly afterwards to the same place, and almost tripped over Catanach's body. They started to run, but were shot down immediately.[2]

These cold-blooded and gruesome murders continued for two weeks, all following the same pattern. They included my Greek companion, Nick Skanziklas, and seven others of the Woodmill Leave Party. Pop Green and Poynter went back to Sagan. Among those shot were Tim Walenn, the Chief Forger, Valenta, Marcinkus, Pat Langford, 'Harry's' trap operator, Birkland and McGill, the two Canadians I had passed on my way out, Tom Kirby-Green and Ian Cross. The last man to be seen alive was James Long at Görlitz on 12th April. He was an old friend from Barth days, and had helped me get out on the incinerator tunnel.

Three got home. Bob van der Stok, a Dutch officer, was Number 18 out of the tunnel. He had papers as a Dutch worker and enough money for long distance train travel. On the platform at Sagan he got into conversation with a girl who startled him by saying that she was a censor and was looking for escaping officers. Van der Stok caught his train; after thirteen hours, three changes and Gestapo document checks every four hours (the German travellers had far more trouble than he did) he reached Holland. Thence the Underground passed him through Belgium and France to Toulouse where he had an anxious moment when he found that he had forgotten the address where he was to make himself known to the Maquis. He remembered that it was something to do with the Dutch Royal Family; as he

[1] Lit. Heaven journey – Ascension.

[2] *Exemplary Justice* by Allen Andrews gives a full account of the official postwar investigation into the shootings.

wandered around fuming, he suddenly spotted the Cafe L'Orangerie, that was it, the contact post for the Maquis. He was soon over the Pyrenees into Spain. He was back on flying and leading a Spitfire squadron on operations within a couple of months.

The two Norwegians Peter Bergsland[1] and Jens Muller travelled by train to Stettin. Here they met some Swedish sailors who hid them aboard their ship that evening; it sailed at once for Sweden where they arrived at dawn the following day – twenty-four hours after leaving the tunnel.

It seemed a high price to pay; three men gained their freedom, fifty were murdered, eight incarcerated in Concentration Camps and gaols, and only fifteen returned to Sagan. It must be remembered, however, that it caused the Germans to divert about five million of their population, directly and indirectly, in the search for the escapers over a period of about three weeks. This was our contribution to the war effort.

The Commandant, Major Broili and nine others of the staff at Sagan were court-martialled and received prison sentences (Appendix B). Three electricians were shot. The Gestapo wondered how 800 feet of cable happened to be down 'Harry' for the lighting system. It had been stolen from the electricians and they were too scared to report the loss, but they were assumed to be traitors by the Gestapo and paid with their lives.

[1] Always known in the camp as 'Rocky' Rockland probably to protect his family in Norway.

CHAPTER ELEVEN

The Gestapo Strikes

At the Police Station Nick and I were taken upstairs to the offices of the KRIPO (Criminal Police) and made to stand under guard in a small outer office. After a few minutes a man in plain clothes came in, pushed two pieces of paper in front of us and said, shortly, '*Ihre richtigen Namen*,' the time for bluffing was past, and we wrote down our names. We were then taken into a passage outside and made to sit on a bench, while watched by two policemen.

Very soon other members of the woodmill party began to appear. First Pop Green who had been caught in Boberöhrsdorf soon after leaving the station. Then the Dodger and his partner Jimmy Wernham who had been caught on Hirschberg main station at 3.30 that afternoon. Their Yugoslav passes would have been accepted if there had not been a Yugoslav nearby who was called to talk to them in Serbo-Croat which they had never heard before; small wonder our passes had been pocketed so swiftly by the policeman who had apprehended us at Hirschberg West. They were followed by the two Polish officers, arrested shortly before, while walking through the town. Finally, at 8 o'clock Doug Poynter was brought in. He had been arrested on a train going to Polaun.

There were now eight of us sitting in a row on the bench waiting for the unknown. We had been beaten by the elements, but there was one more task before *Nacht und Nebel* closed in. We managed to hide our maps and money behind a narrow cabinet standing against the wall behind us.

The interrogations soon began. I was called first. I found myself in a large office with a desk behind which sat a small, bald-headed, mean-looking man in horn-rimmed spectacles, the interrogator. I was made to stand in front of him and through an interpreter, with a typist taking down the transcript, he started firing questions at me.

'At what time did you get out of the tunnel?'

'I don't know.'

'Why do you not know?'

'Because I didn't have a watch.'

'How did you get here? Did you come by train?'

'You should be able to figure that one out.'

'How many went out with you?'

'I really don't know,' which happened to be true.

'What was your number out of the tunnel?'

'I can't tell you.'

'Why can you not tell me?'

'Because it was a military operation and, as a British officer I can give you no information about it.'

'Military operation,' with a sarcastic laugh, 'Boy scouts!' Then, still hoping to get me rattled, 'You say you are an officer; you do not look like an officer in those clothes.'

'Nor would you if you had done what I have been doing.'

'Where did you get those clothes?'

'They are my uniform.'

'They are civilian clothes.'

There followed questions on the construction of the tunnel, the number of people employed, length of time to build and so on, to which I gave uniformly negative replies. My interrogator and sometimes the interpreter raged and threatened. Now and again they tried more subtle methods. Finally the typescript taken down by the girl was pushed in front of me to sign. When I refused, the mean man jumped up and, boiling with rage, went towards the door.

'*Komm mit*,' he shouted, beckoning me to follow him.

I went outside with him into the passage and down to the end where he opened a door into a dark, narrow cell. He unlocked an iron grill pushed me inside, slammed it shut and went out closing the door behind him. A dim light filtered through the glazed window above the door and showed up the outline of a low wooden seat. It appeared to be a converted lavatory.

I sat down on the seat wondering, wearily, how long I was going to be left there. The fact that eight of us had been caught within a short time in the vicinity of Hirschberg indicated that a very intensive search must have been initiated in the Sagan area, if not all over Germany. My present situation was most unusual, if not unprecedented, for an ordinary British 'kriegie' recaptured after escape. I felt it boded ill for all of us. However I was far too tired to worry about it. Having had no sleep for two days, I was overcome with fatigue and dropped off into a deep slumber.

I was awakened by the noise of the grill opening. There was my inquisitor again. '*Heraus!*' I got up and followed him back down the passage.

I found myself back in the office. It was now filled up with bedizened and black-uniformed SS and Gestapo officers wearing bright red armbands with black swastikas prominently displayed. I glanced at the clock; it was midnight. Dazed with sleep and blinded by the electric light after the dark cell, conscious also of the grim and threatening figures behind me, I was subjected to another interrogation by the little Gestapo man. Bellowing, screaming and brow-beating went on for about half an hour. My attitude was the same as before. Suddenly it stopped. I was sent outside with a policeman who pushed me roughly into a corner of the passageway in which the seven other members of my party were sitting. When I tried to communicate with them, I was stopped with a cry of:

'*Unterhaltung verboten,*'[1] and pushed closer into the corner face inwards.

After about twenty minutes we were all lined up one behind the other. Each manacled to a policeman, who secured our left wrists with a chain and twist grip, we stumbled out into the night and, like a chain gang, shuffled through the dimly lit snowy streets to the gaol. It was a large, gloomy old building where we were all crammed into a small dank cell. In wet, steaming clothes we fell asleep on the dirty stone floor.

In the early morning the cell door was flung open to cries, of '*Aufstehen, aufstehen,*'[2] our first introduction to the Meister, the small, sallow complexioned Chief Warder, with aquiline nose and rather piercing cold blue eyes behind rimless spectacles. He wore riding breeches and a sort of smock, and, I'm sure carried a whip sometimes, his manner was at once ingratiating and bullying. I think he was one of the most unpleasant Germans I ever met.

This rude awakening was followed by breakfast brought to the cell door by an attractive Polish girl, the sight of whom made more palatable the meagre fare of ersatz coffee and black bread with a scrape of jam. Even the forbidding presence of the Meister could not detract from the pleasure of my first contact with the opposite sex for four years.

We spent most of the morning swapping escape stories with their interminable 'ifs'. We all agreed that if the weather had not been so appalling we would have made it at least into Czechoslovakia where

---

[1] 'Conversation forbidden.'
[2] 'Get up, Get up.'

we were all heading, and we hoped that the other four members[1] of
the party had had more luck.

Our Polish girl friend came round with the Sunday lunch which
even contained a morsel of meat among the cabbage and spuds. This
constrained the Dodger to lead us in a sing-song. He had been
singing when he was arrested by the OGPU in south Russia in 1921,
while strumming a ukelele on the back of a camel. Now he was
singing in another repressive regime. The French in neighbouring
cells responded and, for a while, the gloomy prison resounded to
songs like 'The White Cliffs of Dover', 'La mer,' and 'Alouette' –
Anglo-French 'Son et Lumière'.

John Dodge was the first to be taken away. They came for him the
next morning.

The 'moving finger' was beginning to write. If any of us suspected
that our destiny was other than to return to Sagan, it was hidden
beneath a facade of bonhomie and good natured badinage. Jimmy
Wernham, the cheery Scots-Canadian, was outlining schemes for
becoming a millionaire on his return to Canada after the war. The
Poles, Kiewnarski and Pawluk, were diverting themselves hanging
through the bars of the cell window talking to Polish and Russian
women prisoners walking in the yard two floors below, until the
Meister rushed out into the yard threatening. A little while later he
came into the cell, grabbed hold of the naval pilot, Doug Poynter,
who spoke good German, and dragged him outside. In a few minutes
the Senior Service returned looking none the worse after the
engagement. The Meister had pointed a revolver at him and
shouted, but Poynter had merely waved the revolver away and told
him not to be so stupid; then, with the gun back in its holster, he had
pressed home his advantage and demanded to see the Police
Commandant, a request that was granted.

The Police Commandant, a Prussian-looking type, stalked into
the cell that afternoon. The interview was brief. We asked him why
we were being kept in prison, and how long we were going to be
there. We asked for exercise, razors and more food. Simple requests
which seemed to make him quite angry. Finally, when we suggested
that British officers should be housed under better conditions, he
shouted at the top of his voice and stormed away in a rage.

One request, at least, was granted. On Tuesday morning the cell
door opened and there was the Meister peering at us like a weasel

---

[1] Bull, Kierath, Mondschein and Williams had stayed together and were caught
south of Hirschberg by a mountain patrol. They were all shot on 29th March.

looking at its prey. '*Spazieren*', he rapped.

So started daily walks in the small, dark courtyard of the prison. They were more in the nature of a half hour shuffle around every day, speed was so reduced by the press of captive humanity.

Around 2.30 that afternoon, the Meister appeared again, this time accompanied by a police official who was holding some documents.

'When I call the names,' said the policeman, 'the person must take his things and come.'

He then called, in a sonorous voice, with an interval to allow each to collect his few possessions and leave the cell: 'Kiewnarski – Pawluk – Wernham – Skanziklas.'

It was the last time that any of their comrades were to see them on earth. They were all shot by the Gestapo.

Two days later the Meister came into the cell with two pink slips of paper – one for Pop Green, the other for Poynter.

Now, where were they all going? I thought. If we had all been going back to Sagan, surely they would have transported us together. Why had I been left alone? For how long? I could only speculate on the answers to these questions, but I felt ill at ease.

Then I had my first shave for a week. Having pestered the Meister for a razor, he finally brought me in a cut-throat razor; at the same time a huge Alsatian police dog bounded into the cell and, even more to my alarm, was left in the cell with me! I have a rapport with dogs and was able to establish friendly relations with my canine visitor, but I have often wondered why he was left alone with me. Perhaps he was trained to attack prisoners if they tried to cut their throats, or it may have been to remind me that they had dogs if I tried to escape.

The next day I was removed to another cell on the next floor up. It was evidently a converted kitchen and was about twice the size of the normal cell. It was right in the centre of the building and so had no windows abutting on the outside. The light came from a skylight in the roof and a barred window which looked out onto the landing. An old range was in a corner of the room underneath the skylight.

The possibility of escape struck me. By standing on the range I could reach the wire mesh grill nailed onto the ceiling beneath the skylight. Through the glass which was extremely dirty, I thought I could detect the faint outline of bars across the top; however, I decided that I would try to prise the grill off anyway. Looking round, I spotted the iron handle of the stove door – an ideal 'pranger'[1]. The

---

[1] POW slang for any handy blunt instrument.

next job was to get it off – for hours I tried without success. The only tool I had was a table knife. I might have saved myself the trouble. Two days later the skylight glass was cleaned and the faint outline of bars became a very definite reality. However it had given me something to do.

During my daily shuffles round the courtyard I used my French, German and Russian to talk to the other prisoners who came from nearly every country in Europe. Although the place was supposed to be a transit prison, many had been there for quite a long time; one of the Russians had been there for a year. All complained of hunger. Most had been slave workers in Germany and had been arrested for various offences unpalatable to the Third Reich, such as sabotage, desertion or consorting with German women. Most were executed later.

As the days passed, I became restless. There was nothing to read, and I paced up and down my cell, sometimes round and round on a left-hand circuit following airfield flying procedure – at least I could pretend I was flying – sometimes on a right hand circuit. Meal times were welcome interludes when the Polish girl appeared with the meagre rations, although always accompanied by a guard. Occasionally I was able to talk to one of the prisoners through the barred window. He was a former German officer who had been put to work on the landing making wooden sign boards for the prison. He told me that he was a communist and was expecting to be executed.

One day the Gestapo paid a surprise visit. The news of their arrival was circulated almost immediately by that rather mysterious prison bush telegraph. I was told by the German officer on the landing. I was alarmed, however, when the two Gestapo men in belted raincoats and carrying briefcases walked into my cell. There was enough room there for some muscular interrogation. However, they had come to see some other unfortunates. I was removed to another cell occupied by some Frenchmen who were among those to be interrogated. They told me that they had been working in the Hirschberg area when they were arrested for sabotage. After an hour the Gestapo left taking with them a Belgian prisoner, and I was returned to my cell.

Very early one morning I was awakened by the sound of my cell door opening, the light was switched on and through half-closed eyes I saw the Meister peering at me with his cold blue eyes. He was beckoning to me.

'*Komm, komm, steh auf,*' he said.

'*Warum?*' I asked.

'Get up and dress and you'll see,' he replied.

On the way downstairs, the Polish girl waved good-bye, and came to the top of the stairs to watch rather apprehensively as another prisoner vanished into the grey dawn. It was 6th April and the time must have been about 4.30 a.m. The date was of no consequence, but the time could have been significant in such circumstances.

In the entrance hall I was handed over to two men in plain clothes, one the Inspector who had asked for our names when we were first taken to the police station, and the other a much younger man in his early twenties. The Inspector pulled a revolver from his raincoat and giving me a hard stare, said

'*Mach keine Dummheit,*' (Don't do anything stupid.)

I was handed back my haversack, the iron grill at the door was swung open, and we were out on the street.

I was marched several paces ahead of the Gestapo men to the main railway station. They refused to give any information about our destination. When the train came in we got into a reserved compartment. A powerful electric engine pulled us away and steadily up and around the big bowl in which lay the grey old Gothic-spired city of Hirschberg.[1] We headed west through the hills on which the snow was melting in the spring sunshine – if only the moonless night had been two weeks later!

After a while the two men relaxed, and the Inspector showed me a photograph of his son who had been fighting on the Russian front and was then going to an officers' school. I asked them how the war was going.

'For whom?' asked the Inspector.

'For Germany,' I replied.

He shrugged his shoulders, and said that although the East Front might not be going too well at the moment, the Allies could never land in the west as the Atlantic Wall was too strong, but he seemed unconvinced, and lapsed into silence. A little later he offered me a cigarette – he smoked continually although at that time cigarettes were rationed to four a day – and giving me the *SS News* to read, shook his head and said, 'Bad politics, war.' This was not the time for me to start a discussion on the causes of the war, so I settled down to smoke my cigarette and read the *SS News*, which, of course, reported

---

[1] Now in Polish territory and known as Jelenia Gora.

the latest German successes on the East Front where they had been retreating for the previous eighteen months.

As the train crossed a bridge over another railway line, the younger man pointed north and said, 'That goes to Sagan.' It was one way of telling me that I was not returning to Stalag Luft III. Then what hell-hole was I bound for?

At Görlitz we changed onto a train going north, and I knew we were headed for Berlin. There was little hope of escape, even had I been in good condition and fully prepared. Every time I went to the toilet the Inspector came with me and I was also obliged to leave the door open. The train was packed, with people standing and sitting on suitcases in the corridor.

The face of Berlin had been considerably altered by Bomber Command since I was first marched through the city nearly four years previously. It lay in ruins, and as we approached the centre there seemed to be hardly a house standing. There was not a pane of glass to be seen, and most of the windows were boarded up. During the last year or so of the war, the Berliners lived almost constantly in electric light – provided it was working.

As we pulled into the terminus, the Inspector dangled a pair of handcuffs in front of me, 'If you will give me your *Ehrenwort* not to escape, I shall not make you wear these,' he said.

I agreed. Either way there was no escape.

Outside the station a girl driver was waiting beside a car. Within fifteen minutes I knew where I was going. I saw the sign 'Albrechtstrasse' as we turned into a street and then entered the courtyard of a bomb-damaged building. This was Gestapo Headquarters. Was I to join the tortured victims in the basement cells? I was taken upstairs and down some passages with sagging floors and tottering walls, symbolic of Hitler's crumbling Third Reich, and into a large general office where I was told to sit down on a chair in the corner of the room.

There followed an interminable wait. An attractive young girl secretary gazed at me with unconcealed amusement. A trampish-looking *englischer Flieger* unshaven and dirty was a new and diverting experience for her. I ignored her and picked up a police magazine to read, but was promptly told to put it down by an SD man, as it was for internal consumption only.

I sat on and waited. The secretary typed, occasionally looking up to gape at me; the two men who had brought me from Hirschberg ate a cooked lunch with beer, a fat, bald, square-headed Major was helped on with his overcoat and waddled out, undoubtedly to lunch. There was no lunch for the prisoner; inured to short rations for so long I didn't really care, I was only curious to know what my fate was to be.

At last an SD Captain of bombastic mien appeared, asked my name and rank, and then went back to his office. Some minutes later he appeared again, beckoned me to follow him and we walked down the rickety corridors to the courtyard below where a car was waiting. I was put in the back with another SD man while the Captain sat in front with the driver.

It was a dull day and I had no idea in which direction we were going as we threaded our way through the blitzed city and out into the suburbs. The SD man beside me was talkative and intelligent and we passed the time talking about everything from education to the area bombing of Germany about which he seemed resigned but not unduly worried.

We had been driving in the country for a little while when we entered a dark pine forest. Suddenly, a high wall rose up on one side of the road; it was camouflaged in dull black and green and ran along in front of us for some distance. Electrified wire ran along the top; at intervals there were guard towers with sentries and heavy machine guns. A chill ran down my spine as I surveyed this sinister barrier. Even the SD man fell silent for a while, then he rubbed his hands together and said, 'Aha, this is a nice place,' a phrase which he repeated, almost gleefully, several times.

We stopped at a door in the wall. The Captain turned round and spoke for the first time, 'Well, Herr James, no more tunnelling for you – it is impossible to escape from here.'

The door in the wall opened, an SS Unterscharführer stepped out and came towards us, grinning and displaying a row of chrome teeth.

I was escorted through the door into a small guard room and out into a little compound surrounded on all sides by high walls; within this was a smaller compound, bounded by a tall electrified wire fence, containing two wooden barrack huts. I was taken through a gate in the wire past the entrance to the first hut where stood several inmates watching my arrival with interest; one of them, a tall, rather swarthy, dark-haired man with horn-rimmed spectacles said, 'Welcome to your new home. My name is Peter Churchill.'

I was taken on down to the end hut where I came face to face with the sole occupant – Wings Day. I was certainly glad to see him again.

After the Germans had gone, I asked him hopefully if we

happened to be in Colditz, being unaware of any other 'strafe' camps to which RAF escapers were sent.

'No,' he growled. 'I wish to hell it was. This is Sachsenhausen concentration camp, and the only way out of here is up the chimney. This is Sonderlager A,' Wings went on, 'and over there is the main compound.' He pointed at the ten foot wall outside the window. 'Sometimes you can hear the screams of the poor devils when they are being beaten up. Here we are treated as political prisoners and are not allowed to write home or receive letters. They count us morning and evening, otherwise they seem to leave us alone.'

'How many are there here?' I asked.

'About eighteen odds and bods, including some Russians, Poles and Irish, and here is one that you know,' said Wings as Major Dodge's tall figure was framed in the doorway. The Dodger came forward, hand outstretched,

'Jimmy,' he said beaming, 'I'm so glad to see you.'

CHAPTER TWELVE

Sachsenhausen

Peter Churchill and Johnny Dodge roomed together in the first barrack hut I had passed on my arrival. Wings and I joined them for meals and formed the British Officers' Mess, Sonderlager A. We were looked after by two splendid Italian soldiers who had been orderlies to the Italian Naval, Military and Air Attachés who had been removed from the compound following the Italian surrender; Bartoli, formerly a pastry cook in Rome, performed daily miracles with German rations and the limited Red Cross parcels, with Amici, a cousin of the Hollywood actor Don Amici.

Like all old prisoners we had become indifferent to surroundings or personal comfort and, in a new milieu, were mainly interested in those with whom we should have to continue our indeterminate and apparently endless incarceration. Listening to one another's accounts of his journey to this point in time we felt, for a space, timeless, and forgot our narrow confines – the high sullen walls restricting our vision to the tops of the pine trees, and the lowering faces of the SS guards patrolling, dog at heel, between the wall and the electrified fence.

Wings' renegade officer plan with Tobolski as German escort had gone awry. Their Berlin contact had failed and they had travelled on to Stettin by train. They had the address of a brothel which had been used as a stopping point on an escape route, but they found it dark and empty; they could not know that all brothels had been closed in 1943 and prostitution made illegal. Tobolski had a sister in Stettin married to a German, but she had begged him to try to get help elsewhere when he approached her. They had, therefore, tried prostitutes before family, but now they went to the tool shed at the bottom of the garden behind the sister's house, which she said could be used as a one night shelter if they insisted. They found eggs, bread and milk left out for them. The next day they managed to infiltrate themselves into a dockside barrack housing a working party of French prisoners of war who agreed to help them board a neutral ship for Sweden. However, they were betrayed by an informer and arrested by the German police the next morning.

'I'd like to wring his bloody neck,' Wings had told the police officer who was interrogating him.

'Don't worry,' the policeman replied. 'Of course this little lot will be worth about a thousand Reichsmarks to him, but when he is of no further use to us we shall see that his activities are made known to his comrades. Then, no doubt, his body will be found floating in the harbour.'

Wings was separated from Tobolski at Gestapo Headquarters in Berlin. He was told by General Nebe[1], Head of the Kripo, that he had become a serious nuisance and was to be sent to a place from which there was no escape. Tobolski was shot.

All things are relative. To Captain Peter Churchill, after eight months in Fresnes Prison in Paris under threat of torture and death, the Sonderlager seemed like a reprieve. A degree in modern languages at Cambridge followed by years of residence in France had made him a natural selection for SOE (Special Operations Executive) who had been exhorted by Winston Churchill to 'set Europe ablaze'. Arriving by parachute, Lysander and submarine, returning by steep Pyrenean paths, he had been caught on his fourth mission with his courier Odette at Annecy.

The name of Churchill[2] and his claim to kinship with the great man had saved Peter from torture and probable execution. Their pose as a married couple had saved Odette from execution but not from torture; courageously claiming to be the head of the south-east network of agents, she had taken the heat off Peter and brought upon herself the searing pain of a red hot iron on her back, the extraction of all her toe nails, and incarceration in the Concentration Camp at Ravensbruck.

The four Irish soldiers, with the extrovert charm of their race, soon made themselves known to me.

'Welcome, Sorr, and a pleasure to meet you. 'Tis bad luck you had getting caught after that great tunnel, but we'll soon get you settled down here in Himmler's home from home.'

'Thank you, Sergeant,' I replied to Sergeant Thomas Cushing, Irish American soldier of fortune with a record of service in the United States and in several other armies, including action in the Spanish Civil War (I forget which side), currently serving in the

---

[1] Nebe selected the names of the fifty officers to be shot after the Sagan escape (Appendix A) He himself was to be executed in Sachsenhausen later.

[2] Winston Churchill once remarked that he had no idea he had so many relatives until the war!

British Army. 'And what about yourselves? How did you happen to
land up in this cage?' I continued, looking round at his comrades,
Corporal Andy Walsh of the King's Royal Rifles, Lance Bombardier
Judd of the Royal Artillery and Private Pat O'Brien.

Their unusual and bizarre story then unfolded. Captured at
Dunkirk, they had been consigned to the usual POW Camps until
about 1942 when the Germans asked for Irish volunteers to train as
saboteurs for the purpose of attacking targets in the United
Kingdom, giving out that this was a heaven-sent opportunity to
strike a blow at the Saxon foe. Some two hundred Irish soldiers had
gone to a camp at Friesack regarding this as a splendid opportunity
to escape. Colonel McGrath had been despatched by General
Fortune, who had commanded the 51st Highland Division, to brief
the men on this exercise. Walsh was already on a plane at
Trondheim in Norway ready to take off for a drop over Scotland
where he was to blow up the Fort William Power Station which he
had helped to build before the war. The Germans suddenly became
suspicious, took him off the aeroplane and threw him into the
Sonderlager together with the other three with whom he had trained.

About a week after my arrival there came another Sagan escaper,
Flight Lieutenant Sydney Dowse; he and his companion, Stanislaw
'Danny' Krol, a Polish officer, had walked resolutely eastwards
through the snow towards Poland for twelve days. On the thirteenth
day they were seen by a Hitler Youth who called out the Home
Guard and they were recaptured. The Gestapo from Breslau were
soon on the spot. They took Danny Krol away and Dowse was told
that his friend was going back to Sagan – his ashes went back, a bit
later. Sydney Dowse, the 'laughing boy' who had been my next door
neighbour at Stalag Luft III, went to Sachsenhausen. His jovial and
easy-going bonhomie belied a tough and determined PRU Spitfire
pilot who had already made four escape attempts, and was one of the
chief diggers on 'Harry'. His long walk had left him with holes in his
heels two inches in diameter.

Major General Ivan Bessanov was delivering his weekly exposition
on the new constitution he intended to impose on Russia after he had
'put the skids' under Stalin.

'Ja ... *Jedermann hat sein Acker*[1] ... in my plan for farming

---

[1] 'Yes. . . . Each man has his acre.'

cooperatives controlled by the Regional Administration under the strict supervision of the Agriculture Ministry to whom I, as Head of State, would issue clear instructions to follow a policy designed for maximum crop production, particularly in the black earth region of the Ukraine.'

He spat purposefully and accurately into a corner of his room. The British officers were gathered as usual to listen at the General's insistent invitation. It was my task to interpret this diatribe, delivered in execrable German, sorting out as best I could the stream of words strung together with little regard for gender or tense.

Not all his utterances were as doctrinaire as the above might suggest. After his capture in the initial stages of the German advance into Russia in 1941, when he was commanding NKVD Frontier troops, his glib tongue saved him from immediate extinction by the SS. His expeditious adoption of an anti-communist, anti-Stalin pose, suggested to the Nazi hierarchy that he might be used as a puppet dictator of the new order in the Soviet Union under the Third Reich. He was given a degree of freedom which allowed him to see most of Western Europe bringing home to him the backwardness of his own country. As a result he had been motivated to write a political thesis setting out his ideas for a new constitution introducing genuine liberal reforms, with a copy weekly to Göring as he progressed. One stipulation was that the Ukraine must be ceded to Germany on the successful conclusion of hostilities.

One night, at a party at the Adlon Hotel in Berlin he had been heard to remark, under the influence of a surfeit of Vodka; 'As if I'd give the Ukraine to these bastards.'

Finally, he had ordered the summary execution of the known Gestapo agents in his private, mostly airborne army, recruited from the ranks of the million or so Soviet defectors under General Vlassov. After this episode he had been despatched speedily to Sachsenhausen.

Bessanov was about thirty-eight years of age, the son of a railway porter, short and stocky, arrogant and extrovert to a degree, and very intelligent. Although crude in his habits, his leathery face often creased into a smile which masked the ruthless Mongol bandit lurking beneath.

Lieutenant General Piotr Privalov, wounded eleven times and decorated with the star of Lenin, was a former Tsarist NCO and a Russian of quite a different kind. Although he was the highest ranking officer in the Sonderlager and had commanded an Army

Corps at Stalingrad, he was quiet and modest, a complete contrast to Bessanov. He told us that he tried to escape several times and had been sent to Sachsenhausen as a result.

Then there was the amusing and eccentric Brodnikov, a bearded 45-year-old lieutenant-colonel who had been an officer cadet in the Tsar's Army in 1917. Although he had fought with the Reds against Whites in the Civil War and subsequently became an officer in the Soviet Army, he was no communist; the excesses and mass purges of the Stalin era had sickened him and turned him against the regime. When he became a prisoner of war he wasted no time in joining the Vlassov Army, and then the Bessanov Circus; hence his presence in the Sonderlager.

Fiodr Ceridilin was a cheerful young Soviet soldier, a simple, laughing peasant with the indefinable 'sympatichny' aura of many Russians, he might have stepped out of the pages of one of Tolstoy's novels. He was one of the few survivors of 20,000 Red Army soldiers consigned to Sachsenhausen in 1941 of whom, in the course of three months, 18,000 had been shot by the SS. Ceridilin, therefore, had something to laugh about. When the Soviet officers arrived in the Sonderlager, he had been sent over to act as their batman. He had been in a slave labour camp in the Soviet Union for two years.

Another Russian officer had been in the Sonderlager shortly before the arrival of the British officers. After hearing about the massacre of 10,000 Polish officers at Katyn, attributed by the Germans to the Soviets – correctly as it happened – he had become extremely agitated; he rushed onto the electrified wire where the lingering life in his twitching body was extinguished by a bullet from an SS guard. His name was Jakob Djugashvili, son of Josef Stalin.

The Russians occupied the rooms at one end of Peter Churchill's hut. In the next room were two friendly Polish officers serving in the RAF, Warrant Officer Stanislaw Jensen and Flying Officer Jan Izycki, respectively the pilot and navigator of a Wellington shot down over France the previous year on a supply-dropping mission to the French Resistance. They had been badly burnt and taken to hospital, but the Gestapo had, nevertheless, removed them and beaten them up thoroughly before sending them to Sachsenhausen.

Sydney Dowse and I shared a room next to Wings at the end of the hut furthest from the gate which was otherwise unoccupied. Very soon we were considering the possibility of escape. The skull and crossbones[1] signs placed along the warning fence were a grim reminder of what might be expected in the event of recapture. Any thoughts we might have had about the consequences remained unspoken. We approached the problem as we had always done in previous camps. We were faced with a problem, the most difficult challenge to date – but there had to be a way out.

Wings, the Dodger, Sydney and I were pacing round the small compound one day weighing up the chances of breaking out. It was obviously not possible to go either through or over the wire, and a walkout through the gate and the little guard room offered a very poor chance of success. There were two watches of nine guards, each commanded by an Unterscharführer – one we called 'Jim', the man who had met me, an unpleasant fellow, and the other 'George' who was reasonable. That meant about one guard to every prisoner.

That left the underground method, and it looked as though a tunnel might be possible. The main problem would be dispersal of the earth, but the sides of the huts below floor level were enclosed on the outside. This was a luxury we never had at Sagan and provided there was sufficient clearance underneath the floor boards, we should be able to pack plenty of soil in there without being seen.

'I think the main thing we have to consider,' said Wings, 'is security with all the odd bods in this small compound. The Poles are certainly all right; the Russians might be, but I wouldn't trust Bessanov. Judd is the trouble. Cushing told me that he is a Gestapo informer. Think about a tunnel, but we'll lie low for a few weeks, watch the other inmates, and see whether the Germans make any searches.'

In the meantime we continued the business of existence in this little cage. By now we would be presumed to be dead by our relatives and friends, vanished into *Nacht und Nebel*; our existence was known only to the Sachsenhausen SS and Gestapo Headquarters where our files could have been, at any moment, dropped into the liquidation tray.

The Russians always walked up and down so if we wanted to vary our exercise we joined them. We found the bearded Brodnikov a stimulating and amusing companion, regaling us in good German with tales of life in the 'People's Paradise', always giving an amusing or quixotic twist to the most horrific stories of racketeering or

[1] Death's Head symbol of the Allgemeinen or Totenkopf SS who ran the concentration camps, and supervised Himmler's policy of racial extermination. The Waffen SS were the SS armed forces.

oppression by the NKVD. It was evident that his sense of humour had kept him going under Stalin's brutal dictatorship.

Once a week we were taken into the main compound for a shower. A ten minute walk down the road running parallel to the camp wall and round the corner at the end brought us into the Kommandantur, and I shall not forget my first sight of the inside of a Nazi concentration camp. Facing us was the notorious exhortation, '*Arbeit macht Frei*,' emblazoned in large letters above the archway formed by the administrative block; passing through we found ourselves in the large semi-circular *Appell Platz* around which were grouped the first semi-circle of twenty barrack huts the ends facing into the exercise area.

About thirty *Sträflinge*, gaunt, half-starved figures in striped suits, were being marched around the area, on their backs were heavy packs containing 30 pounds of bricks; truncheon-wielding SS guards ensured that they kept up a smart pace and sang when required to do so. They were testing boots for the Russian Front and had to cover about 25 miles daily. As an added refinement of torture some were forced to wear boots which were too small for them.

A gallows stood obscenely at the apex of the *Appell Platz*, a grisly reminder of the fate awaiting those who tried to escape. All the inmates were paraded immediately an escape was discovered and made to stand, sometimes for many hours, until the escaper was recaptured; they were then forced to watch while he was publicly despatched on the gallows. Jan Telling, a Dutch resistance fighter who was in Sachsenhausen for four years, remembers being forced to watch a Ukrainian being hanged in August 1942 for appropriating a little leather for his worn-out shoes, and before he was executed he was given twenty-five lashes.

We hurried on past the gibbet to the showers; had we known that shower rooms were often used for gassing, our pace might have been a bit slower. The only threat of death we encountered at this time was a large notice on the wall of the shower house which read; '*Ein Laus dein Tod*'.[1]

About three weeks later Sydney Dowse decided to forego his shower and stay behind in the Sonderlager. When we returned an ugly situation had developed. Sydney had reversed all the skull and crossbones signs so that they faced the guards on the wire. This had infuriated 'Jim', the red-haired Unterscharführer – puce in the face, he was shouting and screaming at Dowse who was giving as good as

---

[1] A louse means your death – a reference to typhus.

he got. Wings managed to calm things down, but he was soon called
to see the Commandant.

SS Standartenführer Anton Kaindl was an Austrian who had been
Commandant since 1942. He was coldly efficient in the disposal of
human bodies dead or alive; among other things, he had abolished
movement at the double, so that prisoners could stay on their feet
longer to slave for the Fatherland (Appendix 'E'). He harangued
Wings on Dowse's rash insolence which, if repeated, would lead to
severe disciplinary action. He reminded Wings of the impossibility of
escape from the camp, patrols and police dogs were everywhere, and
guards shot to kill. Then he abruptly dismissed him.

Wings was furious. He called the small Sagan group together and,
pacing round the compound, he told us that the time had come to
start the tunnel and show the SS we could outwit them. If Kaindl got
fired or shot in the process he had no objection.

Sydney and I had already decided on the general plan for the
tunnel. The trap was to be made in our room, the shaft sunk at the far
corner of the hut nearest the wire and dug out under the wire and
wall to a length of about 120 feet to break on the far side of the road.
This way all tunnel workings would be as far removed from the
guard room as possible.

The biggest factor, and it was a very big factor indeed, was going
to be security. The tunnel must be kept a close secret, known only to
the British officers and to the two Italians who cleaned our rooms. It
seemed a daunting task to keep hidden perhaps for months an
ambitious tunnel not only from our captors, but from the dozen or so
persons with whom we shared the same small living space,
measuring only some 70 yards by 30 yards – particularly when one
was an informer.

A home-made saw (a table knife with a serrated cutting edge) was the
only tool we had to build a tunnel one-third the length of 'Harry',
and Sydney and I were the only workers in the escape organisation.
The Dodger had wanted to help but his absence from the hut where
Judd lived would have been too marked, besides he was too big.
Peter Churchill did not wish to be involved as he thought he would
certainly be shot in the event of escape and recapture. Wings, of
course, could not work underground; being the SBO his absence
would most certainly have been noticed, and he had trouble with his
knee, due to a football injury years before.

We sawed laboriously through the floorboards near the wall under my bed. When we were, at last, able to lift them we found, to our dismay, that there was only six inches clearance between the ground and the floor. There was going to be a big dispersal problem. It was a disappointing start. We should have to dig a hole big enough to get into under the trap, and then push out inspection trenches to find out the extent of the problem.

We completed the trap, breaking off the ends of the nails which had been prised out of the cross beam underneath the boards, and pushed the end near the wall under the skirting where the boards had been cut. After sweeping dust into the cracks we felt we had a trap which might even have stood up to a ferret search at Sagan. It was easily opened by inserting the knife into the end opposite the wall and lifting.

Wings had kept watch for us during this operation. From now on only one of us must work at any one time, while the other kept a sort of circulating watch – a static watch in a compound this size would raise suspicion. We must also limit our working hours to about four a day so that the digger was not missing for too long.

It took us about a week to dig a large enough hole and push out a couple of inspection trenches; these were enough to confirm our worst fears. There was nowhere more than six inches clearance in any direction. Trenches for dispersal would have to be dug. There was another problem; a beam resting on stakes driven into the ground ran down the centre of the hut, and the effective dispersal on our side of the beam appeared to be blocked off by the concrete base of the wash house in the middle of the hut.

The wash house seemed to stand in the way of success. Then Sydney had an idea. 'Let's have a look at the passage,' he said, and we hastened out to look at the wooden floor running past the wash room. We got hold of a piece of wire and pushed it down between the boards. It went down about a foot, and there was our by-pass to the other side of the hut.

We were now assured of sufficient dispersal space to take the soil from the tunnel. With an average cross section of two feet, there would be at least 400 cubic feet to be dispersed.

'We'll have to calculate the length of the trenches pretty accurately,' I said. 'Make them too long and we'll be adding to the security risk, too short and we'll be stymied on the last green.'

'That's right,' replied Sydney, 'and there'll be no chance of doing a penguin act here or building up the flower beds.'

'We'll certainly need two trenches,' I went on. 'If we make one on each side of the beam, start digging the tunnel and fill up the trench on our side up to the wash house, we'll be able to figure out how long the other trench will have to be.'

We were ready to start undermining the SS defences. Working shifts of about two hours at a time while the other kept watch, we laboured on our bellies clad only in underpants, with a knotted handkerchief on the head and another one tied around mouth and nose as a mask against the dust which hung in clouds in this dim, constricted underworld, as we scooped the soil out and packed it each side of the trench beneath the floor boards.

When I heard Sydney's voice raised in the chosen warning song, usually the South African War song, 'Hold him down, you Zulu Warrior,' I lay still. On the occasions when I had to sing it, my rendering was not as melodious as Sydney's, but I was told it was recognizable!

In order to make faster progress we started to work in the early morning between the count and breakfast. This way we could get some time in before characters like Judd were astir. We also thought we could dispense with the usual watcher at that hour. One morning we had just removed the trap and I was climbing down into the hole underneath, when we heard the sound of heavy boots approaching in the passage. I leapt out of the hole and we pushed the trap hastily back into position. We had barely scrambled under the blankets when the door opened and 'Jim' appeared.

'*Morgen*,' he rasped, flashing his chrome teeth.

'*Morgen*, Jim,' we chanted, putting down the books we had hastily grabbed before his entrance.

'*Noch nicht aufgestanden?*'[1]

I assured him that it was our usual practice to lie late abed, on account of the general lack of amusements in the Sonderlager.

He had only come to tell us that there would be no showers that week as they were out of order.

We quickly cancelled the early morning shift and reverted to day-time working only. At the same time we took care to enter into compound activities as much as possible, and to be seen to be doing so; volley ball games, a little jogging and walking. It was natural that we should wish to retire to our room after such activity considering the inadequate diet.

I found sufficiently challenging intellectual stimulus in the German lessons I was giving to General Privalov and Fiodr

---

[1] 'Not up yet?'

Ceridilin. I used the only available text book which was in French, *Allemand sans Peine*, trying to explain any knotty points of grammar in Russian. Ceridilin, who was of course a lot younger, was a more apt pupil than the General, but I think I learnt more than they did! Sydney was learning Italian from Peter Churchill, who spoke it like a native, and was also teaching German to Wings and the Major. I continued my Russian with Colonel Brodnikov. He conducted his lessons entirely in Russian, often accompanying his explanations with much arm waving, beard pulling and leaping about the room. These pantomimes were vastly amusing, and compensated for the fact that he used some sort of lotion, which smelt like scent, for his hair, which was usually in a net in the manner of former Imperial officers, keeping the window shut even on the warmest summer day.

The RAF night raids on Berlin had finished just before our arrival in the Sonderlager. The American daylight raids were now in full swing and, being only 17 miles from Berlin, we had a Grandstand view. Once or twice a week the sirens would wail, the guards would disappear quickly into their shelters which had firing slits so that they could still keep the compound covered, and the prisoners would jump onto the window sills to obtain a better view as a thousand Fortresses swept in from the west. The fighters peeled off to dog-fight in the skies above us; the Forts went in to bomb, thousands of flak guns barked and roared, burning aircraft fell out of the sky as the white parachute canopies blossomed around them, the huts shook and vibrated and the air was full of whining shrapnel – then a huge pall of smoke and dust would rise many hundreds of feet above the doomed city. The great armada would wheel round to the north-west and thunder, formation after formation, directly over the camp on their way home. We sincerely hoped that they had dropped all their bombs – Bessanov used to jump up and down with excitement shouting *'Kak parad – kak parad!'* (It's like a ceremonial flypast.)

There was a little compound adjoining ours, accessible only through a door in the wall dividing us. Here lived Field Marshal Papagos, later to become Prime Minister of Greece, and four Generals of the Greek General Staff. We never saw them. Whenever they were taken for showers, we were locked in our huts under guard.

The long awaited and exciting news of the D-Day landings was a tremendous morale booster. German Army reports relayed through a loudspeaker, at first seemed to be confused as to whether the landings were taking placing in Normandy or in the Calais and Dunkirk area where parachute troops and naval units were reported, testifying to the success of the brilliant electronic diversionary measures carried out. There was soon no doubt that vast armies were ashore in Normandy. An operational map was put up in our Mess and Sergeant Cushing came into his own as an amateur strategist keeping it up to date. He used to breeze into our room after the evening meal and, with a running commentary and the air of having done it all himself, move the appropriate pins on the map. Then he would often regale us with a highly embellished account of soldiering in some foreign army. It was light relief from the political and philosophical discussions often instigated by Johnny Dodge who was no doubt keeping in practice for his post-war political platform at Gillingham.

Our busy little routine in the Sonderlager could not dispel the evil atmosphere which pervaded this dreadful place. We were reminded weekly when we saw the marching *Sträflinge* and passed under the shadow of the gallows on our way to the showers. Screams and groans could be heard in the night, frequently a burst of machine gun fire as some poor devil was caught in the searchlights attempting the impossible task of getting through the wire or, more likely, committing suicide. By day smoke from the crematorium chimney would signal that more brave souls who had opposed Hitler were out of their misery.

One day in June the smell of death became more personal. Wings was reading a copy of the *Völkischer Beobachter*' (the official Nazi Party Newspaper) when he spotted a paragraph which momentarily transfixed him with horror; he went through it again to make sure his translation had been correct. It reported a speech by Anthony Eden in the House of Commons condemning the brutal massacre by the Germans of fifty Royal Air Force prisoners who had taken part in a mass escape. It could only refer to the mass execution of our comrades who had escaped with us through the Sagan tunnel – after recapture.

Wings at once called the Dodger, Sydney and me to his room and broke the sad news to us. The implications were obvious should we manage to complete our tunnel successfully. After a short discussion we decided unanimously that we should carry on with our escape plans. We had made good progress with the dispersal trenches, there had been no searches to date, and we felt we had a good chance of digging the first tunnel from a concentration camp which the Germans considered escape proof. Besides, somebody might get home and report the existence of those in the Sonderlager and anyone else in Sachsenhausen known to us.

The Author, in front of his Hawker Hart at Evanton, Cromarty in December 1939.

Course photograph No.11 Operational Training Unit, RAF Bassingbourne, April 1940. The Author is seated fourth from the right.

Wellington bomber, the mainstay of RAF Bomber Command in the first two years of the war. The Author was flying a Wellington when he was shot down, 5 June 1940.

The entrance to Oflag XXIB, Szubin, with guards lined up to receive prisoners.

Recaptured. Major Dodge, related to Winston Churchill, back in German hands after jumping from a train.

West Block (foreground), Barth, 1941.

Room 25, East Block, Barth, November 1941. Left to right: Tony Trench, the Author, 'Cookie' Long (executed after The Great Escape), Gilson.

The Author, shortly after capture in June 1940.

Wing Commander HMA (Wings) Day, the highly respected SBO.

Squadron Leader Roger Bushell (Big X), executed by the Gestapo after The Great Escape.

Peter Churchill, SOE agent, a fellow prisoner at Sachsenhausen.

NCO prisoners at Barth. 'Dixie' Deans is standing second from right.

Best of enemies. Left to right: Roger Bushell, Eberhardt, German Security Officer, and Paddy Bryne.

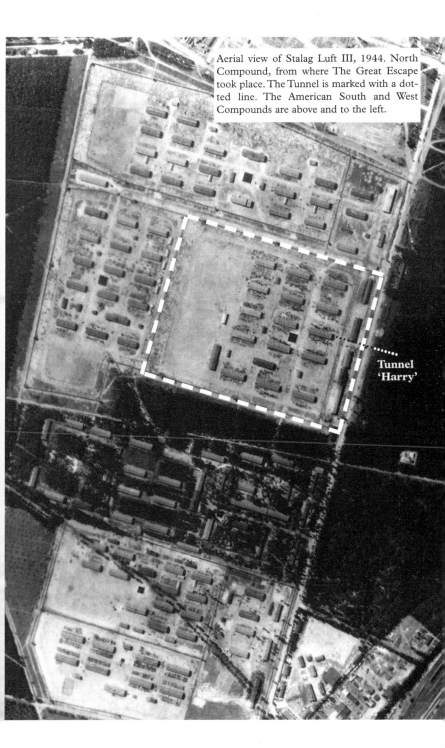

Aerial view of Stalag Luft III, 1944. North Compound, from where The Great Escape took place. The Tunnel is marked with a dotted line. The American South and West Compounds are above and to the left.

Tunnel 'Harry'

Above: Trap door and entrance to shaft leading to escape tunnel.

Left: Stove in Hut 104 which concealed the trap door.

Below: Escape tunnel 'Harry' with wooden trolley for removing the spoil.

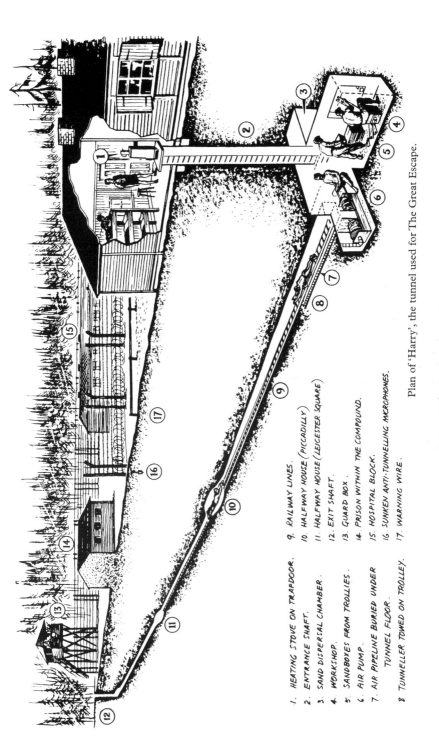

1. HEATING STOVE ON TRAPDOOR.
2. ENTRANCE SHAFT.
3. SAND DISPERSAL CHAMBER.
4. WORKSHOP.
5. SANDBOXES FROM TROLLIES.
6. AIR PUMP.
7. AIR PIPELINE BURIED UNDER TUNNEL FLOOR.
8. TUNNELLER TOWED ON TROLLEY.
9. RAILWAY LINES.
10. HALFWAY HOUSE (PICCADILLY)
11. HALFWAY HOUSE (LEICESTER SQUARE)
12. EXIT SHAFT.
13. GUARD BOX.
14. PRISON WITHIN THE COMPOUND.
15. HOSPITAL BLOCK.
16. SUNKEN ANTI-TUNNELLING MICROPHONES.
17. WARNING WIRE.

Plan of 'Harry', the tunnel used for The Great Escape.

Inmates of Sachsenhausen.

Plan of Sachsenhausen Concentration Camp, showing the Author's escape route. He escaped with Jack Churchill, Sydney Dowse, 'Wings' Day and Johnny Dodge.

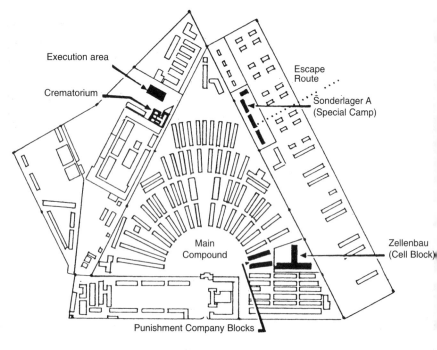

Execution area

Crematorium

Escape Route

Sonderlager A (Special Camp)

Main Compound

Zellenbau (Cell Block)

Punishment Company Blocks

Left: Dr J. C. van Dijk, former Dutch Minister of Defence (left), and Pastor Martin Niemöller. Both were prisoners at Reichenau, 1945, and previously Dachau and Sachsenhausen.

Scene of Liberation. The Author was attending early Mass at this chapel in the Dolomites when the Americans arrived 4 May 1945.

The Author and Madge at their wedding 26 July 1946.

Opposite: The Author, 1946.

Colonel Jack Churchill and the Author revisit Sachsenhausen, 1975, the scene of their escape. The wreath was laid in memory of the seven Commandos executed for their role in Operation MUSKETOON (Norway).

From left to right: The Author, Dick Churchill, Peter Fanshawe and Bob Nelson (who designed the air pump for 'Harry') at the RAF Museum, Hendon on the 45th Anniversary of The Great Escape.

Concentration Camps Memorial, Epinal-Alsace. A brooding and awesome sculpture evoking both horror and fear – bearing the names of Sachsenhausen, Dachau, Buchenwald, Mauthausen, Auschwitz and the other main Concentration Camps.

Memorial to those who died at Sachsenhausen Concentration Camp in the Père Lachaise Cemetery, Paris.

CHAPTER THIRTEEN

The Lonely Dig

Two colourful but contrasting personalities arrived in July. The first was initially an embarrassment, as he was a Russian who was put into the room next to ours.

Nikolai Rutschenko, son of a Ukrainian landowner shot by the Bolsheviks, had been a lecturer in history at Leningrad University. A lieutenant in the Reserve pre-war, he had been propelled at the outbreak of hostilities into some extraordinary adventures. First, the bitter Arctic warfare against the Finns who had a habit of burning unattended Russian skis, thus virtually sentencing their owners to a frozen death. Then the siege of Leningrad where he was captured by the Germans at the end of 1941. He existed for a while in a prison camp where there was no shelter except the holes dug in the ground by the Russian prisoners, and no food except, occasionally, raw horse meat thrown over the wire by their captors. Nikolai escaped in a mass breakout in which hundreds were shot, joined up with some Russians partisans in the woods and got back to the Soviet Army. He was not allowed any leave to see his wife, but was immediately trained as a parachutist and dropped behind the German lines; after many adventures, he was caught, interrogated and tortured by the Gestapo in Berlin and then sent to Sachsenhausen.

He turned out to be a most intelligent and likable fellow, and we need not have worried about security. He tended to keep to himself, doing much reading and writing in his room, although he enjoyed playing volley ball, and the rest of the time he spent with the other Russians. So we were able to continue operations 'below decks', muffling our movements as far as possible immediately under his floor area.

The next arrival was a bonus for our escape plans. One night at eleven o'clock, a stocky, rugged, fair-haired man was escorted into our block. He was wearing khaki shorts and bore the insignia of a lieutenant-colonel on the shoulder straps of his tropical shirt. He was Jack Churchill, the dashing Commando leader, holder of the DSO and bar and MC, whose name was a legend in the Italian theatre of war.

He had been stationed on the island of Lissa off the Dalmatian coast of Yugoslavia, where his brother Tom was commanding the Commando brigade, and had led his battalion in an attack on the neighbouring island of Brac, playing his men into battle on the bagpipes, as was his custom. They captured the hill which was their objective, but the Germans counter-attacked and Jack was captured after everybody around him had been killed. The Germans suspected that he was related to the Prime Minister and had kept him for several weeks in one of the houses just beyond the north wall of our compound. He told us that the occupants of the other houses were Dr Kurt von Schuschnigg, late Chancellor of Austria, his wife and young daughter, who had been there since 1938, Fritz Thyssen, the industrialist and his wife, and, in the fourth house, the Prince of Bourbon-Parma, his wife, a son of twelve and a young child.

The Colonel was, of course, delighted to become a party to our tunnel scheme and, as he was put into a room in the same hut, he became a very useful addition to our small operational team. If the reasons of the old prisoners for an escape that would obviously try Hitler's patience, not to mention Himmler and the SS, were perhaps a little nebulous, and certainly unspoken, compounded as they were of duty, the desire for freedom and the acceptance of a challenge, tempered with caution, our new arrival had no such reservations; for 'Mad Jack'[1] this was another adventure, a continuation of the infantry battle. In fact Wings had some difficulty in restraining him from trying schemes which included edging along the tops of walls somehow at night, and dropping off outside.

Churchill was able to confirm that fifty officers had indeed been shot after the Sagan escape, and told us of the horror and anger felt at home when this brutal massacre of prisoners of war became known.

We found Jack Churchill to be a most amusing and entertaining raconteur; for at least a week he enlivened our meal times with a nonstop flow of news and anecdotes about the war. It was a breath of fresh air for old prisoners shut off from the world for months which had rolled into years, until the surging tide of war seemed a far off murmur. He brought the din of battle into the room and even Cushing was silenced for a short while.

The camp strategists were busy forecasting the end of the war. The gloomier maintained that the Germans might have sufficient reserves to throw the Allied armies back into the sea. However, after

[1] As he was known in Commando circles.

the breakthrough at Falaise and further big advances by the Russians on the East Front, the issue was no longer in doubt, it was just a question of time. Bessanov could often be seen outside his hut demonstrating loudly with stick and stones how battles could be won and German armies surrounded and annihilated, while the taciturn Privalov, who had taken a leading part in forcing the German surrender at Stalingrad, looked on without comment. The Russians were all a little wary of Bessanov – after all, he had been high up in the NKVD.

As the Allied Armies advanced towards Germany, we did not expect any outward manifestation of despair from the SS. It was, therefore, a surprise when 'Jim' in the course of a few exchanges about the war, asked if I would be able to find him a job with the Allies after the war – he would be prepared to do anything, black boots, if necessary. In a POW camp an approach such as this would have been an opening for bribery, but an SS corporal was not to be trusted. 'Jim' was a typical product of the Hitler Youth who had jumped on the SS bandwagon. He was a bully by nature, and this was the reaction of the bully in the face of strength. 'George', the other corporal, was quite different; an older man drafted into the SS, he had a sense of humour and treated us in a civilized manner.

The dispersal trenches were finished by the end of July, work having been speeded up with Jack Churchill's help. We then sunk the tunnel shaft in the corner of the hut, as planned, to a depth of about five feet. No shoring was necessary as the soil was firm. We did not bother to make a trap for the shaft; if the SS happened to suspect a tunnel they would tear the hut apart and find it whatever we did to try to conceal it.

Sydney Dowse and I, as the diggers, started to push the tunnel out towards the wire. We had to work alone and in complete darkness. The 'mod cons' of POW camps were simply not available. Air holes could not be made for security reasons and so fat lamps would not burn; there was just enough air to sustain one sweating digger, ventilation got worse and dispersal more difficult as the tunnel lengthened. When sufficient earth had been loosened by our knife and pulled away from the face, we would slither backwards scrabbling the pile of earth along with arms extended in front until we reached the shaft where the soil was thrown up to Jack who did sterling work pulling it down the trenches with his steel helmet.

The tunnel edged on towards the wire. Then one day we noticed that bits of the roof were falling off just below the path, which received quite a pounding from the inmates taking exercise, and very soon it began to show signs of collapse. We managed to collect sufficient wood, mainly bed boards, and shored up the tunnel just in time.

Keeping the tunnel straight and at an even depth was a problem in the dark. Sydney seemed to have a built-in spirit level, and now and again accused me of digging like a 'dog's hind leg'; although my professional pride was injured, I usually had to agree. We had many arguments and discussions, but we got on well and formed a good partnership for this particular job.

In June the shower parties had been stopped without explanation. This was a blow to our plans. A new compound was being built just outside the Sonderlager and much of the enclosing wall had already been built. Our escape route could be cut off. We simply had to see over our wall. Then, one day, Wings had a brain-wave. He wrote to the Commandant to say that British officers liked to keep fit, and could they please have some parallel bars to assist them in this admirable aim. Surprisingly the request was granted. We used the parallel bars to good purpose; besides exercising dutifully and regularly on them, we extended them to their full height, then by standing on top of the bars were able to see over the top of the Sonderlager wall and observe the progress of the new compound.

As the tunnel approached the wire we had to consider the possibility of encountering seismographs, alarms or even electrified wire extended below the surface. Johnny Dodge had been told by the SS, on arrival, that these existed and that lights would flash in the guard room if the wire were tampered with. He volunteered to dig the section of tunnel under the wire, but was told firmly by Wings to stay above ground.

To minimize the risk of hitting unpleasant obstacles Dowse and I increased the depth of the tunnel to about eight feet as we dug below the wire and wall. At this depth, one hundred feet from the shaft, even for a lone digger, the air was putrid, it was pitch black and claustrophobic.

It was about the second week in September we calculated that the tunnel was outside the wall with a length of about 110 feet. We had to decide whether to break the tunnel on this side of the tarmac road, into the rough verge between the nearside of the road and the Sonderlager wall, with some risk of the guard and dog being alerted, or to continue under the road for another 10 or 15 feet; the length of the dispersal trenches had been accurately calculated and there would have been enough room for the extra soil. The view from the parallel bars was not encouraging; at any moment electrified wire could be placed on top of the new wall. There was also the extra security risk involved in spending more time on digging operations.

We were all aware of the risk of siting the exit hole near the wall; the dog's sharp hearing and acute sense of smell could 'put paid' to the escape before it had started, and caught outside the wall the SS could shoot us without any questions asked. Wings walked each of us round the compound in turn in order to sound us out independently. He got, in effect, the same reply from all: 'Let's go now.'

'Now we're all decided on breaking the tunnel this side of the road, we've got to choose a suitable night.'

Wings was as usual deceptively languid, his six feet four inch frame draped over his bed, he stared grimly at the four of us. His injured knee had swelled up like a balloon and was causing him considerable pain.

'We've also got to get the Dodger over to our hut,' he continued. 'Any ideas, Major?'

Johnny Dodge, behind an innocent facade, had a shrewd brain; he leant forward and, in his earnest way, making each point with a stabbing forefinger, said:

'How would it be if I wrote a nice informal letter to the Commandant – something on these lines – "I am a man of fifty and find the company in my hut rather noisier than I like. I should be most grateful if you would allow me to move over into the other hut where I could have a room to myself."'

'Bloody good idea,' said Wings. 'Go ahead and write it. Now about the tunnel break. When is it to be?'

We certainly needed a dark night. The moon table in the newspaper indicated the next moonless period about the third week in September with the 23rd as the darkest night. Jack Churchill said he hoped that we might get some rain as well. He had noted that the sentry and dog, on a fine night, always took up position at the guard's air raid shelter, almost opposite the point at which we would open the tunnel, with the dog lying on the roof, its nose only a few feet from the top of the wall, while on rainy nights they both retired into the shelter. We also hoped that 'Jim' would be on duty.

'Well, the main thing we want is a moonless night,' said Wings, 'so the 23rd it will be – and let's pray for some rain as well. We've got just over two weeks, that'll give time to get a reply from the Commandant – he replies promptly, I'll say that for him – Sydney and Jimmy can do any finishing touches to the tunnel.'

Our escape plans had already been laid. Wings and Sydney were going together. Attired in civilian suits lent by Bartoli and Amici, and with a little money they had managed to keep, they planned to catch a suburban railway train from Oranienburg Station to Mahlsdorf, a suburb in SE Berlin, where they had the address of a German anti-Nazi black marketeer called Fullert, obtained by chance from Andy Walsh who had met him when he was in Berlin. Fullert was a member of the TODT Organisation, the Nazi Civil Labour and Construction Force, and his lorries were under contract to supply electrical equipment to the German fortifications in the west; they returned to Berlin loaded with cognac, cheese, butter and other black market loot. If Fullert agreed to pack them in with his equipment it would be an easy way to get to France.

Jack Churchill and I were planning to walk at night up the main Berlin-Rostock Railway Line, resting in the day-time, jumping trains whenever possible. We hoped to smuggle ourselves aboard a neutral ship either at Rostock or at some other Baltic port and get to Sweden. With only modified Service uniforms – I still had my faithful old tunic, in which I had been shot down, and the trousers in which I had escaped through the Sagan tunnel – no papers and no maps, except for a very basic newspaper map which showed the railway line, and a sheet of Bessanov's School Atlas 'appropriated' by Jack Churchill, we should have to rely on foot-slogging to get us to our destination.

It fell to the Dodger to be the odd man out; this was not entirely his choice, but we were all of the opinion that three people travelling together might attract too much attention when it was likely that the whole country would be looking for us. His plan was simply to walk west towards the advancing Allied armies. If necessary he would just hide up in some farm and wait for liberation.

In the next fortnight all the loose ends were tied up. Sydney and I made an extra bay at the tunnel face to take the earth from the breakthrough. The Dodger received a letter from the Commandant approving his transfer to our hut and installed himself in one of our rooms. Finally, Wings got treatment for his knee from an SS doctor who drew off the water from the bulbous pouch over the knee cap, bandaged it up and advised rest.

There was still our immediate Russian neighbour Rutschenko.

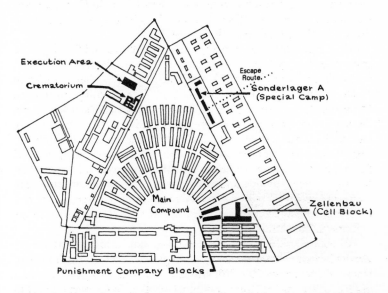

Sachsenhausen concentration camp showing the author's escape route.

Over the preceding weeks we had watched him closely, come to like him and, more important, to trust him. It was a pity not to offer him a chance to leave through a tunnel just under his floorboards. I was deputed to ask him in Russian whether he would like to join us. He seemed to take it as a matter of course that there should be a ready-made exit for him. Russian fatalism or had he suspected something? He thanked us politely for the offer, but excused himself on the grounds that it was too short notice for him to make adequate preparation; in any case, he said that he would probably be shot if recaptured. He had, no doubt, had enough of the Gestapo and their methods.

On the late afternoon of 23rd September we exercised for the last time on the parallel bars. The compound was still empty and unguarded, the high wall remained free of electrified wire and the builder's ladder was conveniently propped against it. Our escape route was ready.

That evening a special escapers' supper was laid on by the Italians. There was cause too for celebration. 'Jim' was on duty. Even better, the sky was dark and overcast with a steady drizzle; it looked as though it would continue when the five of us were locked in our hut at ten o'clock, as usual.

CHAPTER FOURTEEN

Escape from the SS

And God stands winding His lonely horn
And time and the world are ever in flight.

'Into the Twilight' William Butler Yeats

In the inky black void at the tunnel face Dowse and I took it in turns to hack our way up to the surface; earth and stones came showering down and the bay was filling up. After two hours Sydney was standing on my shoulders slashing away with a knife, cursing and muttering, when there was a metallic rasp.

'Hell,' came an agonised gasp.

'What's the matter?' I asked.

'We're under the road. We'll have to start another shaft a bit further back and hope to God there is enough room for dispersal. We must have been ten feet down at least.'

Jack Churchill, who was standing by in case help was needed, went back down the tunnel to tell Wings and Major Dodge, waiting anxiously in the room, that there would be a delay.

As we hacked our way upwards again the minutes dragged on, the air was stale and heavy, the pile of rubble grew until we could stand on it, and there was already a danger that it could block the exit. At last came a sigh of relief from Sydney; his knife had pushed up into the night air, and soon I could see the dull grey light above as the opening widened. Jack took the good news back from tunnel face to entrance shaft, much to the relief of the two who were waiting.

We widened the hole further, in complete silence now, the guard and dog would only be a few feet away on the other side of the wall – Thank God for the rain – then we put a temporary trap in and went back to clean up.

'Congratulations,' said Wings, 'Now we must get going.'

We grabbed our home made packs containing our escape rations, and went down the tunnel one by one. Dowse went first, I followed, then came Churchill, Wings and Dodge. Sydney took my pack from me as I crawled out of the exit hole, and then disappeared over to the far wall while I waited for Jack, I took his pack as he emerged quickly. The rain continued in a steady drizzle.

Far down the camp wall I saw a torch flash momentarily, and was about to join Sydney to relieve the congestion at the exit, when I realized that Wings was having trouble. The pile of rubble and his swollen knee were doing much to impede his progress. After a struggle, pushed from below by Dodge, he got his head and shoulders out, then Jack and I heaved him out the rest of the way. The Dodger had even more trouble. His large frame made it very difficult for him to squeeze over the big pile of rubble which had been made even bigger by the soil dislodged by the four of us out before him. Wings and Jack were whispering advice down to him, as one arm and shoulder appeared they grabbed it and heaved, the Dodger struggled upwards and was out at last.

'Ah, free at last!' he muttered in an imperturbable stage whisper.

I nipped over to the far wall to try to find Sydney. I could not see him anywhere, but I found the ladder and waited for the others who suddenly appeared like ghosts out of the murk, Sydney came from nowhere and I started up the ladder, quickly followed by the other four.

There was a fifteen-foot drop on the other side of the wall. Luckily the ground was soft and we all landed safely. Wishing one another good luck we set off on our separate ways, intent on putting as much distance as possible between ourselves and the SS. It was about 2 a.m.

Jack Churchill and I went off through the trees in a north-westerly direction. We soon came to a built-up area which seemed to lie across our line of advance. Jack was highly elated with the new-found taste of freedom and this obstacle was merely a small challenge to his Commando training. He led the way through silent gardens and back yards; as we dodged behind bushes and crawled along below the shadow of walls, he whispered excitedly,

'This is like an infantry battle!'

Then we came to railway lines running north, but our small map indicated that the main Rostock line lay some miles to the west, so we crossed over the tracks and continued westwards across open country at a fast pace, at one point following a canal. By morning light we reckoned we had covered about twelve miles and we happened on a small coppice where we rested for the day. It was still raining and we were very wet but we did not care, we were too excited at gaining our freedom.

The next night under an overcast sky we plodded on over

ploughed fields, keeping direction by the north-west wind which whipped a chilling rain across our faces and soaked our thin clothing. The heavy soil underfoot and the numerous fences over which we had to climb allowed only slow progress, but soon, carried on the wind, we heard faintly, the low moaning whistle peculiar to German locomotives, and we quickened our pace. The whistling and puffing of steam engines continued all night and grew louder, until at first light we stumbled out onto the main Berlin-Rostock railway line.

There was sparse cover in the neighbourhood, all we could find was a shallow depression among some trees where we lay down to rest. The rain passed but when the sun was up we found that we were uncomfortably near a German army barracks with soldiers passing along a path very close to us, so we covered ourselves with sticks and foliage and lay still all day, the steam rising from our soaked clothing.

As we marched north along the railway, usually on the sleepers between the rails, occasionally on the cinder path beside the track, we reflected that this was a great improvement on ploughed fields. Diving off to the side when trains passed, we continued thus for two nights, with a welcome day's rest in a haystack, until on the fourth night out we reached a little station in a wood. It was called Dannenwald and there were some goods sidings near the station.

We rested in the deserted woodlands not far from the tracks. In the afternoon Jack went off to reconnoitre the station area and returned about an hour later with a load of fresh vegetables, swedes, carrots, leaks, a few potatoes and a lot of elderberries, which he said he had filched from the station allotments.

'How on earth did you get those without being seen?' I enquired.

'Fieldcraft, old boy,' was the laconic reply. 'Anyway, I had a good look round, and I think we ought to stay here tonight and watch the form.'

'Do you think we could jump a train here?'

'Well, there are three goods vans parked over on the far sidings, so goods trains must obviously stop here.'

We managed to light a small fire of sticks and we cooked the vegetables in a rusty tin we had found, making a crude vegetable soup but at least it was hot, and it was a change from our usual diet of hard biscuits, cheese, the odd cube of chocolate (strictly rationed) and swigs of condensed milk out of a tin.

We watched the station all that night but no goods trains stopped. The next day we found a small lake nearby and replenished our water bottles.

The following night Jack decided that he would go over to the three goods vans standing in the siding and try to find out where they were routed from the destination labels, placed in small wire grills on the side.

He padded off across the tracks in his rubber-soled Commando boots merging into the darkened sidings. He returned shortly with the labels. By the light of a match we discovered the destination of all three to be Stettin, a desirable Baltic port. Just at that moment a long goods train steamed into the station from the south and stopped. It backed slowly into the siding where the three vans stood and they were coupled to the end of the train.

The frantic action packed into the next twenty minutes remains in my memory as a nightmarish apograph of one of those speeded up Hollywood films of the twenties and thirties, like the Keystone Cops; at least our antics would have done justice to the Marx Brothers.

As the train began to move forward we tore across the tracks and just managed to throw ourselves over the buffers between two trucks. Before we could ease ourselves into a safer position, the train came to a halt in the station.

At that moment Jack dropped down onto the sleepers between the rails. Thinking that somebody had seen us, I lowered myself quickly down beside him.

'It's all right,' he whispered, 'I've only dropped my water bottle.'

Before we could get up again the train began to move – this time backwards, and over the top of us. There was no choice but to lie flat between the rails while the long line of wagons clattered over us.

Then we heard the clanking of mighty connecting and driving rods as the huge locomotive approached. Lifting our heads slightly we could see the base of the fire box glowing red; low on the track it bore down on us. Motionless we pressed ourselves down on the sleepers and prayed. Belching smoke and hissing steam the monster engine thundered over us and came to a halt about twenty yards down the track. Its forward searchlight shone down on two petrified figures lying prone on the track.

A realisation that we were lying just below the edge of the platform got us quickly to our feet. We walked back down the side of the train as nonchalantly as possible. Some shunters shone their lamps on us but said nothing; there were many odd characters walking about Germany in those days. We slunk back into the shadow of the wood in case somebody had reported our strange behaviour.

Once more the train was moving forward. It must really be on its

way this time. We made another dash across the tracks and managed
to clamber onto a flat truck loaded with very large tree trunks to a
height of about nine feet. Thankfully we climbed up on top of the wet,
slippery timber. But this was not yet the start of our journey.

The cacophony of clashing buffers once more surged down the line
of wagons and the train ground to a halt in the same place. Slowly it
started to back, then a little faster, gathering speed until there was a
sudden stop – the uncoupled truck behind us was shunted off into the
darkness, and Jack Churchill, who was sitting on the edge of the pile
of timber, was catapulted out after the departing truck and landed
heavily on the track twelve feet below.

Groans of discomfiture rose up from the track. I scrambled down
to find that the Colonel had sprained his ankle and could only move
with difficulty. Somehow, by hauling and pushing alternately, I
managed to help him back up to the top of the timber. Surprisingly,
nobody seemed to have noticed these capers, although there was a
good deal of signalling and shouting around us.

A few minutes later the train was moving forward again. Clinging
to the timber we expected another jolting halt, but it was gathering
speed at the station and we knew we were on our way at last. Out on
the open track we felt a sense of relief and exhilaration as the long
goods train pounded north. As I held fast to the chains which secured
the tree trunks high up on the swaying wagon, smoke and sparks
flying past on the wind, my thoughts took me back more than five
years to British Columbia, when I was clinging to the catwalk of a
Canadian National Railways box-car thundering north up the wild
and rugged Fraser Canyon, never dreaming that I was training for a
similar experience in Nazi Germany.

We halted once at some small unlighted sidings, then
steamed on again and stopped at a large marshalling yard bathed in
the light of many arc lamps. Our truck came to rest right beside a
signal box from which the signalman at the window appeared to
have a good view of us on top of the timber. However, he was
engaged in conversation with a mate below – they were talking about
the war and appeared a little depressed about it. The sign on the
signal box indicated that we were at Neustrelitz, so we must have
covered fifty miles during the night. We lay motionless, keeping our
faces and hands covered, and were luckily not spotted.

After about twenty minutes the train moved out into the darkness
and stopped, obviously prior to reversing on another interminable
shunting operation. At this point we decided to get off as we did not

fancy being lighted up by the arc lamps again and, anyway, the night was drawing to a close. I was also feeling unwell as a result of a surfeit of vegetable soup and elderberries and we detrained hastily; we had, furthermore, become extremely cold from the wind on our soaking clothes.

Churchill, with his sprained ankle, was only able to crawl; he took his gaiters off and used them to protect his hands. I took his pack and went ahead to find somewhere to rest that day. I found some undergrowth in a wood and here we settled down thankfully, chewed some biscuits, had a swig of condensed milk and went to sleep. We were awake that afternoon when a young German soldier almost stumbled on us. He circled around doubtfully, watching us, then went off at a fast pace, obviously intent on informing someone in authority. We moved down to the bottom of a deep depression about a hundred yards away and covered ourselves with autumn leaves and sticks. Not long after, hoarse cries and the trampling of heavy boots told that the search party had arrived; they came very close to us, then sounds of the chase died away and peace returned to the woods.

It was not possible for us to continue the journey until Jack's ankle improved. I went off that night to reconnoitre the marshalling yards but they were so brightly lit up that it was very difficult to move about in them without detection. I managed to look at the destination labels of some wagons standing in a siding on the edge, but they were not bound for the Baltic. On the way back I found a haystack which we made our headquarters the following day.

Two days' rest had greatly improved my companion's ankle and that night we were able to go on – it was our eighth night out since leaving Sachsenhausen and we decided to mark the occasion by another visit to the marshalling yards where we altered the destinations of as many wagons as possible by swapping the labels around, hoping this would cause some confusion on the Reichsbahn.

Highly elated, we strode out along the railway line we had left so hurriedly two nights previously. Soon the tracks ran out onto a high embankment. A bright moon lit up the countryside. Then Jack said:

'Jimmy, we're a bit conspicuous up here. I think that we ought to keep direction along the bottom of the embankment in the shadow.'

We moved down to the shaded side on the right. A very long time later the embankment died away and we were back on the line again. After about a mile I stopped.

'I think we're wrong,' I said.

'We can't be,' replied Jack. 'We're still on the railway.'

'Yes, but when we started it was a double track, now it's single.'

'By God,' exclaimed Jack, 'you're right, so there must have been a fork to the left when we were walking along the bottom of the embankment on the right.

A quick star check confirmed that we were heading too far east. It would have lost a lot of time going back to the fork, so we decided to head due west and hoped we'd find the right track again before long.

We turned off to the left and plunged into a pine forest. It was one of the many vast wooded areas of North Germany. All that night we tramped down long rides between the trees, the silence broken only by the barking of the deer. It was daylight before we reached the main line for Rostock.

The next night's march in pouring rain brought us, exhausted, to a small station in another wood. We spent the day in the wood trying to dry out our wet clothes in front of a fire of sticks which we had encouraged with some oil we had taken from a railway signal lamp; we also brewed up some tea. We decided to stay put that night, and Jack went off on a long reconnaissance.

'There's nothing in the train line that I can see,' he said when he came back, 'but I saw a party of wood cutters near some huts, and they seemed to be chatting in Russian.'

The following day we edged around the clearing in which the huts were situated. There were no Germans about and we beckoned to the two young men nearest to us. At first they looked suspicious, then they approached hesitantly.

'*Zdravstvuitye!*[1]' I greeted them in Russian.

'*Zdravstvuitye!*' they replied.

I told them that we were British officers who had been on the run for ten days, we were getting weak and exhausted, and could they please fill our water bottles and give us a little food.

They became friendly and took our bottles, returning with them filled and some bread as well.

'Come back tonight after dark when the German overseer has gone and we'll give you a meal,' they said.

'*Blagodaryu Vas,*'[2] I replied.

We had a cheerful evening with the Russians sitting outside one of

---

[1] 'Greetings' or 'How do you do'.
[2] 'Thank you' in the more fulsome form.

the huts around a roaring log fire above which was suspended a large tureen of steaming soup. It contained a number of vegetables and some meat and after our starvation diet it tasted like nectar. We soon cleared two large bowls of it. Warm and replenished, we turned our attention to our hosts who, faces glowing red in the light of the fire, were gathered around watching us eagerly, anxious that we should be satisfied. There were about twenty-five of them, all civilians, and they told us that they had been captured as young boys in the German advance in 1941; their present ages ranged only from about fifteen to twenty, with a few older ones. Although they were made to work hard, they were not, apparently, badly treated.

I told them I had been a bomber pilot, a statement received with much enthusiasm.

'How many times have you bombed Berlin?' I was asked.

'About ten times,' I replied, embroidering the truth a little, in the hope of raising their morale. I was not disappointed; a great cheer went up.

'How many times has he been over Berlin?' was the next question, indicating the Colonel.

'Tell them thirty times,' replied Churchill without hesitation. This, of course, raised an even bigger cheer.

From them we learnt that there had just been a terrible disaster at Arnhem; they had no details but knew that a great many British paratroopers had died.

All too soon the evening passed and the time came for us to continue our journey. Before we left, with typical Russian generosity, they pressed upon us some gifts, a good general purpose knife for Jack and a fur-lined leather Russian hat for me. In return we gave them a little cocoa and tea from our meagre store of saved up Red Cross rations.

Reluctantly we said farewell and, leaving the friendly circle around the warm fire, we stepped out into the chill autumn night.

Feeling refreshed we made good progress and one night's walking brought us to Waren, a large town situated on one of the Mecklenburg lakes. The following night, to avoid a big detour and to conserve our energy, we walked through the town. We met numerous police and troops, but our trampish appearance brought no comment, although a soldier with a rifle at the ready patrolling near the railway sidings took a long look at us. We hurried on and, after a few wanderings, joined the track again to the north of the town.

It was on this night on a high embankment that we decided incautiously that we wanted some more signal lamp oil to light our fires of wet sticks. Standing on a small wooden platform at the base of the signal, we wound the lamp down with the handle. We were filling our bottle with oil when there was a crunch on the permanent way behind us. We turned to see an elderly railwayman watching us.

'*Guten Abend*,' I greeted him.

'*Abend*,' he muttered.

'*Kalt*,' I continued, trying to introduce some kamaraderie into the conversation, if we could call it that.

'*Wir machen hier eine Kontrolle*,'[1] I went on with as much conviction as I could muster.

'*So*,' he growled and disappeared into the night leaving us a little shaken. It would have been wise to have departed from the scene at once, but we thought we should clear up the mess and we wanted our oil, so we continued fiddling with bits of the lamp and pouring the rest of the oil into our bottle. Before we could finish a howl of rage rent the air and two men wielding long staves were rushing across the track at us.

I grabbed my pack and tore down the embankment. The Colonel, unfortunately, was trapped on the platform and, having the undivided attention of the two enraged Germans who seemed to be beating him to pulp, obviously needed some assistance. I scrambled back up the embankment and caught hold of a handle of the bag one of the men had snatched from Churchill; the blows which he had been aiming at the Colonel now fell on me while he hung onto a bag handle with the other hand. This bizarre tug of war went on for a minute or two until the bag handle the German was holding broke, and I fell head over heels backwards down the embankment, still clutching the bag.

This diversion had allowed Jack to struggle free from the other German, and he came running down after me with black eyes and a bleeding head. We ran on across the fields for some distance and then did a dog-leg back across the track to throw off any pursuers. We went on across country for some three miles; at daybreak, coming by lucky chance on a small lake surrounded by woodland. It seemed a little oasis on the only warm, sunny day of the whole escape; we were able to rest after the alarms and excursions of the night, lick our wounds, wash and shave, and have a good bathe in the lake.

---

[1] 'We're doing an inspection here'.

When we set off again at nightfall, we at first thought it best to avoid the railway and steer a course, as far as possible, parallel to it. In open country on a clear night we 'steered' by the stars, usually the North Star; if it was overcast, we established the direction of the wind before the sun went down, and hoped it wouldn't change. On this night the North Star shone brightly and it was unfortunate that we could not continue to follow it out in the open; after some three hours of slogging over wet sticky ploughland, cakes of mud clinging to our feet at every step, and struggling over or through fences, hedges, ditches and other obstacles we finally gave it up and cut back to the railway.

The relief of feeling the firm wooden sleepers beneath our feet once more put spring into our step, and we covered more miles that night than on any other. The taste of salt air on our lips gave us more encouragement; we were nearing the Baltic, and quite soon, a day or two perhaps, we could be aboard a ship for Sweden.

The early hours of the morning brought mist, swirling around us in patches, it gradually thickened until at daybreak a dense blanket of fog enveloped us. There seemed little possibility of finding a hideout for the day by continuing along the track in such fog, in any case it seemed safer to leave it, so we struck off across a field.

We had walked for only a few minutes, when suddenly and without warning some dim shapes loomed out of the murk, rapidly materializing into a column of women, Polish as it turned out, going off to work in the fields. We found ourselves standing almost face to face with a large German overseer.

'Who are you?' he asked.

'We're French workers,' I replied.

'Where are you going?'

'To Farmer Schmidt's over there,' I invented.

'*Papiere,*' came the usual demand.

'*Nous avons laissé zu Hause,*'[1] I replied trying to imitate a Frenchman in Germany.

The German was unimpressed and called up a young Polish lad of some fourteen years.

'Take this lot back to the house,' he said.

We went off with the boy, and it was then that the fog became our friend. After a short while the column was swallowd up in the mist; we said goodbye to the boy and ran off as fast as we could, and

---

[1] 'We have left (them) at home.'

continued running until we came to a wood. We found that it was a large deciduous wood, the mist was beginning to clear, and under dripping leaves we plunged into its dark depths. Finding a clump of bushes we settled in their midst for the day.

In the afternoon we were stretched out on the ground trying to sleep when, out of the corner of one half open eye, I caught a glimpse of what appeared to be the head and shoulders of a man flitting past the top of a bush – it seemed that there was a gun slung over his shoulder.

I nudged Jack and told him what I'd seen. We started to pack up our gear in readiness for a swift departure.

Suddenly, the bushes parted and we found ourselves looking down the muzzles of three shot guns aimed at us by three very determined looking representatives of the Volksturm (German Dad's Army).

'*Hände hoch!*'

We raised our arms in the air.

'*Wer sind Sie, Russische, Polnische, Französische?*'

No doubt, because I was wearing my Russian hat.

'*Britische Offiziere,*' I replied firmly.

They at once lowered their weapons, relieved that we were not *Untermensch*[1] and allowed us to pack up our things. They escorted us back to the local inn where they sat us down at a table and took our particulars. The atmosphere was relaxed. 'The whole country was looking for you, so you had no chance at all,' said one of them.

While we polished off the remainder of our escape rations, knowing they would be confiscated, we chatted to the inn-keeper and a few locals; they told us it was bad luck we had been caught, but a general alarm had gone out after the farmer had seen us that morning. In the meantime they gave us some good beer.

The SS arrived about nine o'clock that evening. Six of them stamped into the bar. Their screams and shouts silenced our friendly conversation and a hush fell on the inn.

We were bundled into cars and taken to Güstrow where we were lodged in separate cells in the local gaol. Early in the morning we were handcuffed, taken out and put into a Black Maria or '*Grüne Minne*' as the Germans called these prison vans. The one hundred and twenty miles or so we had covered so painfully and perilously from Sachsenhausen was retraced in little over four hours.

---

[1] The Germans regarded all peoples from the Eastern Territories as *Untermensch* (subhuman) and they seemed to regard the British with the most respect.

Perhaps we had not done too badly; with no weather protection, in light clothing, we had been continually wet, cold and hungry during the whole fortnight we were out, although we never got a cold or a cough, and had been caught within a 'sea breeze' of our goal by mischance. We had also done a modest amount of sabotage, but this was nothing compared to the general upset caused by our escape from the Sonderlager (Appendix 'D').

The cell door slammed shut behind me as Jack Churchill was taken further down the passage to another cell. I found myself, still handcuffed, in a small space measuring about eight feet in length by about four feet in width; there was just room for a bed, small table and stool. The only other amenity was a toilet bucket in the corner. There was a barred window about seven feet up in the bare wall opposite the door.

I knew that I was in the notorious Zellenbau (Cell Block or Bunker) in Sachsenhausen, and that few incarcerated therein ever lived to tell their friends about it, and certainly not those who had escaped from the all powerful SS.

I felt curiously detached and lay down to think over what we might have done to avoid recapture, to contemplate what might remain of life, and to give some thought to the life hereafter, with the sanguine hope that my latter period on earth might shorten my stay in purgatory.

CHAPTER FIFTEEN

Zellenbau

'In Nazi Germany – first they put the Communists and Jehovah's Witnesses in Concentration Camps, but I was not a Communist or a Jehovah's Witness so I did nothing – then they arrested the Trade Unionists but I did nothing because I was not one. Then they arrested the Jews and again I did nothing because I was not Jewish – At last they came and arrested me, but then it was too late; there was no one left to speak for me.'

Pastor Niemoller

I was lying handcuffed on my bed the first afternoon speculating on an uncertain future, when the cell door suddenly opened and the sinister face of SS Oberscharführer Eccarius was looking down at me, with cold pitiless eyes and his cruel mouth drawn tight.

'It is forbidden to lie on the bed in the daytime,' he shouted 'Steh auf! Der Kommandant.'

I stood up and, looking past him, saw the Commandant standing in the passage. It was the first time I had seen Kaindl. He was short and squat, and looked quite undistinguished, his rimless spectacles giving him the appearance of a little Himmler. He made no attempt to come in, but just stood at the door and stared at me with an expression compounded of anger and loathing. I think the latter predominated but he was obviously seething with anger. No word was spoken. For a minute or two he glared at me; then he turned abruptly, Eccarius shut the door, and I was once more alone with my thoughts which had now become disturbed.

Kurt Eccarius was the SS Warrant Officer who for long had been in charge of the Cell Block. He was the Beast of the Bunker and something of his notoriety had filtered through to us in the Sonderlager. After the war his full record was revealed as a sadistic torturer who perpetrated the most terrible cruelties on prisoners in the cells. Many were also despatched to the death factory at Station Z for hanging, shooting or gassing (Appendix 'E').

The light was put out at ten o'clock. After two weeks' exposure to the elements with little rest, I fell into a sleep of exhaustion. I was awakened by the sound of the door crashing open, the naked electric light bulb shining down on me and the screams of the SS corporal, whose name I learnt was Unterscharführer Luchs, ordering me to take my bucket down to ablutions. It was 5 a.m. the normal time for 'reveille' in the Bunker.

In the washroom I met Jack Churchill and, to my surprise, Wings Day and Sydney Dowse. We had little time to talk and, indeed, it was officially forbidden, but on this and subsequent meetings in the washroom we learnt that they had reached Mahlsdorf on the S-Bahn, although they had missed the last train and had to wait for an early morning connection. When they reached their contact address, they found that the house had been bombed. Only the cellar remained; they went down into it and slept for two hours or so. On awakening they were nibbling some escape rations considering their next move, when two policemen burst in with pistols and arrested them. They learnt later that they had been seen by the woman next door and reported. It was fortunate, and indeed played a significant role in our survival, that they were in the hands of the police before being returned to Sachsenhausen. As it was, they bore the initial brunt of Gestapo fury and had been chained to the floor of their death cells.

Back in my cell Luchs thrust a broom into my hand shouting at me to sweep it out. The door slammed shut and I was left to reflect on the situation. Wings and Sydney were still on earth. Although this gave one some reason for hope, expectation of life in the Zellenbau was an imponderable, and depended on how the dice fell in the game of death played out in the labyrinthine corridors of Gestapo power. On the second day I was taken out for interrogation, still handcuffed, in some trepidation, but received only a mild questioning from a Doctor of Law attached to the SS from the German Ministry of Foreign Affairs. Fate had made a favourable move. I was to know why later.

In the meantime, I had to face alone for an unknown period the empty monotony of existence in my little hutch; a timeless vacuum broken only by the regular cycle of ablutions, ersatz coffee, mid-day soup and *Abendbrot* – nothing to do, nothing to read and no exercise – stretching out it seemed for eternity. Perhaps the *Genickschuss*[1] would end it all; but this was a nihilistic attitude of mind I knew I must overcome.

An effort of will was required to build a pattern of life within this empty existence. Gradually I established a routine for myself. In the morning after a leisurely mug of ersatz coffee, munching any bits of

[1] Neck shot.

black bread or sausage saved from the night before, I would sit on my little stool with my back to the wall and meditate for some hours. Then it was exercise time for those allowed that privilege. By standing on my bed I could look through the barred window onto the exercise yard which was bound by our wing, the other wing of the 'T' shaped cell block and the enclosing wall. About thirty prisoners of all nationalities, including German, walked round and round in single file, guarded by two SS men. I had to be rather cautious over this as there would be a scream of rage if one of the guards happened to see me; not wanting a bullet between the eyes I had to stand back in the shadows. This passed an hour. I tried to guess their nationalities, something of their backgrounds and the reason for their incarceration – later I came to know all this through the prison grapevine. After this it was about time for mid-day soup and I did not have much difficulty in dallying over the unappetising concoction that was brought round. Provided the guard did not look through the spy hole, I usually managed a nap on my bed in the afternoon.

My exercise period followed; for at least an hour I would walk up and down, up and down, my cell, it was hardly possible to walk round it but I made a pretence of doing so by edging around the walls and the sparse furnishings, sometimes to the left, sometimes to the right. Soon after this was *Abendbrot* black bread with a bit of sausage, blood or liver, or a piece of smelly cheese wrapped in silver paper. I made chessmen out of the silver paper wrappings and in the evenings would play chess with myself on the squares of the check counterpane. I could claim the credit for whichever side won, and so it became a daily morale booster. By the time lights went out I felt that I had had a full day, at least I was tired enough to sleep – an important factor in the circumstances.

I soon began to establish contacts and obtain news through the grape vine common to all prisons. In the Cell Block news was carried mainly by the 'Trusties' who brought the food round. They were Jehovah's Witnesses, one of Hitler's aversions. In the Cell Block there were four of them, arrested in Hamburg in 1940 and kept in Sachsenhausen since then. They were entirely dependable, carried messages for us and passed on items of news.

I came to know those among the walkers in the exercise yard who had been condemned to death. I remember, particularly, one young Norwegian of about twenty, who was to be executed for resistance activities in Norway. I used to see him, tall, proud and unafraid, striding round the circuit on his daily walk – then one day he was no longer there. I learnt that his name was Per Becker Erikson. There were German soldiers, including SS men, caught looting who were also executed, and many others.

Sydney Dowse was the only one of us to occupy a cell on the other side of the passage. He told us one morning at ablutions that a wooden shutter had been placed in front of his window; curious to find out what was going on, he had managed to gouge a small hole in the wood and had seen three men being hanged on a gallows just outside.

Torture and death were all around; cries and screams rent the stillness of the night. I found refuge in my periods of meditation. Free from all distractions I entered new realms of consciousness; poetry and events long forgotten came back to me with extraordinary clarity. I drifted back in time and saw panoramic visions of the past. I was a small child again in India with my parents. Our bungalow was falling down in an earthquake and, as the Indian bearer was carrying me away on his back, I saw my mother coming out of the collapsing building – I was riding with my sister on the trolley to the nearest bazaar – my father's wrath when I ran screaming from the snake charmers as the swaying cobras reared up out of their baskets, it was an outpost of Empire and fear was not to be shown, even in the very young.

The scene would shift to England and my school days in Canterbury, and the vast and beautiful Cathedral which had dominated our lives when I was at the King's School, but taken for granted by most of us boys. Now the great Cathedral rose up before me in all its mediaeval splendour, the lantern pinnacled Bell Harry Tower soaring above the majestic lines of Choir, Nave and Transept and the ruined Benedictine Priory. Built to the glory of God it now seemed to come back out of the past to cast a protective shroud over me in this satanic place. I felt that God was near and for the first time for many years I prayed.

One morning about two weeks after my arrival in the Cell Block Johnny Dodge joined us in the washroom. He was as cheerful as ever after a month hiding in a pig sty. He told us that he had walked north along the main Rostock railway line, jumping a goods train on which he had travelled for about twenty miles, after this he had met some French workers who had hidden him in a barn and then in a hay loft above a large pig sty – rather a smelly retreat, he said, but the

Frenchmen brought him milk and hot food every day and he would
have been quite happy to stay there until liberated by the Allies. His
dream was shattered one day when he found himself looking down
the barrel of a revolver.

'*Komm mit,*' said the German farmer.

The 'Dodger's' spell of freedom was over. At the police station he
was told by the policeman, a Luxemburger, that he had known about
the Dodger's whereabouts for some time and would have been quite
happy to leave him, but somebody had given him away. Before being
taken back to Sachsenhausen, the Major had given the policeman a
list of names of the people in the Sonderlager and asked him to try to
get it back to London.

A month passed and we were allowed out for half an hour's walk
every day except Sunday in the exercise area on the other side of the
wing visible from my cell window. It was laid out as a garden, and
was for the use of staff and certain prisoners like ourselves who were
being 'kept on ice'. The 'Hitlerstrasse' was the main diagonal path
which was flanked by the well kept 'Himmler', 'Göring', and
'Goebbels' flower beds. It was like gangsters running a flower shop;
to say the least, bizarre to find crazy paving, pergolas and a profusion
of flowers in this corner of hell. Perhaps the perpetrators of evil
needed some compensating beauty, like the SS at Auschwitz who
ordered the 'Musicians of Auschwitz' to play Beethoven, Chopin
and Wagner after liquidations. Even more macabre was the Katyn
mass grave memorial in a corner of the garden beside the steel cover
of the dungeon in which Eccarius' victims were consigned to starve
in its black depths.

For a short space the five of us found welcome relief from our
solitary confinement as we walked up and down the 'Hitlerstrasse'
swapping information and experiences and chatting about the war.

Wings told us the full story of events after his recapture with
Dowse. On return to Sachsenhausen he had been thrown into the
death cell, handcuffed and chained to the floor by one leg. He was in
agony from his injured knee.

At midnight the cell door was opened and two guards yanked him
off his pile of dirty bedding on the floor, unchained him and pushed
him out of his cell, as he thought, to his execution; but he was
taken to a cell at the end of the corridor where an SD man was sitting
at a small table. The interrogation went on until dawn, the SD man
covering sheets of paper while he probed for some ulterior motive for
the escape, some connection, for instance, with an outside

organisation – we were well treated – why risk death by escaping from the SS? In spite of his painful knee and utter weariness, Wings' mind was clear. He knew that he must not trip up on his story or give the Germans any legal excuse for pinning a charge of sabotage on us.

The following midnight he was dragged out again. This time he was taken to the administrative building where he found himself facing five interrogators, the President who was in lawyer's garb, an SD man and three senior police officers, Amend, the Director of the CID section of the Kripo, Criminal Commissar Struck, and Inspector Peter Mohr (Appendix 'D'). Wings was encouraged by the presence of the police officers. He knew that if he passed this ordeal it would lessen our chances of being handed over to the Gestapo for extermination. After some preliminary boxing when Wings was querying the exact meaning of words with rather a bad interpreter which gave him more time for thought, he went over to the offensive.

'I told them,' he said, 'that it was disgraceful that officer prisoners should be treated like criminals, handcuffed and chained, in complete disregard of the Geneva Convention. The Prosecutor replied that we could hardly be regarded as POWs when we were accused of sabotage, communicating with the British Secret Service and so on. I plugged the theme that all we were interested in was escaping, and that it was our duty to escape at all times, and so it went on around the same arguments until dawn.'

Wings had four more interrogations in the following week, two with the SD man down the corridor, a conversational approach in both cases, dangerous because he knew he could be trapped into saying something apparently inconsequential which could be used against us. The next midnight interrogation in the Administration Block turned heavily on accusations of spying and sabotage. He was accused, among other things, of spying on the Oranienburg Test Base, a charge easily refuted when Wings referred them to the train timetables and the hour of his recapture with Dowse at Mahlsdorf – leaving no spare time for spying or anything else.

On the last night Wings decided that there was only one course of action left to him; he would go over to the attack.

'I was near breaking point,' he told us. 'It was two or three in the morning, and they had been needling away at me trying to find some obscure reason for our escapes. I suddenly got angry. I got up and, hobbling up and down the room – my knee was giving me hell – I loosed off a broadside at them. I reminded them that I was a professional soldier who had served in both world wars – when this war broke out I had obtained a transfer from the Staff to command a squadron in the air. Shot down at the very beginning I had been vegetating ever since behind barbed wire, while my contemporaries had been promoted to high rank. I ranted on about professional honour as a Royal Air Force officer, and finished by pointing out that their forces contained men of like spirit who would try to escape as we had done, and furthermore would be treated fairly on recapture. This exhausted me and I collapsed into a chair. I was past caring what happened.

'There was complete silence for a minute or two – it was extraordinary, but I knew we were off the hook – then the President said, "We understand, Wing Commander."'

We now knew why we were walking in the flower garden, saved for the time being at any rate from the execution squad. Sydney Dowse had also contributed to this during severe interrogation when he had invented a story that he had posted letters to the Swiss Red Cross and to the Luftwaffe Kommandantur at Sagan giving an account of our recapture after the Sagan escape, our incarceration in the Sonderlager, and our subsequent escape.

We did not know at that time that Himmler had given an order, immediately our escape was reported, that we were to be handed over to the Gestapo on recapture for *Verschäfte Vernehmung* (Interrogation under torture) and then liquidated, to be reported 'escaped but not recaptured'. The same procedure had been adopted with the seven Commandos captured in the Musketoon Operation, a sabotage attack on a hydro-electric station in Norway; put in the Cell Block one afternoon, they were shot before dawn the following morning. By early morning roll call their bodies had been cremated.

In our case the intervention of the police had undoubtedly saved us.

We were now allowed books – one at a time from the camp library. Although they were all in German, I knew enough of the language to enjoy reading, for instance, *Ben Hur* in which I was able to compare my lot favourably with that of Ben Hur's mother and sister who were entombed for eight years in their dungeon. German newspapers, chiefly the *Völkischer Beobachter* were passed around. I was kept very busy translating articles on the war and drawing up operational maps showing the progress of the Allied armies. This material I circulated to the British officers through the 'Trusties'.

The other inmates of the Cell Block were becoming known to us. Jack Churchill was exchanging a weekly letter with Lieutenant

Commander Cumberledge RNVR through a Polish agent called
Jacubiance. Cumberledge, with three sergeants who included
Sergeant Davis from Marendallas, South Africa, had been left
behind after the retreat from Greece in 1941 to blow up the Corinth
Canal. After capture they were subjected to diabolic interrogation
for some months, and then ensconced in the Cell Block.

Sydney Dowse who had been moved to a cell overlooking the
Hitlerstrasse area, managed a short conversation through his
window with a tall, distinguished-looking man of about sixty who
was tending the flower beds. He turned out to be Captain S. Payne
Best, former British Intelligence Chief in Holland, who had been
kidnapped by the Gestapo at Venlo in November 1939, with his
Deputy Major Stevens; the latter had been transferred to Dachau,
but Best, after much verbal duelling with the Gestapo had been kept
in solitary confinement ever since at Sachsenhausen, but always with
a guard present in his cell.

Dowse had also contacted Dr and Frau Vermehren, whose son Dr
Erich Vermehren, a German Intelligence Officer in Sofia, had
defected, with his wife, to the British via Turkey; another son was
also in the Cell Block, and a daughter, Isa, in Ravensbruck.

In the cell opposite mine was an Austrian General arrested in
1938. I remember seeing him once, bent and old-looking, no doubt
beyond his years. We never knew his name and he just vanished like
many others. Then there were the former German Ambassador to
Spain and his wife, Dr and Frau Heberlein, considered unreliable
and kidnapped by the Gestapo in Madrid, the Duke of Mecklenburg,
and there was Pastor Niemoller who had been arrested in 1937.

Georg Elser was an anti-Nazi carpenter arrested in 1937 and sent
to Dachau. He had been forced to construct and conceal a bomb in a
pillar of the Munich Beer Cellar where Hitler was to speak on 8th
November 1939, the object being to kill a group of conspirators who
wanted to shoot Hitler. The bomb was exploded after Hitler had left
the beer cellar, with the desired result. Elser was given his 'freedom'
but was arrested on the Swiss Frontier and sent to Sachsenhausen.
His name had been linked publicly with that of Captain Best who
was supposed to have given him instructions to plant the bomb
which, of course, was seen as a plot against Hitler. Best had seen
Elser once in the washroom, a wiry shock-haired little man, with
intensely bright eyes. We had news of him later in Dachau.

The weeks passed. My relations with Unterscharführer Luchs
remained uniformly bad. His early morning shouting at ablution

time caused me considerable irritation. One morning I shouted back, and had an *Anschnautzer* (Literally 'snort', or shouting match) with him. It was, perhaps, a calculated risk; I knew the Germans understood this, and I thought the SS might in my sort of situation where the scales were weighted temporarily in favour of the British officers, as I suspected we might be in the hostage category. Anyway Luchs quietened down and behaved in a civilized manner thereafter. The other SS corporals, Hartmann, Beck and Meyer were quiet and impassive. Happily we saw little of Eccarius.

The Dodger had acquired a pair of wooden clogs. As his cell was not far from mine I always knew when he was taking his exercise; the sound of the clogs could probably be heard over most of the building as he marched up and down, usually for an hour or more, with his voice raised in song.

Jack Churchill also sang, often hymns he remembered; but he had another novel way of passing the time. He managed to collect a number of small tins and receptacles; into these he poured his midday soup and, supping one at a time at half hourly intervals, he was able to extend his lunch over most of the afternoon.

Christmas 1944 came. As most of the guards were off duty we were denied our usual walk and had to solace ourselves with the Christmas fare provided by the SS, stew with a small piece of pork, a doughy lump of pudding and a sweet biscuit with an extra ration of jam, rather better than the usual diet of vegetable or sauerkraut soup with lumps of fat floating in it. We exchanged Christmas Cards made up from toilet paper.

On Christmas night the loudspeakers blared out Christmas Carols, and the haunting strains of 'Stille Nacht, Heilige Nacht' floated incongruously over this unholy place; these mingled with the moans and sobs of those about to die, among them a young SS conscript – he had deserted and was passing his last moments before being despatched.

'I hear that Bhuddists ring a bell to warn animals in the wood so that they come to no harm. I must pass a law after the war to enforce kindness to all animals,' observed Himmler on one occasion to his masseur, Felix Kersten.

The previous Commandant at Sachsenhausen, Lohritz, had indeed been kind to animals. He had kept a menagerie in the camp and, for his bears alone, he had reluctantly had to dock the prisoners about one and a half hundredweight of their rations weekly!

'To make a flower garden I must pull out the weeds,' Himmler said on another occasion to his Masseur, who was also his confidant. 'The Jews must be exterminated. The German people must learn to kill without flinching – to look upon tens, hundreds, thousands, yes tens of thousands of dead bodies – pressed so close in the gas chambers that they cannot fall when life expires – then to get them out to the crematorium. Yes! We Germans must be strong – what we have to endure!'

The motivation for mass murder in Hitler's Third Reich was, perhaps, encapsulated in this observation. It was an element of Nazi ideology which was communicated to thousands of Gestapo and SS men who obeyed orders to kill without question and without pity. It was one of the reasons why men like Eccarius had plied their gruesome trade for so long.

Unknown to us, Eccarius had received orders in the New Year to reduce the number of prisoners in the Zellenbau by intensified liquidation. We knew that something was afoot when our contacts started to disappear. Cumberledge and his Army sergeants were among the first to go and were despatched in Station Z. Two SOE agents, Charles Grover-Williams (Sebastien) a former racing driver with a French wife, and Francis Suttill, a former barrister with a French mother, both of whom had been in the Cell Block for a year, were also executed about this time.

Numerous resistance fighters from all over Europe were executed. The Russians were high on the priority list. Wings met five of them early one morning as they were being lined up to be sent off to the death factory. Large groups were usually gassed.

General Arthur Nebe, who had despatched Wings to Sachsenhausen was arrested after the 20th July Plot against Hitler and brought into the Zellenbau to die the agonising death decreed by Hitler for higher enemies of the State. They were hoisted up by the neck on piano wire and, if they were 20th July plotters, deprived of belt or braces so that their trousers fell off. Hitler delighted in watching the films made of these sadistic killings; Goebbels watched once and fainted.

By April 1945 the population of the Zellenbau had been decreased from about 100 to 13.

The Battle of the Bulge in the Ardennes had placed the American, British and Canadian armies securely on Germany's western borders ready for the spring crossing of the Rhine. The walls of the

Bunker shook regularly with the continual air raids on Berlin. At night the Pathfinders dropped the red fires to mark the boundaries of the camp; they would be followed by a large force of Mosquitos, and the target area in Berlin would be obliterated by the four thousand pound bombs that came crashing down, huge crimson flashes lighting up the night sky. In the daytime the American Fortress raids continued, and one raid on 3rd February almost finished off what was left of Berlin.

What frightened the Germans, however, was the Russian winter offensive. On 12th January about 250 divisions, with numerous tanks, covered by an unbroken line of thundering artillery, supported by 7,500 tactical aircraft, erupted from the East Prussian, Neva, Warka and Baranov bridgeheads and swept across Poland in little more than two weeks. They comprised the 1st and 2nd Belorussian Fronts under Marshal Zhukov and Rokossovsky and the 1st Ukrainian Front under Marshal Koniev, altogether 2,500,000 men. The Germans were heavily outnumbered in everything. In the south the Oder had been reached, Breslau was threatened, and it could only be a matter of time before the Red Army captured Berlin.

Winston Churchill had stipulated unconditional surrender for Germany but if he could be persuaded, with Roosevelt, to make a separate peace with Germany in the west, it would give the Germans a chance to halt the Russians in their eastern frontiers.

This was why Sydney Dowse, early in February, received a visitor in civilian clothes who asked him if he would be prepared to be allowed to escape to Sweden, so that he could carry a message to the Prime Minister asking for peace terms. Sydney could not think why he should have been asked; he thought it was probably because his mother was partly German descended from a distinguished German family as had been noted in his records. He turned down the proposition; it had a machiavellian flavour and could have rebounded unfavourably on himself.

Johnny Dodge was approached with the same proposition which he quickly accepted. Distantly related to the Prime Minister, experienced in politics, he was sure of himself and of what he was being asked to do – besides he wanted to get home before the war finished. He suddenly disappeared the second week in February. I remember hearing his clogs clatter past my door and die away at the end of the passage – but he never came back. Nobody knew where he had gone, and we were worried about him. After many adventures, including close proximity to Allied bombs in the

Dresden raid, he reached England about the end of April, but by the time he had managed to see Churchill, the surrender of the German armies was already being accepted by Montgomery on Luneberg Heath.

The door of my cell opened on 15th February.

'*Pack ein und komm mit*,' said the guard. Was this finally the end of the road?

It did not take me long to gather up my few belongings.

In the passage I met Wings, Churchill and Dowse. We were taken up to the end of the corridor and into a cell where Kaindl was standing waiting for us. He looked almost benevolent.

'You are free to go now. You are going back to your comrades in the Sonderlager. But no more escaping – next time you will certainly be shot.'

It seemed like a miracle as we filed off under guard on our way back to the Sonderlager.

We saw our friends lined up just inside the gate; it looked like a guard of honour. As we entered, Peter Churchill stepped forward and said:

'Welcome back. We thought you were all dead – we salute you.'

As we passed down the line shaking each by the hand we felt like ghosts returned to the land of the living, but the handshakes we received were firm enough.

CHAPTER SIXTEEN

Corridor of Death

The god of war is drunk with blood,
The earth doth faint and fail;
The stench of blood makes sick the heavens;
Ghosts glut the throat of hell.

'Gwin, King of Norway,' William Blake

The guards had doubled in the Sonderlager since our escape. There was now a total of thirty-six guards, about two guards to every prisoner, and it was noticeable that a number of them were non-German conscripts into the SS. The amiable 'George' was still there, but 'Jim' had been posted to the East Front, following our escape, as we had hoped.

A new arrival in the compound was Lieutenant R.N. van Wymeersch, a French pilot attached to the RAF, who had been one of the Sagan escapers. While travelling to Paris on the train he had been arrested at Metz due to a defect in his papers, a recent change of format, the Gestapo officers were chatty enough to explain, which our forgery department couldn't possibly have known about. He was brought back to the Albrechtstrasse in Berlin; while waiting in a passage he sensed impending doom and stepped into a line of passing prisoners, after a railway journey in cattle trucks he found himself in Buchenwald – not quite where he wanted to be, but it probably saved his life. He spent nine months there before his identity was discovered, and then he was sent to Sachsenhausen.

A startling phenomenon in the skies was a type of aeroplane having engines without propellers. These aircraft passed low overhead at tremendous speed and we thought at first that our five months in solitary confinement had brought on hallucinations, until we were told that these were the new jet propelled fighters, Me 262's and Me163's, which were operating against the Russians in a ground attack role on the front near Kustrin.

On the afternoon of 15th March the air raid sirens sounded, the guards scuttled for their shelters and the inmates, as usual, climbed up onto the window sills to watch the final death throes of Berlin. As we watched the approaching bomber stream we suddenly realized that it was not heading for Berlin – it was on course for the Sonderlager, or so it seemed! Fascinated, we waited. The roar of the engines grew to a crescendo, and the first formation was almost overhead, then the leading aircraft released a smoke marker bomb and, like a thousand screaming banshees, the bombs from the formation came rushing down. For the next half hour the huts shook to their foundations as high explosive rained down on the town of Oranienburg just over the far wall of the main camp. This was precision bombing from 12,000 feet by the American Air Force, in two waves of B17's and B24's totalling about 800 aircraft. The Allies knew the locations of all the main prison camps in Germany.

That night, far off, we heard our Mosquitos approaching as always from the north. We were very conscious of the still burning Heinkel factory so close to the camp, and an obvious target to finish off. We waited uneasily as the distinctive whine of the powerful Rolls Royce Merlin engines grew louder. The outer flak defences of Berlin roared into action around us. The marker flares burst out of the black sky far above. Were they going to drop in the right place? We watched anxiously as they slowly fanned out and dropped like a multi-coloured umbrella to the south of the camp. It was almost an anti-climax when the shattering explosions and blinding flashes of the 4,000 lb bombs tore the night apart. Suddenly it was over and the huts were still. The factory had been destroyed. The hum of the Mosquitos faded away into the distance as their crews set course for England and bacon and eggs in little over an hour.

The curtain was going up on the last act. The fire curtain had long been raised; now fire and slaughter raged unchecked, and what remained of Hitler's Germany was fast crashing in ruins. Following a secret order from Hitler that all political prisoners were to be executed on day X, to be determined by the Führer himself, the Gestapo were preparing to make the final blood sacrifice of concentration camp prisoners.

Fräulein Hiltgunt Sassenhaus, a courageous young German woman, whose self-imposed mission during the war had been to visit Scandinavian prisoners in Gestapo prisons giving them medicines, food and news from home, had got wind of Hitler's secret order and she managed to get word to Sweden. Count Folke Bernadotte, President of the Swedish Red Cross, intervened in Berlin with the result that Himmler agreed to release the Scandinavian prisoners. Swedish Red Cross Buses collected them from all camps in Germany, including Sachsenhausen. Shortly after this tens of thousands of prisoners of all nationalities were exterminated in Gestapo prisons and in SS concentration camps all over Germany.

On 1st February 1945 Gruppenführer Heinrich Muller, head of the Gestapo, passed to Kaindl an order from Himmler to destroy the camp and its inmates '*mit Artilleriebeschuss, Luftangriff oder Vergasung*'[1]. Kaindl refused, not on humanitarian grounds, but because such measures would obviously have killed a lot of civilians, not to mention the SS. Instead he drew up his own plans for liquidation designed to dispose more efficiently of unwanted bodies.

The camp now contained nearly 45,000 prisoners, swelled to overflowing by the starved and beaten remnants of humanity evacuated from camps which had been located in the eastern territories, such as Auschwitz, Treblinka and Belzec. It was expedient to reduce the numbers as quickly as possible. On 2nd February, the first 150 prisoners were shot, these included two British airmen, nineteen former resistance fighters from Luxembourg – and Lieutenant John Godwin[2] RN who wrested a pistol from the guard commander and shot him on the way to execution. Up to the end of March about 5,000 prisoners were executed in various ways.

However, time was pressing and the Russians were getting close. Kaindl started drawing up a plan for mass liquidation. Those remaining in April, about 30,000, would be marched to the Baltic where they would be loaded onto vessels which would be towed out to sea and then sunk.

The inmates of the Sonderlager watched and waited – and listened as the sound of battle in the East rolled ever nearer, first a faint rumble, barely audible, growing daily louder until the thunder of the guns was clearly heard as the Red Army reached the Oder ready for the final onslaught on Berlin. Patton was racing for Prague which he was prevented from liberating for political reasons, while Montgomery's British and Canadian Army Group was thrusting towards Hamburg. Hitler with Eva Braun and his personal staff including Goebbels, his wife Magda and six children[3], had retired to the Berlin Bunker where he stormed and ranted about secret weapons and final victory, while the capital of his Third Reich crumbled in flames, smoke and ashes above his head. The boundaries of the Nazi Empire were fast contracting into a narrow corridor of death and destruction. East and West Fronts held

---

[1] By artillery fire, air attack or gassing.

[2] Godwin was captured in Norway with a commando sergeant, two petty officers and three seamen. They spent 15 months in Sachsenhausen before being executed.

[3] All poisoned with their mother and father shortly after Hitler and Eva Braun had committed suicide in the early morning of 30th April 1945.

tenuously apart by remnants of the once mighty Wehrmacht, Volksturm and Hitler Youth, propped up under threat of death by fanatical SS units. The Gestapo still exercised its iron grip on the bomb-shattered population, to which corpses of deserting soldiers hanging from lamp posts bore grim witness; attached to their bodies were notices proclaiming them to be 'Deserters' and 'Traitors'.

In this atmosphere of death and destruction it was evident that our lives hung on a thread, on Hitler's whim, perhaps, or the death accounting of Kaindl, we could even be victims of some hate-crazed SS man. We were not to know that we were deemed too important to die just then.

Very early on 3rd April we were awakened and told to pack, as the compound was being evacuated. Wings was reassured to see his old friend Inspector Peter Mohr who told him that he was accompanying us on the first stage of a journey to the south, but would give no further details. Bessanov and the other Russians were visibly relieved as we were loaded onto two buses and then taken to Oranienburg Station. For the first time we met our neighbours, the Greek Generals, who were travelling with us. Closely guarded by the SS there began a journey we would long remember.

In the main compound preparations were also being made for the evacuation of the prisoners who were to go in the opposite direction. There were several more air raids in the vicinity before they left. In one raid some bombs fell inside the camp boundary and about 300 prisoners were killed. A British airman came down by parachute and had the bad luck to land in the SS quarters. He was immediately seized by an SS officer who began screaming at him, threatening and calling him a '*Terrorflieger*'. The airman pulled away and asked, '*Sind Sie Offizier?*' On getting a loud affirmative he landed the SS man a hard right to the chin which knocked him to the ground. Unfortunately the SS man had the last word with his revolver which he drew and shot the airman dead.

Early on 21st April the evacuation began. In groups of 500 escorted by heavily armed SS men over 30,000 prisoners, who included a number of women, were marched out of the camp. For five days they were driven like cattle towards the Baltic and the ships waiting to send them to a watery grave – Kaindl's 'final solution' for Sachsenhausen. Without food and without rest they were made to cover about thirty kilometres a day, remaining in the open at night. Gaunt and ragged, already starved and overworked, many fell out from exhaustion, and were at once shot in the back of the head by the

SS – it mattered not if they happened to be women – their bodies left on the side of the road.

One of the prisoners, Peder Soegerd, a young Danish medical student, helped men on the point of collapse and, with his comrades hardly less exhausted, almost dragged them along until the last vestige of strength ebbed away from emaciated bodies, and they had to be left – to be destroyed like animals, by an SS bullet. At one infrequent stopping place, Soegerd saw men being shot for trying to take potatoes off a pile on the side of the road.

In the death wood at Below, near Wittstock, they stopped for three days; here many died from hunger and exhaustion. Charles Desirat[1], former French resistance fighter, spent much of his time burying his comrades. The excesses of the SS were often curbed by units of the Wehrmacht who saved many from being shot.

The Allied armies were now closing in rapidly and the survivors of this death march were liberated by the Russians on 30th April. The 3,000 sick who had remained at Sachsenhausen were freed earlier on 22nd April, also by the Soviet Army.

Everywhere prisoners were on the move. Back at Stalag Luft III, Sagan, they had been evacuated earlier when the massive onslaught of ninety Soviet infantry divisions and fifteen tank corps threatened to engulf Silesia.

On the evening of 27th January 1945, the Adjutant of the British North Compound suddenly appeared in the theatre where they were rehearsing *The Wind and the Rain* and announced, 'We're being moved out. Pack up and be ready to move in an hour's time.' The Americans in the South Compound had even less notice. In the theatre a yet more appropriate play was being shown, *You can't take it with you*, when Colonel Spivey, the Senior American Officer, ascended the stage and announced, 'The goons have just come and given us thirty minutes to be at the front gate.'

Throughout that night and the following day the British and American prisoners from East, West, North and South Compounds and from Bellaria were marched out into the bitter weather carrying only the barest necessities. The long columns of prisoners, 2,500 men straggling over twenty miles, were forced marched through snow, ice and blizzards for days on end. The Americans from South Compound, who were in the lead, were made to cover fifty-five

---

[1] Now President of the International Sachsenhausen Committee.

kilometres in the first twenty-seven hours, and the other columns not much less. Thereafter, with no food except what they had brought with them, and little water, they marched about twenty-five kilometres a day – westwards, away from the Russians. George Parker still had his pram 'Speriamo' from Szubin days – there was still hope – and he pushed it gloomily along the snowbound roads for many miles. Others pulled their few possessions along on hastily constructed sledges or handcarts.

The temperatures dropped to zero fahrenheit and below. Many collapsed and had to be left behind. A German guard died of pneumonia, another had to have both legs amputated because of frostbite. In some cases prisoners were carrying the guards' rifles and equipment.

They were driven on. At night they slept in barns and often in the open. At one stop all the guards had found shelter leaving most of the prisoners out in the snow, but Glemnitz, with the RAF prisoners since 1940, stayed up all night and got nearly all of them under cover. The civilian population were generally friendly disposed, the more so as many of them had even less food than the prisoners, and they offered various forms of barter in exchange for odd pieces of chocolate and tea from Red Cross parcels. In one village the prisoners were taken into the villagers' houses for the night but, almost at once, ordered out again by SS and police and forced to spend the night in the open.

The arctic weather and weakened condition of the prisoners made escape inexpedient and impracticable. An order had also been received over the BBC advising against it and recommending that everybody stay together. This did not reach the men from South Compound and Bellaria, and a number of prisoners broke away from these columns. All were recaptured – except two. Wing Commander Bob Tuck and Zbishek Kustrzynski, a Polish officer in the RAF, stayed hidden in a barn when their column was marched off one morning. After trudging for weeks through snow and blizzards, and some incredible adventures, they reached the Soviet lines and the British Embassy in Moscow in early spring.

At Spremberg the columns separated. The Americans went southwest towards Munich where most of them were liberated by their own troops. The British went north, Bellaria to Luckenwalde near Berlin where they were liberated by the Russians, and the rest were marched up through the narrowing corridor in which tens of thousands of prisoners of all ranks and all nationalities were being herded by frightened guards to unknown destinations in an increasingly confused and ephemeral situation.[1]

At the beginning of April the majority of British prisoners from Sagan had reached Tarnstedt, thirty-seven kilometres north of Bremen, where they stayed for a week in a wrecked naval POW camp in terrible conditions.

On 10th April they were moved off again towards Lübeck. On the way they were strafed by RAF Tempests and some Naval personnel were killed. Their blue uniforms led the pilots to think they were Germans. On 2nd May they were liberated by a spearhead of tanks from the 11th Armoured Division.

The NCOs had to make a much earlier move from their camp at Heydekrug out on the Memel Peninsula in Lithuania. In July 1944 the Russian guns could be heard and they began their long and arduous journey westwards. One group moved by train, 3,000 men crammed into wired-off sections of cattle trucks built to hold a third as many. Suffocating and unutterably cramped, they arrived at Thorn in Poland, hardly able to walk when they detrained.

It was much worse for the group who went by ship. Battened down in overcrowded holds in the sultry July heat, the wounded, who included many Americans shot down in daylight raids, left on deck unattended with only paper bandages, it took them four days to reach Swinemunde. They continued by rail in cattle trucks to Kiefheide near Stettin, where they were met by an officer and a squad of guards with dogs to shouts of '*Terrorflieger*'. They were made to run the three miles to the camp at Gross Tychow; those who fell were attacked with bayonets and rifle butts and bitten by dogs.

Eventually they all went to Fallingbostel near Hannover. They were joined by Sergeant Major Bill Lord with the survivors of Arnhem who marched into camp, carrying their wounded, as though still on the parade ground. At the end of March 1945, like everybody

---

[1] 'Spud' Murphy who had put wheels on his sledge when the snow melted was in the Luckenwalde group. The Russians were low grade troops, uncooperative and suspicious, with an admixture of political commissars who insisted on taking particulars of all the prisoners in accordance with the Geneva Convention which the Soviet Union had never recognised. Murphy, with about fifty others, broke away and reached the Americans who had already been trying to negotiate for the release of the prisoners. In the event about five hundred British prisoners were held for months and eventually reached home *via* Odessa on the Black Sea.

else in the corridor, they were on the move. As they marched north the smoke from bombed and burning cities rose up around them and the sound of battle was ever present. 'Dixie' Deans acquired a bicycle and kept continuous contact with the marching columns, doing a tremendous job encouraging everybody and keeping up morale.

They crossed the Elbe, then tragedy struck. Four RAF Typhoons attacked the columns and left 100 casualties, including thirty dead. Deans got the Commandant's permission to cross the lines with an escort. He contacted the nearest Allied Brigade HQ who passed an urgent message to 2nd Tactical Air Force about the prisoners. The Brigadier wanted Deans to stay, but he kept his word to the German Commandant and returned across the lines with his German escort. On 2nd May they were contacted by a fighting patrol of the Queens and they were free.

The train carrying the Sonderlager inmates picked its way slowly through the desert of rubble which formed the western outskirts of Berlin[1], clattering and thumping over bent points and twisted crossings.

The bomb-cratered roads were jammed with tanks and troops, in places inextricably mixed with refugees fleeing from the eastern territories, old men, women, ragged bare-footed children and battered prams, half-starved horses drawing carts carrying their few remaining possessions, cattle, sheep, chickens and pigs. Well-dressed women scrambled for coal that had fallen off a lorry or fought with peasant women for a few potatoes lying on the road. Grandmothers clasped starved and frightened grandchildren to them. Many transported their recent dead in home-made coffins; the Berlin authorities insisted on immediate burial, and confiscated coffins for reissue, so the black market price of coffins soared.

These were some of the 672,000 refugees – like us the flotsam of war – who passed through Berlin from east to west from the

---

[1] Ten square miles of Berlin had been flattened, less than one third of the buildings had escaped damage, there was no gas and only fluctuating electricity. The Reichsbahn estimated there was enough rubble to fill 4 million freight cars or, if piled in one place, to make an artificial mountain higher than the Brocken, 3,747 feet a.s.l. in the Harz Mountains.

In spite of this, it was a remarkable fact that, almost to the end, 600,000 Berliners had essential wartime jobs and could still be fired for being late. Factories, even in mid-April 1945, were producing 74% of top capacity. Rations suddenly doubled in the last fortnight – *Himmelfahrt* rations (Ascension Thursday) announcing the end.

beginning of 1945 to the end of the war.

We speculated on the outcome of this extraordinary train journey through the crumbling corridor which was all that was left of Hitler's mad dream. There was a strong rumour that we were being taken to a mountain redoubt, perhaps in the Bavarian Alps, to be held as hostages. Bessanov was loudest in his elaboration of this theory, '*Ja*, then when the Allies will not meet their demands, they will shoot us,' he postulated with Russian realism.

Beyond Berlin to the south we gazed out on shattered towns and military airfields on which were parked squadrons of fighters, immobile for lack of fuel, while Allied aircraft flew unscathed overhead. Communications were so disrupted by bombing that it was impossible to get the petrol to the airfields. Dresden, where we stopped in the main station, lay in ruins around us. The city had been destroyed in the Anglo-American raids of 12th to 14th. February in an attempt to bomb two German Panzer Armies as they passed through by rail from the west to the south east fronts. In fact they had already passed through during the first week in February, but this intelligence reached the Allies too late; as a result 35,000 civilians, mostly refugees, had been killed and one of the most beautiful mediaeval cities in Europe destroyed – to no purpose.

That night, as the train stood in the sidings at Plauen, there was an air raid alert; the guards got out and ran for shelter, but we were left locked in the carriage covered from every angle by tommy guns.

The following day a change at Weiden onto a narrow gauge railway carried us up into the attractive rolling hills of the Bavarian Oberpfalz near the Czech border. However, we were not to experience a Bohemian idyll. Towards evening Peter Mohr and 'George', the SS Corporal who had treated us in a civilized manner on the journey, told us that we were approaching our destination. Very soon we trundled into a bowl in the hills; gashed out of a hillside was a quarry with a large hutted camp sprawling around it. Surrounding this was a high fence of electrified barbed wire through which we could see, in striped prison clothing, the same gaunt figures we had seen at Sachsenhausen. Another Nazi educational camp.

When we got off the train we were handed over to the local SS who greeted us with shouts of, ''*Raus! Los! Los! Schnell!*[1]' as they herded us, as through the gates of hell, into the camp and to the quarters reserved for us, a ward of the hospital block. We were correct in

---

[1] 'Out! Get on! Fast!'

assuming that the cells were full.

We had said good-bye to Peter Mohr, but he was, once more, unknown to us, saving us from execution – an agent of fate sent, for some reason, to ensure our survival in this chilling twilight world whose gods were falling in a final Wagnerian holocaust.

'You have, of course, brought these men here to be executed, Inspektor,' barked the Commandant, SS Obersturmbannführer Stavitsky, when Mohr reported to him.

'They are not to be shot, Herr Kommandant. I have orders to leave them here in your custody until further notice.'

'What!' bellowed the Commandant. 'They are not to be shot? But the camp is overcrowded, the normal death rate does not take care of the overflow, and special executions cannot be carried out fast enough.'

Such was the Commandant's casual acceptance of the policy of implementation of mass liquidation in a concentration camp.

Mohr explained firmly to the Commandant that the prisoners he had been charged by Berlin to deliver could be of great importance to Germany in any negotiations with the Western Allies, and these could be jeopardised if it was learnt that certain prisoners had been liquidated. Additionally it would not bode well for the Commandant.

We had not long arrived in our new quarters when the Commandant burst into the ward knocking down a medical orderly who got in his way. A stout, thick set, bull-necked man, the SS Colonel was in a furious temper and proceeded to harangue us about good behaviour and the dire consequences of escaping; we would be shot immediately and, in any case, the camp was mined around the perimeter.

As he turned to leave, Wings asked him politely in German if he would tell us the name of the camp.

The Commandant scowled and then snarled, 'You will find that out soon enough,' and stamped out of the ward.

We found out very soon that we were in Flossenburg Concentration Camp, a labour camp where conditions were exceptionally harsh, even by SS standards. Although not geared to systematic extermination like Auschwitz, the distinction in terms of human life was academic. Flossenburg was a death camp, like Sachsenhausen, Dachau, Belsen and many others in Germany where thousands of men were done to death in cruel and barbaric ways (Appendix 'F').

The hospital stood in a raised position overlooking the camp. On a hill opposite, the brooding ruins of a fourteenth-century castle looked down, as we did, on barbarities hardly paralleled in mediaeval times indeed, in the words of Winston Churchill 'surpassing anything that has been known since the darkest and most bestial ages of mankind.' Hundreds of starved and emaciated prisoners were daily kicked and beaten to work in the quarry by sadistic SS guards, there to break stones for twelve hours until, exhausted, they were driven back to their huts in the evening. Death released about fifty a day. The crematorium, which lay beside us, belched smoke continually but was unable to burn all the bodies, the remainder were piled up in pyramids on the camp perimeter and either used for fuel, of which they were short, or burnt in bonfires – and on the spring air was carried the smell of burning flesh.

Those not already expired but unable to work we met in the hospital washroom, the grey yellow skin stretched around shaven heads, sunken cheeks and glazed tortured eyes in hollow sockets, sores covering matchstick limbs, walking skeletons proclaiming the imminence of death. The French doctor told us that the worst cases were on the slab about to die; on starvation rations and with minimal medicaments there was little the doctor could do for them.

The murder machine was fed by human fodder regularly supplied by the Gestapo, now often from evacuated camps in the eastern territories. We watched one day as an intake of some 500 prisoners stripped naked after delousing, ribs protruding from wasted bodies, limped and staggered across the compound just below our windows, the weaker clinging to the stronger, those who fell kicked upright by the guards – slowly and painfully this dance of death disappeared from view, its participants to be used for breaking stones for a few more days before their bodies were finally broken and burned.

The macabre traffic between the cell block and the crematorium also passed across our vision. About five days after our arrival Wings who happened to be standing at the window gave an exclamation of horror. The rest of us crowded up in time to see three blanket-covered stretchers being carried to the crematorium. The blankets were covered with fresh blood and smeared with flesh and brain fragments. On that day three prominent Germans had been executed; the courageous Pastor Dietrich Bonhoeffer, Admiral Canaris, the former Chief of German Intelligence and his Chief of Staff General Hans Oster. The two latter had been strung up on nooses of piano wire. It was 9th April.

On the evening of that day we walked the short distance to the death house; it was the usual concentration camp cell block and we were locked up two to a cell. In the morning our group was allowed to walk in the corridor for a few hours. On this and on subsequent days we learnt, from snatches of conversation through still locked cell doors, that a mass execution had taken place on the day of our arrival in the cell block. Besides the three already mentioned there were three more Germans, General von Rabenau, Captain Gehrer and Rechtsanwalt Sack, all implicated in the plot against Hitler. Then there were thirteen SOE agents, mostly French and Belgian, but including two British, held for eighteen months after their capture in France. The death message was tapped out one to the other on the central heating pipes. As each one was taken out for execution, he or she was made to undress to save the clothes for the Third Reich, then naked[1] they went singing, often their own national anthem, on their last few steps on earth to the execution shed. The *Genickschuss* or guillotine sprawled their bodies onto a blood-stained stretcher ready for removal to the crematorium. We had moved into their cells.

Two outstanding SOE agents were executed at Flossenburg in late March 1945. Brian Rafferty (Dominique), an Irishman, had been arrested near Clermont Ferrand, and Flight Lieutenant Jack Agazarian, an Englishman who had tossed a coin with Bodington, the head of F Section at Baker Street, to determine who should check a suspect address in France. Agazarian lost. Both these agents behaved subsequently with exemplary courage.

A number of British parachutists and Commandos had also been executed in Flossenburg, following Hitler's murderous Commando Order of 18th October 1942 which laid down that all sabotage parties, whether in or out of uniform, were to be slaughtered to the last man. They were nearly always brought in to the camp in the evening, given comfortable quarters, a good dinner with wine, then led out to be shot in the early morning. Even the SS sometimes honoured brave men.

As we walked the dark corridors of the grey cell block, we absorbed the gruesome atmosphere of this slaughter house almost unconsciously. It was as though we had become inured to the pall of evil which encompassed Nazi Germany and now, shut away in one of its darker corners awaiting the executioner, had become

---

[1] 'The girl was beautiful and walked like a queen,' said one of the inmates who had watched through a slit in his cell door.

unconcerned about our fate. Sydney Dowse, ebullient as ever, had contacted some of the girls in the SS brothel which was visible through the wire from the window at the end of the corridor. They were of various nationalities, including French, German, Polish, and even one British. One of the French girls was the widow of a British Major killed while fighting with the Maquis in France. I can remember some of them now in their clinging summer dresses with haunted, wistful faces, the first women some of us had seen for years. It seemed an oasis of femininity in this waste of barbarism; most of them, no doubt, had been forced into this way of life with execution as the only alternative.

The wooden shed at one end of the exercise yard looked as though it contained gardening tools. It was the execution station for the camp, housing a variety of apparatus for the termination of human life. Wings was standing one day beside a tall young SS Unterscharführer, blond and Aryan-looking; he was in charge of the execution squad.

'The Allies are not going to like what you are doing in that little shed,' said Wings, pointing up at a formation of American aircraft flying overhead.

'*Befehl ist Befehl*[1], shrugged the SS man. This was a phrase heard so many times at the War Crimes Trials at Nuremburg.

As the din of battle drew nearer and it was obvious that it was only a matter of time before Patton's tanks burst through, the shed was hastily cleared of its grisly contents.

There were other ways of liquidating people. One day the Adjutant opened the food hatch of one of the cells and shot the occupant between the eyes; the occupant was a doctor named Rascher, a former concentration camp Medical Officer who experimented on the inmates, but made the mistake of sending the results of his experiments to Swiss colleagues thinking this would help him after the Allied Victory.

Peter Churchill knocked on one of the cell doors to be told, 'I am Josef Muller, a Bavarian lawyer. I hope the Americans come soon because I am sure they will shoot me. They took me twice to the execution shed and both times I said I refused to be executed without a proper trial.'

A lawyer's persuasive tongue had saved him on both occasions.

---

[1] 'Orders are orders.'

On the evening of 15th April we were told to collect our belongings and get ready for a move. As the Sonderlager group was herded outside we were joined by another group who appeared to be of various nationalities. Waiting in the yard were a Black Maria and two canvas-topped lorries.

Wings chose this moment to make a protest.

'This is disgraceful,' he told the SS officer in charge. 'As a prisoner of the Luftwaffe I never travelled in such inferior transport. Go and tell the Commandant that I object. We are not criminals.'

Wings' air of authority and the proximity of the American guns moved the SS man, rather unexpectedly, to comply with this demand.

While we were waiting, I noticed an emaciated figure, who had been standing with some prisoners watching our departure, edging slowly towards us, when he reached our group he whispered, 'I am Wadim Grenewich, British Embassy, Sofia.' Quickly, Wings, Sydney Dowse and I drew him into our midst, threw a Polish army greatcoat over him, placed an RAF cap on his head and pulled it down over his eyes. It was none too soon. The SS officer returned at this moment with a message from the Commandant that if we did not get into the vehicles immediately, force would be used.

During the night one of the lorries broke down, half its occupants were piled into the Black Maria and the other half into the lorry in which I was travelling. We continued the journey in conditions of some discomfort. The Black Maria designed for eight persons now had about twenty crammed into it; they included Peter Churchill, Dowse, Cushing, Walsh, Prince Philip of Hesse, Baron Wilhelm von Flugge, a business man, and Josef Muller whose face was still bruised and puffy from blows with a truncheon. The heat was stifling and after a while the Prince fainted and Dowse who was standing beside him insisted that the vehicle stop. Shoved disdainfully out of the door by a guard, Dowse got some water from a villager and brought the Prince round.

We were no less cramped in our lorry. In contrast, of course, we were freezing cold and got covered in dust, but we had the advantage of being able to see out behind us. I was sitting near the tailboard with Jack Churchill, but we also had two SS guards with Tommy guns at the ready sitting on each side of us. In the same lorry were Wings, some of the Russians, the Greek Generals and Wadim Grenewich. During the journey Grenewich told us that he had been in concentration camps for five years and would have been shot at Flossenburg if he had not joined our party. In the growing confusion the SS had not missed him.

The wretched, cramped and bone-shaking night passed. At morning light, bleary-eyed and white with dust we perceived that we were travelling south. Then the ground strafing by Allied aircraft started. Every time the Spitfires and Mustangs swooped low over the trees, the guards leapt out to make a dash for the ditch where they kept us covered with their fire arms. We were moving down in the immediate rear of the German forces still holding out in the west; military targets were all around us, and so were bullets and cannon shells from attacking fighters.

In one village we stopped near a Command Post where a German officer was consulting a map beside his headquarters vehicle. He looked worried as despatch riders rode to and fro at high speed. A glimpse of Hitler's last-ditch stand. The Russians could not be far distant to the east. What then was the purpose of this closely guarded little convoy through this narrow devastated 'no man's land' – and whither were we bound? Jack Churchill had been throwing out, at intervals, chits of paper on which were written his name, Commando number and information that he with others had been moved from Sachsenhausen by the SS, and that we were being transported south to an unknown destination. One of these chits was picked up and reported in *The Times*.

We crossed the Danube at Regensburg. Shortly afterwards we witnessed quite a heavy Fortress raid on the town. Again we passed airfields with dozens of aircraft sitting immobile, easy targets for Allied aircraft who now had total command of the air – but there was little point in bombing them at this stage, as the petrol could not reach them.

Late that night we pulled up at the flood-lighted entrance to a large and sinister looking establishment. The hard, brittle pool of light spilled out onto high walls topped with electrified wire, the dim outlines of guard towers and guns visible beyond.

Wiping the dust from my eyes, I saw the familiar sign, '*Arbeit macht frei*'.

'*Wie heisst dieser Konzentrationslager?*'[1] I asked the friendlier of the two guards beside us.

'*Ja – hier ist Dachau*,' he answered cheerfully.

---

[1] 'What is the name of this Concentration Camp?'

This was one we had heard about.

There was some delay about our reception. While we were waiting, a sing-song led by Thomas Cushing, the Irish soldier of fortune who had sung in armies all over the world, started up in the Black Maria, ably supported by Wing Commander Dragic of Yugoslavia. Soon the dust-laden lorry contingent joined in, and for the next fifteen minutes melodies like 'Boulevard of Broken Dreams' floated over the grim portals of Dachau.

Flanked by guards holding back snarling police dogs and accompanied by the usual SS exhortations we were taken through the gate to a well-appointed hut which, we learnt, had been the SS brothel.

In this unlikely setting it was soon apparent that we were in the midst of a number of prominent persons, princes and potentates, bishops, generals, ambassadors and important functionaries of all nationalities. They gave us a friendly welcome. In our weary condition it seemed just a sea of faces, but two colourful personalities stand out in my memory of that evening, General Garibaldi, the grandson of the liberator of Italy, and Colonel Ferraro, a much decorated French Foreign Legion officer. Both had been captured fighting the Germans, Garibaldi with the French Resistance, and Ferraro with the Italian partisans. Colonel John McGrath soon made himself known to us; he was the officer sent to organise the Irish at Friesack, but when the Germans realized that he was working against them and organising escapes they put him in Dachau. That night there was a thunderous air raid on Munich, and the hut seemed about to collapse but I was too tired to care.

In the morning after a cup of ersatz coffee and a piece of black bread, we met and talked with a number of the *Prominenten*. When I shook hands with Pastor Martin Niemoller I felt both warmth and strength. Suspended by the Nazis for his opposition to Hitler he, nevertheless, continued to preach to packed congregations at his church in Dahlem until he was arrested in 1937 and sent to Sachsenhausen. A World War I U-Boat Commander, he had a tough and athletic appearance, although his years of solitary confinement had obviously taken their toll.

We met our former unseen neighbours in the Zellenbau at Sachsenhausen, Dr and Frau Heberlein. Dr Richard Schmitz had been Mayor of Vienna at the time of the Anschluss to which he had objected. There were Prince Frederick Leopold of Prussia, a Hohenzollern, and Prince Xavier de Bourbon who nearly died from the treatment he had received at Dachau; after his recovery the Commandant had given him lighter work as servant to the women in the brothel.

Some eminent clerics included Gabriel Piguet, Bishop of Clermont-Ferrand, and Johann Neuhäusler, Canon of Munich, both of whom had been put in the brothel block presumably as an affront to their cloth. They had overcome this by sprinkling Holy Water everywhere, and a room was sanctified in which Mass was celebrated daily.

During the day it was rumoured that we were moving on. Wings and Sydney collected some extra bread from the British, and clambered up through the trap in the washroom into the roof space above the ceiling, intending to sit it out until the Allies arrived.

The seasoned soldier and experienced KZ inmate Colonel Ferraro thought this scheme highly dangerous.

'For God's sake, tell them to come down,' he said to Peter Churchill. 'The dogs will sniff them out in no time; if not they will die of the typhus epidemic which is almost bound to break out. I've heard it on good authority that we are going to Italy where the Partisans will liberate us.'

Peter relayed this message to the men in the roof, adding his own endorsement. Reluctantly they climbed down. It is very probable that they would not have survived. There was a severe outbreak of typhus in the last days at Dachau, and Wings and Sydney could well have joined the Russians who, with temperatures of 105°, were carried out to the crematorium on stretchers to be shot there.

As at Sachsenhausen the Germans also had plans to destroy the camp and all the prisoners. At Dachau the *Wolkenbrand* (literally cloud fire) plan was being considered. Operation Fire Cloud was the code name for a plan to poison all non-Aryan prisoners on the orders of Kaltenbrunner.

CHAPTER SEVENTEEN

The Road to Liberation

I saw the Powers of Darkness take their flight
I saw the morning break.

Sir Owen Seaman

SS Hauptsturmführer Stiller was in charge of the brothel block and this meant that he also attended to any executions deemed necessary among the *Prominenten*. His most recent essay in this field had been the liquidation of Georg Elser whom we met in the Zellenbau at Sachsenhausen. A secret message from Gestapo HQ in Berlin, sent direct to Stiller, had ordered that Elser be disposed of as discreetly as possible. Accordingly Stiller had taken Elser out into the garden where he had been shot in the back of the neck by another prisoner who was himself immediately liquidated.

Stiller was now to be the SS man in charge of our move, and he had already given us a warning, tapping his revolver, that 'orders must be obeyed'. On our way to the main entrance we passed a massive parade of prisoners lined up for *Appell*. From out of the vast throng of starved and ill-used humanity came the cry 'Raoul'. This was Peter Churchill's code name in SOE. Almost simultaneously there arose a mute collective murmur like waves breaking on a distant sea shore. Peter turned and gave the thumbs up sign. At once several thousand thumbs were raised above the sea of shaven heads. The moment had passed and Peter never discovered his former colleague buried in the depersonalised anonymity of Dachau.

Three buses set off from Dachau carrying the *Prominenten*, including the Sonderlager group, on the early evening of 17th April. It was my birthday, my fifth in captivity, and there seemed every prospect that it could be my last. Whichever way the dice fell, the end was near; either the Allies would liberate us, or the SS would liquidate us in a final massacre to mark the end of their blood-stained record.

I found myself sitting next to a Wehrmacht officer. Count Fabian von Schlabrendorff. He told me that he had been a lawyer before the war, and been implicated in the plot against Hitler. More than this he would not tell me, but I sensed that his aristocratic reserve concealed a story of suffering. He had indeed suffered. We learnt later that he had been one of the resistance leaders in General Beck's organisation. On 13th March 1943 he had concealed a time bomb in a brandy bottle, which he had sent on the aircraft on which Hitler was travelling after a visit to the East Front, supposedly as a present to a friend in Berlin, but the bomb had failed to explode due to a faulty fuse. After the 20th July Plot had failed, Schlabrendorff was arrested and tried by the People's Court. He had been acquitted but was immediately rearrested by the Gestapo who were always above the law; after six months of interrogation and terrible torture he was told that he would be shot. There was still time.

We passed slowly through the bomb shattered still smoking ruins of Munich, and took the road to the south. It was rumoured that we were going to Innsbruck. Darkness fell, and the continual rumble of battle to the west was now accompanied by the flashes of bombs and gunfire which illuminated the horizon in a flickering pattern of light. The mountains closed in, and silence fell; a prelude, it seemed, to our incarceration in a dark fortress set in some inaccessible ravine, our fate dependent on the gang of fanatical SS men awaiting orders from Berlin – perhaps they already had them. The night passed in uneasy and fitful slumber.

The dawn light tinged the Alpine peaks with a pinkish glow which slowly suffused the glaciers and upper snow fields until they were bathed in the morning sunlight, the dark pine forests in the valley standing out stark against the snows above. Beside the road a dark, swift river materialized out of the morning mists. It was recognized by somebody as the Inn. A little while later we reached Innsbruck and about three miles to the south halted at the entrance to a hutted camp surrounded by the familiar barbed wire defences. A sign advertised this as 'Police Education Camp – Reichenau' although it appeared to be staffed by the SS who, no doubt, did the educating.

It was a punishment camp where prisoners were driven out at dawn on working parties to return exhausted after dark; its open cesspits festering in the spring sunshine, it seemed incongruous that such a place should be situated amidst the grandeur of the Austrian Tyrol so near the beautiful and historic town of Innsbruck.

The British officers and a few others who were in the Sonderlager were together in one of the large barrack rooms; our room-mates included the Greek Generals with Field Marshal Papagos, a tall and remote figure, and some former members of the Hungarian Cabinet, the Prime Minister Miklos von Kallay whose *Schaukelpolitik*, when he had tried to make a separate peace with the Allies, had displeased

Hitler and resulted in his arrest, together with Baron von Schell his Minister of the Interior and the others, in March 1944.

More convoys arrived from Dachau and similar places containing prominent resistance fighters of all nationalities, and our numbers increased to around 150. We met for the first time our near neighbours at Sachsenhausen, Dr Kurt von Schuschnigg, his wife who had joined him voluntarily in captivity and his little daughter born in Sachsenhausen. He had become Chancellor of Austria at the age of thirty-six following the murder of Dolfuss. After the infiltration of Nazis into Austria, he·had been summoned to Berchtesgarten by Hitler in 1938 and given an ultimatum, which included *inter alia* the appointment of Seyss-Inquart, a notorious Nazi sympathiser, as Police Chief. Schuschnigg returned to Vienna and called a referendum on the issue. This so enraged Hitler that he forced the Anschluss on 12 March 1938, and Schuschnigg and many others were arrested.

Another married couple who had been neighbours at Sachsenhausen, Fritz Thyssen and his wife, also appeared. Other Germans included high ranking Army Officers, Field Marshal von Falkenhausen, late C-in-C Belgium and Northern France, who had refused to shoot hostages, Colonel General Franz Halder, former Chief of the General Staff, and his wife, all arrested after the July Plot, and Colonel Bogislav von Bonin who had ordered withdrawal of German troops from Warsaw against Hitler's wishes, when he was chief of operations on the General Staff in 1944. About forty *Sippenhäftlinge*, or Family Hostages, added some colour and gaiety to our drab existence. They were relatives, men women and children, of those implicated in the July Plot, mainly members of the Goerdeler and von Stauffenberg families. A girl called Heidi with the *Heute Nacht oder nie* air of a former night club hostess was also with us; one of her admirers was Wassili Molotov, a Soviet Army lieutenant and nephew of the Soviet Foreign Minister, who followed her about with dog-like devotion but without much success, as she was casting her favours elsewhere.

Numbered among us now were Danes, including two Merchant Navy captains, Norwegians, Czechs, Yugoslavs, a Lettish professor called Gustav Celmins, and even a Swedish company director and a Swiss engineer, Armand Mottet, at one time condemned to death.

One of the most outstanding personalities now among us was Leon Blum, ex-Prime Minister of France and Leader of the Front Populaire. Although he was Jewish he had refused to leave France when the Germans invaded. In a rigged trial at Riom the Vichy Government had accused Blum of leading France into war but, as a former lawyer, he had conducted his defence so brilliantly that the Germans had stopped the trial and had Blum deported to Buchenwald. He was joined voluntarily by his companion of many years, Jeanne Reichenbach, and they were married there. It is surprising that he survived.[1] Now over seventy, with walrus moustache and thatch of white hair, he and his wife were courteous and friendly to everybody.

A prominent Dutchman was the seventy-year-old Dr J.C. van Dijk, Minister of Defence in Holland from 1937 to 1939; he had been arrested in 1941 and sent to a concentration camp.

We met the other three British officers who had survived the Zellenbau at Sachsenhausen. Captain Sigismund Payne Best, whom Sydney Dowse had contacted through his cell window, still looking the caricature of the aristocratic Englishman after more than five years in solitary confinement, tall and lean with monocle fixed in his right eye. His companion in the Venlo Incident had a similar period of incarceration and, although subdued, was cheerful enough and the former Indian Army officer was still recognizable. Squadron Leader Hugh Falconer was a wireless expert who had been caught on a secret mission in Tunisia in 1943; after severe interrogation from the Gestapo he had been sent to the Bunker at Sachsenhausen where, for eighteen months, he knew his survival to be in doubt; later he was transferred to Buchenwald.

Food was scarce, usually only a bowl of vegetable soup at mid-day for which a long queue hurriedly formed. In spite of the knowledge that the Allies were pressing in from east and west, the frequent bombing attacks on the Brenner Pass, clearly visible from our camp, and a few on Innsbruck, a gloomy reaction seemed to descend on our party.

'The war could drag on, and we could be here for months,' remarked a rather excitable Yugoslav.

'Don't worry, they will shoot us before that,' replied one of the Germans, Wilhelm Visentainer, a circus clown at one time. He had also been a ship's cook. He had been arrested in Vichy France for smuggling food to English women and children in an internment camp. After this he spent four years in Dachau, where, among other

---

[1] Georges Mandel, another politician, with whom Blum shared a house at Buchenwald, had been taken back to France and shot by the Germans.

degradations, he was beaten unconscious while hanging from a rafter, spent six months in a dark cell fed only three days a week on bread, and had all his teeth knocked out by the Commandant for daring to say he had received 75 lashes for nothing, instead of admitting his 'offence'.

Visentainer had, therefore, spoken with some authority, and some weight was given to his remark shortly afterwards with the arrival of SS Obersturmführer Bader and a detachment of twenty SS killers. The same afternoon three men died.

'*Los! Los! Hinein, schnell!*' shouted the SS guards as they drove us into our barracks and locked the doors. For two hours a hush fell on the camp. A tribute to the three Austrian resistance fighters who were being hanged on this sunny afternoon in the shadow of their native mountains.

It was another late evening move. The mountains silhouetted against the blood-red western sky were merging into the night when the convoy of seven buses carrying the *Prominenten* Party of about 150, with fifty SS guards, set off from Reichenau. Taking up the rear was a supply lorry containing boxes of hand grenades.

At this late hour – it was 27th April – the iron grip of the SS had been tightened by the addition of Bader and his squad. Although junior in rank to Stiller, he was vested with more authority which, in SS terms, meant that he was a professional killer and could be trusted to carry out any liquidation orders without demur. After all, the motto of the SS was, 'Loyalty is my Honour.'

Slowly the convoy wound up the twisting road leading to the Brenner Pass. Ferraro had been right, we were going to Italy – if we happened to get that far.

At midnight we reached the Brenner frontier post and stopped. It was a moonless night but clear enough to see the shapes of concrete block houses and the ragged outlines of ruined buildings. A line of ghostly figures was moving along the road in the direction of Italy. Some were pushing carts, others were driving a few cattle, pigs or donkeys. They were Italians returning home. Most of the SS had got out and disappeared into the darkness. The singing in the next bus, led as usual by Cushing and accompanied on the accordion by Isa Vermehren, suddenly faded. Schuschnigg had remarked angrily, 'How can you sing in this grave hour?'

Tension built up as an uneasy silence descended on the halted convoy. What were the SS planning in the shadows? There was some desultory conversation in our bus. I discovered that Colonel Stevens had an interpretership in Russian, so we passed some time speaking in Russian trying to forget the unnamed horror which could spring out of the darkness at any moment. One of the Germans was more articulate, 'Perhaps they are going to use the hand grenades if there is an air raid,' he said.

At last, as the dawn lighted the mountain tops, Stiller, Bader and the SS guards returned to the buses, and the convoy moved on.

At the head of the convoy was an SS man on a motor cycle. We could observe him as he weaved about, went ahead to reconnoitre, or stopped the convoy at a cross roads where he would be joined by Bader and Stiller when there would be much pointing, head-shaking and shoulder-shrugging. It was evident that they had only a vague idea of where we were heading. Uncertainty could bode ill where a man like Bader had lost touch with his headquarters.

We turned east down the Pustertal, a beautiful South Tyrolean valley flanked by the rocky snow-capped Dolomites. In the early morning, after bumping over a level crossing, the convoy ground to a halt. It appeared that two of the buses were out of petrol and another had a flat tyre.

The SS guards got out and some sentries were posted along the road, but most of them appeared to be in a group conferring with Stiller and Bader. This was a flashpoint. With the buses out of action, Bader's final solution could be a massacre with Tommy guns and hand grenades in the peaceful Alpine meadows.

Hesitantly the prisoners started to leave the buses and soon we were milling around meeting and talking to friends. Then a number of significant, separate but interrelated events were set in train over the next twenty four hours, leading up to a dramatic climax.

First, Wings and Colonel Churchill were surprised to be asked by Bartoli to attend a meeting with Garibaldi in the level crossing keeper's lodge, when they could manage to slip away.

Inside the lodge Wings and Churchill found Garibaldi sitting at a table which seemed to be groaning with food and wine; with him were Peter Churchill, Ferraro, Bartoli, Amici and the level crossing keeper who was introduced as a sergeant in the local partisan group whose Headquarters was in Niederdorf[1] the neighbouring village.

[1] The official name was Villabassa as this part of the South Tyrol was then Italian, but the majority of the population were Austrian and called the village Niederdorf.

'I'm glad you've come, Wing Commander,' said the General.

'Please sit down both of you and join us in a little lamb, and this chianti is excellent.'

With Peter Churchill interpreting, he continued, 'I have a plan to put to you. In the woods behind us are some units of the Italian Partisans of whom I have assumed command at their invitation. They are ready to surround the convoy at any time and liberate the prisoners. I should be prepared to lead the attack with Colonel Ferraro, and I suggest that you, Colonel Churchill, Dowse, James and the other British join us in this operation, unless of course, you think that your absence from the convoy would be noticed by the SS.'

This immediately appealed to Wings' fighting spirit. The prospect of striking a blow at the enemy after years of inactivity was, at first, exhilarating. But a little reflection told him that this dashing plan must be tempered with a little discretion.

'I congratulate you, General, on the audacity of your plan,' he replied. 'We all want to be free of these SS swine, but we must remember that we have a number of women and children with us, and also some elderly people in their seventies. They must be protected from harm, I feel, therefore, that we should stay with the convoy so that we can overpower the SS when your partisans attack.'

'All right,' said Garibaldi. 'And when do you think the Partisans should attack?'

'I feel that it should be a night attack, not tonight, perhaps tomorrow night when we might be in a more sheltered position and we shall have had an opportunity of watching the movements of the SS.'

'All agreed?' Garibaldi's eyes swept round the meeting.

'*Bene*, then we'll be in touch later on regarding details and timing.'

When Wings and Jack Churchill got back to the convoy, things had been moving.

Payne Best had got into conversation with Stiller.

'Now where are you taking us?' he asked the SS captain.

'I was going to take you to a hotel, but that is occupied by Luftwaffe staff. I can't do anything without petrol, and I really don't know what to do next.'

Best's impression was that Stiller did not want to do anything and would be agreeable to any plan which Bader might have to liquidate us. He, therefore, sought out Thyssen, the industrialist, and Hjalmar Schacht, the former President of the Reichsbank, and suggested that some pressure be put on Stiller in the form of a bribe to take us to the Swiss Frontier. Although the two Germans were willing to offer 100,000 Swiss francs, they did not wish to approach Stiller about it, nor would they go with Best while he put forward the offer.

In the meantime Dr Schuschnigg, who was a Tyrolean, had been recognized, and there soon appeared on the spot a Dr Tony Ducia, a youngish, alert-looking man who introduced himself as the billeting officer for the area. He also happened to be the local South Tyrolean Resistance leader who, with his colleagues, had been informed as soon as the convoy entered the Pustertal. Stiller thought he was an emissary from the area Gauleiter Hofer, and agreed to the offer of accommodation for the group in Niederdorf.

The Schuschniggs, Best, von Bonin, General Thomas and some others then set off to walk the short distance to Niederdorf to have a look at the accommodation available. Meanwhile, Bader and some of the SS men had been drinking since dawn and were weaving about drunkenly, clutching bottles of schnapps and wine.

'*Schlecht*,' muttered Niemoller. 'From my long experience of the SS, these drinking bouts are often the prelude to the shooting of prisoners, the build up to a killing.'

Bader stumbled to the roadside and collapsed in a drunken stupor.

'Give him some more refreshment,' whispered Hugh Falconer. 'Then we can get hold of his wallet.'

One of the Germans fed him some more schnapps, loosened his tunic and extracted his pocket book. Inside was found an order signed by Himmler for the execution of twenty-eight persons, including all the British officers, should there be any danger of their falling into Allied hands. 'If possible it should be made to appear as the result of an air attack.'

Word was sent at once to the VIPs who had left for Niederdorf.

As Payne Best, Thomas and the others were passing the post office in Niederdorf, there was a cry of 'Thomas' and a German officer in the uniform of a Major-General rushed forward to greet his old friend General Thomas. He turned out to be the administrative commander of the area with a small headquarters in the post office where all lines had been requisitioned for military purposes. He led the party which included most of the VIP's, such as the Blums, Thyssens, Schuschniggs, the Greek Generals and the Hungarians, to the Hotel Bachman, the best hotel in town, where they sat down to a tremendous meal.

The execution order found in Bader's pocket overshadowed complete enjoyment of the meal and gave some urgency to the problem of getting rid of the SS. Colonel von Bonin who, up to that time, could have been persuaded to cooperate with the Partisans in attacking the SS hit upon a more peaceful solution upon hearing that his old friend General von Vietinghoff was in command of Army Group C in Italy with HQ at Bolzano. He went off at once to put a phone call through to his HQ, from the post office. He could not contact Vietinghoff but spoke to General Roettiger, the Chief of Staff, whom he also knew, and put to him our grave situation, requesting immediate protection for our group in the form of an officer and a company of infantry. Roettiger promised to get hold of Vietinghoff as soon as possible and phone back.

As von Bonin put the receiver down, Stiller and another SS man burst into the office,

'Don't you realize that you are a prisoner,' screamed Stiller. 'Whatever your rank and honours, you cannot do as you like when you are in the hands of the SS.'

Von Bonin, a most impressive type of German officer, in the uniform of a Colonel, towered authoritatively over the SS man, and in language indicating that Stiller was very much a subordinate told him he was a fool if he could not recognize the changed situation and ordered him to leave the premises immediately. Stiller went pale, and, with an angry glance at the four administrative orderlies standing stiffly to attention behind Bonin, stamped out of the room.

The rest of the party had been straggling into Niederdorf. We were first given a splendid meal in the 'Goldener Stern'; the main course, I can remember now, was excellent spaghetti and as much as we wanted. After my five years on prison camp rations, moreover eating in civilized surroundings, it seemed like manna from heaven for which we had to thank our generous Austrian hosts.

Tony Ducia had been busy and accommodation had been found for the whole party in two hotels and in the Town Hall. The British, Poles, Russians and a few others were to sleep on straw in a large room on the first floor of the Town Hall. The affable Baron von Schell, who could have joined his Prime Minister in more comfortable quarters, elected to join us on the straw. He spoke perfect English, having spent his early years with an English Nanny.

The SS had brought their vehicles into Niederdorf and had established their HQ in the town square around the supply lorry containing the hand grenades. They did not interfere with our movements. They knew, and we knew, that this was now an open prison in which seventeen different nationalities were held together in a close association acknowledging a common danger. Now the guards were patrolling again, their schmeissers at the ready, sullen and brooding. They had heard about von Bonin's phone call, and their mood could be summed up in a remark made by one of Bader's sergeants, a man called Fritz; 'We should have shot that traitor first.'

On the top floor of the town hall, Garibaldi had established his own headquarters. Having discarded his Dachau striped prison garb, he was now resplendent in a General's uniform and quite openly the commander in the field directing his partisans who, thinly disguised as civilians paying their respects to the General, were excitedly rushing in and out looking like the bandits some of them probably were, ready at any moment to shoot or knife the SS.

Garibaldi, however, had been told of von Bonin's phone call and had agreed to postpone the attack on the SS. For the moment he would have to restrain his guerilla force, and this included Ferraro who was furious at the prospect of missing the opportunity of leading a dashing attack on his erstwhile oppressors.

The British were in favour of keeping the partisan plan 'on ice' but only briefly. An attack by the Partisans who could certainly have overpowered the SS by weight of numbers alone perhaps with minimum loss of life, was preferable to sitting around waiting to be massacred by the Bader gang. Besides we should have the satisfaction of freeing ourselves without German help.

This was the situation on 28th April as dusk was gathering over the ancient roofs and carved gables of this little Tyrolean town which now harboured a human tinder box needing only a spark to set it ablaze.

Night fell, and most of the hostages were drifting off to their beds, between clean sheets in the best hotels if they were VIP's, or just happened to be lucky, or on beds of straw in the big room in the Town Hall as in our case.

Jack Churchill sitting on a pile of straw on one side of me, suddenly said, 'I'm off, Jimmy, I've had enough of this lot. You coming?'

'No, not this time,' I replied. 'I think the war would be over by the time one managed to stumble over the mountains – if one got that far.'

But Jack was restless. He was tired of Best and his faction and considered they spent too much time talking and too little time acting. After nine months as a prisoner, most of it in solitary confinement, following an active and distinguished war, he felt that he wanted to get back into the battle before it was all over. He obtained Wings' approval, and we got him extra clothing and some food. Wings took him to the edge of the town and watched him disappear into the forest on a journey quite as dangerous as staying in Niederdorf. It was arranged that, if there was any danger of the British being shot, Wings was to say, 'Colonel Churchill who escaped had with him your name, Bader, and that of every man in your squad, and if you do anything so stupid as to shoot us you will all be executed, the moment you become prisoners, as murdering war criminals, killing defenceless hostages.' All in the hearing of his squad.

When Wings got back to the Town Hall there seemed to be SS guards everywhere, but he was disturbed to see Bader pacing up and down in the entrance hall, edgy and irascible.

Bader walked up to Wings and said, 'We have a special room for you British in a nice hotel across the square.'

Wings sensed immediate danger. 'We don't want a special room. We'll be quite happy to doss down with the others upstairs.'

Bader hesitated for a moment, then moved away. Baron von Schell, who had overheard this conversation, whispered to Wings:

'For God's sake don't go to any special room. The SS are gunning for you British.'

SS guards were posted to all parts of the building. There were two of them, Schmeissers slung across their knees at the ready, sitting one at each end of our room. The SS had not been unaware of the activity around Garibaldi's HQ that day; now there was no sign of any Italians in the town hall. But the woods were full of them; at any moment they could pour out of the darkness, guns blazing. In the stillness the SS watched and waited. The tension mounted as, on our beds of straw, we waited, watching the motionless shadowy figures of the two guards, weapons ready for action. Would they use them in indiscriminate slaughter before the morning – even without a Partisan attack – at a word from Bader? The night of the long knives had begun.

In the Hotel Bachman, shortly after midnight, the drunken SS man was muttering, 'Shoot them all down -bum-bum-bum-bump them all off is best.'

Payne Best had been talking to him and to the equally drunk Fritz, who had just shown him a copy of the execution order for a number of prisoners.

'You don't mean to tell me that Stiller would be such a fool as to carry out this order,' said Best. 'He assured me that he would hand us over safely to the Americans when they reach us.'

'Well,' replied Fritz, 'it is Bader who runs this show, and he says that he is going to liquidate all the prisoners. He has had his orders for the past three months, and he always carries out his orders.'

'Now, Fritz, we have just drunk *Bruderschaft* and surely you will not take any part in killing me.'

'*Ja, Herr Best*, but what can I do? You are all going to a Hotel in the mountains tomorrow. You will all be shot and then the hotel will be set on fire. I don't like it because these tommy guns don't kill people properly. The bullets are too small, so a lot of people won't be dead when the place is set on fire.' He thought deeply for a while. 'I tell you what I'll do, I'll give you a sign before they start shooting and you can come and stand near me, so I can give you a shot in the back of the head (*Nacken* or *Genickschuss*) – that is the best way to die, I am a dead shot.'

He drew his revolver, 'Just turn round, and I'll show you.'

'Don't be silly,' countered Best. 'How can I see what you are doing behind my back. Why, you might have an accident and shoot me!'

Whereupon Fritz turned to his pal and requested him to turn his head for a demonstration of the *Nackenschuss*, but the man just stared glassily, still muttering about bumping them off, and finally passed out, sweeping bottle and glasses off the table. Fritz became more and more melancholy and lachrymose. There followed a catalogue of his shooting of hundreds, thousands of people, of which his wife and children had no inkling, but war was terrible – all the fault of the Jews and plutocrats in England and America. The Führer was good and wanted only peace.

Best went off to bed. At 3 a.m. he was awakened by General Thomas to be told that he and von Bonin had at last received a telephone call from Roettiger saying that Vietinghoff would at once send an officer with a company of infantry to ensure our safety. He also promised to notify the Americans of our whereabouts and ask them to regard Niederdorf as a neutral zone.

As the early morning light filtered through the windows of the long room in the town hall onto our beds of straw, I awoke from an uneasy sleep and noticed that the guards were no longer there. Thomas Cushing, who was beside me, had also woken up and he started to whistle Reveille announcing loudly:

'Everybody up. The SS bastards have gone. We've got our own parade this morning.'

Roused from an exhausted slumber, we were all up in no time in the clothes we had slept in, and stumbled down the stairs in time to see the final demise of the SS.

Across the square the SS men were grouped uncertainly around their vehicles, Bader standing in front exuding hatred and defiance. Facing them was a Wehrmacht unit of about fifteen men commanded by a young lieutenant. The SS were having a heated discussion among themselves and were obviously unwilling to surrender to a Wehrmacht unit whose commander, Lieutenant von Alvensleben, seemed uncertain of taking any definite action.[1] Wings had anticipated something like this and had gone off for a talk with Best, von Bonin and Korvettenkapitän Liedig to tell them of the Garibaldi plan which horrified them, as they thought it would lead to too much unnecessary bloodshed. They told Wings that they had already had a formal talk with Stiller who had been ordered to hand over his command, nominally to the British since they were the representatives of the nearest Allied Forces; he had been encouraged to comply with this order by von Bonin's newly acquired revolver.

I could see von Bonin, very much in command of the situation, standing beside the Wehrmacht platoon. He now told von

---

[1] This was not surprising as von Avensleben had received on the telephone some rather vague orders from General Roettiger who had merely said, 'There's a convoy of *Prominenten* in Niederdorf. Go and find out what the trouble is. If necessary find food and shelter for them.' Nothing more. It was perhaps ironic at this stage of the war that Roettiger should have been afraid that his telephone was tapped by the Gestapo. One reason may have been that he was conducting, with SS General Wolff commanding all SS and police in Italy, secret peace negotiations with Field Marshal Alexander's HQ in Italy through Allen Dulles, CIA director in Switzerland.

In the circumstances von Alvensleben had acted with considerable initiative and displayed more courage than he had appeared to have on the town square. He had arrived in Niederdorf the previous evening and had strolled into town on his own to find out what was going on, as ordered. He happened to bump into Stiller and they had a coffee together in a local inn; he soon grasped the situation when he heard the names of some of the personalities in the group; and that Bader, the killer from Buchenwald, and his squad were among the SS. 'My mission is complete when they are all dead,' Bader had said. Von Alvensleben then resolved to get his men up to the main square in the early morning and get rid of the SS.

Alvensleben that he would accept full responsibility for the actions of his unit, and that he should get on with the job of disarming the SS. Orders were barked out by Hauptfeldwebel Mutscheller and two heavy machine guns were mounted quickly and trained on the SS.

Colonel von Bonin strode across the square to Bader and told him that the SS must throw down their arms. If they refused, he warned, the machine guns would open up on them. There was a moment's hesitation then the weapons were dropped.

'Now get the hand grenades, *schnell*,' ordered von Bonin.

They were added to the other weapons which were being snatched up and whisked away by the red-scarved Partisans, many of whom had been standing round watching the proceedings.

Bader was soon pleading for petrol so that he could drive off with his men. Not only was this refused but von Bonin could barely be restrained from shooting all the SS men on the spot.

When the SS lorry was searched it was found to contain 120 Red Cross parcels; these were distributed among the prisoners. Meanwhile von Alvensleben had phoned General Roettiger to tell him that the SS had all been dealt with and what was he to do with them. Roettiger, still in dread of the Gestapo, was horrified.

'Are you mad?' he exclaimed. 'How could you do this? It will be your head or mine.' SS General Wolff, however, was a good deal more decisive, he picked up the phone and told von Alvensleben, 'Send the fellows down here to me.'

Bader got some petrol and drove off with his men in the lorry and a bus. The Partisans did not allow them to get very far. Their bodies were found later hanging from telegraph poles at the side of the road. Stiller, with ten men, decided it would be safer to stay and take their chance with the Allies.

It was Sunday, 29th April. That morning Mass was concelebrated, appropriately, by the Bishop of Clermont Ferrand and Canon Neuhäusler in the ancient church with its beautiful frescoed ceiling. The church was packed with members of our group, of all denominations giving thanks in the hour of our deliverance.

At midday Payne Best and von Bonin were standing on a table in the Cafe Bachman addressing members of our party – von Bonin in German and Best in French and English. They were leading members of a committee which had been formed to look after our interests. They told us of arrangements that had been made by Tony Ducia to get us transferred to a hotel 5,000 feet up in the mountains where we were to await the arrival of the Allies.

With the demise of the SS, the whole village relaxed and took on a festive air. Certainly the inhabitants could not have been more generous or hospitable. Quantities of food, wine, cognac and schnapps were produced from their undoubtedly limited stocks which they would find impossible to replenish for a long time.

That afternoon, Sydney Dowse and I went for a walk down the sunlit valley with Baron Schell, Isa Vermehren and her cousin Countess Gisela von Plettenberg, both of whom had been in Ravensbruck together. A stream of vehicles passed us in varying degrees of mobility, most of them filled with soldiers of the retreating and disintegrating German armies, some packed with loot of all kinds, others with excited Italians shouting '*La guerra e finita.*'

The Pragser Wildsee Hotel, called Hotel Lago di Braies after this part of the Tyrol became Italian in 1918, lay high up in the mountains on the edge of a small lake, tree-girt shores flanked by rocky precipices which soared up to the sharp, craggy heights of the Dolomites reflected in the gently rippling, turquoise waters below.

On 30th April when we arrived at the hotel by bus, in my case on foot after the bus had broken down half-way up the steep road, it was snowing; we were 5,000 feet above sea level and had left the spring behind in the valley. Then the sun came out to reveal a fairyland of dazzling white snow crystals enhancing the beauty of this silent amphitheatre in the mountains. After my years of viewing barbed wire, guard towers and cell walls, it seemed like a wonderful dream.

Human memory is short; most of us lived from day to day. Very soon, it seemed, the common suffering and danger of only yesterday were forgotten in the scramble for comforts in the 200 room hotel which had been closed for five years. There was no heating, as most of the pipes had burst and this led to the incident of the blankets and eiderdowns missing on the second day from rooms on the second and third floors. After a number of complaints they were found stacked up in the luxurious first floor room of a senior member of the party who wanted to make quite sure of his own comfort!

Then there was the disappearing wine. Frau Emma Heiss, the proprietress, generously invited everybody down to the cellars for a wine party. Afterwards fifteen gallons of wine were found to be missing from the wine cellar which had been left unlocked.

In mitigation of these unfortunate incidents, it might be said that the 'magpie' instinct acquired by most prisoners died hard.

A volunteer staff of ladies from the *Sippenhäftlinge* produced meals, sorted out bedding and attended to various chores.

Hugh Falconer, the wireless expert, got hold of an old radio and made it work; on this we listened to regular BBC broadcasts. One of the SS men protested but he was soon put in his place by von Bonin. After the news of Hitler's suicide on 30th April, the SS kept very much in the background.

Although the threat of sudden extinction had passed, there was danger still in the air. The Wehrmacht platoon led by von Alvensleben had been withdrawn. The woods harboured deserters drifting back from the Italian front, many of whom would have slit a throat for a suit of clothes or some food. Ducia reported that the Italian Partisans operating behind the German lines were becoming an increasing threat to law and order, and the different factions, Communist, Italian Nationalist and pro-Austrian were even beginning to fight among themselves. Furthermore a strong force of SS under the South Tyrolean Gauleiter Hofer was reported to be nearby at Bolzano.

It was against this uncertain background that Wings and Tony Ducia left on 2nd May in the latter's battered Volkswagen on a hazardous journey across the mountainous North Italian battle zone to try to reach the Americans who were near Trento.

There were some other departures from the group. I was surprised when young Vassili Molotov came up to me in the lounge and asked in Russian, 'What will the Allies do to me when they arrive?'

'*Nichevo*,' I replied, 'If you want to go home, they will send you back to the Soviet Union,' assuming that he would wish to be where Uncle could assure him of a good career.

He appeared satisfied. Later that day four red-scarved partisans, armed with sub-machine guns, swaggered into the hotel and claimed they had received orders to give Vassili special protection. In spite of every effort by the British and others to dissuade him, he insisted on going with the Italians. That was the last we saw of him; he was taken up to the mountains where he died from gangrene which developed in feet already frostbitten on the Russian Front.

Another Russian decided that he had stayed long enough. General Bessanov, having announced that the Soviets did not recognize prisoners, said that he was not going to hang around and wait for the Allies to return him to the Soviet Union to be shot by 'Uncle' Joe Stalin. He disappeared into the mountains with a Luger and some ammunition he had found. There he stayed for some years until he was able to get himself to South America. He was a great survivor.

General Garibaldi had remained in his HQ at Niederdorf. With Colonel Farraro, he was busily engaged in disarming German troops retreating down the valley. He sent a message to Peter Churchill requesting his presence as an interpreter. The problem of transport was solved by Hugh Falconer who found an old banger in a garage, and got it working. He and Peter drove off down the mountain in it to help Garibaldi sort out the remnants of the German Army.

Sydney Dowse and I found ourselves included in a lunch party held at a local Gasthaus in honour of the Schuschniggs. I happened to be sitting next to Hjalmar Schacht. After some attention to the splendid meal which included some of the best Tyrolean wines, I broke through a somewhat forbidding reserve by venturing that I had also worked in a bank when I was in Canada, albeit in a somewhat junior capacity.

'We can't all be Bank Presidents,' he replied rather loftily.

Thereafter I found him a pleasant enough lunchtime companion. Another point of contact was that we had both been in Flossenburg at the same time. Schacht had been suspected of complicity in the plot against Hitler; arrested after the 20th July he was to have been murdered by Stavitsky, the last Commandant at Flossenburg. Although somewhat of an enigma, his anti-Nazi stand considered equivocal by post-war German Nazi trials courts (he was also anti-Semitic), he had, nevertheless, resigned as Minister of Finance in 1937 because he refused to cooperate with Göring in his extravagant economic plans, which of course covered rearmament, and had been dismissed as President of the Reichsbank by Hitler in 1939.

I looked round the table at the courteous, smiling Dr Schuschnigg, the scholarly General Halder, von Falkenhausen who had refused to shoot hostages, von Bonin who had saved us from the SS, and others who had defied Hitler. I remembered the relatively gentlemanly treatment we had received in Prisoner of War Camps, the humanity of Commandants like Rumpel at Dulag Luft, Burchardt who had congratulated me on our tunnel at Stalag Luft I through which Shore had escaped, Lindeiner at Stalag Luft III, Feldwebel Glemnitz, through the horrors of the concentration camps – yet even here was a glimmer of light, Corporal 'George' in the Sonderlager – the death cells, the walking skeletons at Flossenburg, the SS killer squad from which we had barely escaped. As suddenly as the pall of death had lifted the scene had shifted to this convivial lunch, and I was sitting beside Hitler's former financial wizard with other leading representatives of all the millions in Europe who had resisted the

Nazi Terror. The wheel had turned full circle, I knew I was beyond hatred.

On 3rd May leaflets were dropped by Allied aircraft with an announcement from Field Marshal Alexander that the German armies in Italy had surrendered and instructing all military units in the area to cease firing. Early on the same day a Wehrmacht company under Captain von Alvensleben, a cousin of the lieutenant who had been with us in Niederdorf, arrived to ensure our safety until an Allied unit could reach us. They did not have long to wait.

The next morning, as I walked back with some of our group from an early Mass in the little chapel on the lake shore it was evident that there was great activity around the hotel. As we approached we saw a line of vehicles parked on the road in front and there were soldiers, unmistakably American soldiers. It seemed unbelievable. Captain John Attwell had arrived with a company from the 339th Infantry Regiment. They had been travelling all night and looked exhausted. Wings and Tony Ducia had got through and we were really free at last.

In no time the Americans were sharing their rations of chocolate and cigarettes with us, a mobile laundry had been set up on the lawn and nets were erected for handball and other games. Our rations were supplemented by such mouth-watering and long-forgotten items as waffles and syrup, eggs and bacon, while they apologized for having only front line rations!

It was not long before the Press and Newsreel cameras were with us. The most important among the *Prominenten* had to submit to a good deal of interviewing and photographing, particularly Blum, Schuschnigg and Niemoller, the latter in various poses both with and without Bible. But the four-year-old daughter of the Schuschniggs, little Cissy, born in a concentration camp, upstaged the whole group!

Leon Blum was bubbling with excitement as the Press descended on him. '*C'est magnifique!*' he exclaimed and insisted on shaking each one by the hand. He maintained that he had no political ambitions at that moment and would only say, 'De Gaulle is the great, great good fortune of France. De Gaulle means a guarantee of a united France.'

There was great relief and joy, but after the years of imprisonment most of us had suffered, often with little hope of survival, it was difficult to grasp the reality of freedom. When the first flush of excitement and exaltation had subsided, and the great aftermath of peace and an uncertain future began to loom in the consciousness of the many different nationalities present, feelings of anti-climax were inescapable.

Many of us had had no communication with home for years and did not know what was waiting for us. The Russians feared being sent back. Those from the countries overrun by the Soviet Army did not wish to go home either. For the Germans there was only a country laid in ruins to which to return. It was, perhaps, because of this that some of the German *Prominenten* and their wives wept when the Wehrmacht soldiers were taken off to prison camps in American transport that evening. It was the final indignity for a nation destroyed by Hitler.

On 6th May Brigadier-General Gerow and his adjutant arrived to make arrangements for our evacuation. He told us that communications to the north had been disrupted, and so we should have to be taken south to Naples by road and air. The party was to be moved in two convoys on different days; all Allied personnel were to be in the first convoy.

After breakfast on 8th May the first convoy was ready to move. About twenty staff cars, light tanks to front and rear, were lined up in front of the hotel, ready to move off at nine o'clock. At five minutes to nine there was no sign of any movement. Then, with deceptively casual American efficiency the drivers appeared, the passengers were in their seats, and the whole convoy moved off exactly at O – nine hundred hours, with the minimum of fuss and almost no shouted orders – incomprehensible to the Germans among us!

I was in a car with Peter Churchill and Josef Muller. It was a beautiful spring day and as we drove down the lovely valley of the Piave our spirits were high. The warm and fragrant air of the Mediterranean came to meet us, washing away gruesome and painful memories of the immediate past and giving us an exhilarating sense of freedom. The journey down the valley was slow. The devastation of war was everywhere visible; wrecked and burnt-out vehicles and tanks, ruined buildings, the rutted and cratered road with sometimes only the river bed to follow, as few bridges were left standing.

Josef Muller was a lively and interesting companion, and on the journey he told us something of his past. Born in Bavaria in 1898 at Ochsenfurt, hence his name the 'Ox', he trained as a lawyer and became a leading legal and economic adviser in Catholic Church affairs, gaining the confidence of the Pope. He had always been anti-Nazi. Drafted into the Army when war broke out he worked in the

Abwehr (Intelligence) under Canaris, who was a close friend, and
General Beck. He was instructed by Beck to undertake peace
negotiations through the Vatican. He was able to do this under his
Intelligence cover and he had an old Jesuit friend, Peter Laiber, who
was the Pope's confidential secretary. Some outline peace proposals
were drawn up but these, unfortunately, fell into the hands of the
Gestapo. Arrested in 1943 on a charge of treason, Muller's defence
rested on his stand that as an Army officer he was entitled to talk
about peace but had not undertaken any peace negotiations. He was
acquitted, but immediately rearrested by the Gestapo and
interrogated under torture for 220 hours, then chained up for six
months. As we know, he barely avoided execution at Flossenburg.

There was a stop for lunch at an attractive restaurant where trestle
tables laden with food and wine had been set out for us in the
sunshine. Then we drove on to Verona. Although it was after
midnight when we arrived, we were given a large chicken supper in
an hotel, and then I was taken with some others to an American
mobile field hospital where we were comfortably quartered in a large
heated tent.

The next morning, sustained by a splendid breakfast, and laden
with gifts from the PX, we were driven to an airfield where a small
fleet of Dakotas was waiting to fly us to Naples. It seemed strange to be
in the air again and yet, when I went up to the cockpit and looked at
the controls and instrument panel, it all came back again and I felt I
could sit down in the pilot's seat and fly the plane to Naples – landing
might have been another matter! We passed over Rome and a short
while later the pilot flew low over Monte Cassino so that we could
clearly see the ruins of the monastery and the scars of the bitter battle
fought for control of the heights from March to May 1944; a Pyrrhic
victory resulting in 115,000 Allied dead, wounded and missing, of
whom over 100,000 were Americans.

At Naples the British were taken over by a British Army Transit
Centre where we met Wings and Jack Churchill. Wings told us that
he and Tony Ducia had had an adventurous journey after leaving us.
The old Volkswagen had soon broken down, but they went on in a
succession of old and battered vehicles and finally on foot over the
mountains, helped by wild Partisans, through the German lines, and
then on through a number of American and Allied headquarters
which had at last resulted in the despatch of Captain Attwell and his
company at two o'clock in the morning. Jack Churchill had also had
an eventful time. He made contact in due course with the American

88th Division who sent him to General Truscott's Corps HQ. At dinner the first evening the General asked so many questions about Tito, Sachsenhausen and the SS, that Jack had no time to eat as his plates were being whisked away by the waiters – until the General realized that this was Jack's first proper meal since he was captured!

The Germans who had been in our group were all taken to Capri where they were lodged in a large hotel at Anacapri to be vetted by the Americans before being repatriated to Germany.

Peter Churchill spent some time and effort trying to get Nikolai Rutschenko repatriated with us instead of joining the queue to go back to the Soviet Union. All his pleas to top brass, including two Generals, were to no avail. One of the Generals said that all Rutschenko had to do was to report to the Russian Consul in Rome.

'You know what will happen if he does that,' replied Peter.

'Oh, nothing will happen,' said the General airily. 'It's just a formality.'

Such formalities cost tens of thousands of Russian lives at that time. Many of them Cossacks, who hated Communism, they committed suicide rather than return to the Soviet Union, and those who were forced into cattle trucks at the point of a bayonet were all executed on arrival. It was a black page in British history.

General Privalov and Colonel Brodnikov returned to the Soviet Union but, sadly, were both shot on arrival. Fiodr Ceredilin we heard went free after a period of 'decontamination' in Siberia.

On 13th May, Wings, Sydney Dowse and I were flown back to England in a Royal Air Force Warwick, a transport version of the Wellington in which I had been shot down nearly five years previously. We passed over the sunlit white cliffs of the South Coast and landed at Blackbushe. We stepped out onto the soil of our native land and with tremendous relief and joy breathed in the air of freedom. Many times in the past years we had doubted whether this moment would ever come. Whatever the peace might bring, we could face it. We had passed through a nightmare experience of what can happen, in any country, when the forces of totalitarianism prevail.

Mass Escape from Sagan

Aftermath

There was uproar in the North Compound after discovery of the tunnel. An immediate *Appell* was called. Block 104 was ringed around by machine guns and ferrets, and prisoners were chased out onto the parade ground by trigger-happy guards. They were made to stand in the snow for three hours while a photographic check was made of every prisoner in the compound.

A camp officer was putting through a large number of telephone calls to offices in the POW Luftwaffe Command, railway stations, aerodromes and the Police, the most important of these was to SS Obersturmbannführer Max Wielen, the head of the Breslau KRIPO, in whose district Sagan was located. He ordered a *Kriegsfahndung*, a war emergency manhunt. When the full extent of the escape became known, he upgraded this to a *Grossfahndung*, a national alert. This meant that the Security Service (Reichssicherheitsdienst) was brought into action with its vast reserves of police, SS, the armed forces and the Hitler Youth, in addition there were hundreds of thousands of male auxiliaries who, for the period of the emergency, were taken from their ordinary work in fields and factories. The search operation was exclusively in the hands of Himmler, and millions of people were involved directly and indirectly.

After Hitler had given the order to shoot more than half the recaptured officers, Field Marshal Wilhelm Keitel, Chief of the High Command, summoned General von Graevenitz, chief of the POW Department of the OKW and Major General Westhoff, head of the General Section (Allgemeine Abteilung) of the POW Organisation, on the evening of 25th March and told them of the meeting with Hitler.

Keitel said, 'Gentlemen, these escapes must stop. We must set an example. We shall take very severe measures. I can only tell you that the men who have escaped will be shot; probably the majority are already.' Von Graevenitz and Westhoff both objected that this was contrary to the Geneva Convention. Keitel replied, 'I don't give a damn, we discussed it in the Führer's presence and it cannot be altered.' (Westhoff's statement, 15th June 1945.)

Having established the number of officers to be shot as 50, Himmler set up the machinery for their execution. He instructed Kaltenbrunner to issue what has become known as the Sagan Order, the approximate text of which follows:

The increase of escapes by officer prisoners of war is a menace to internal security. I am disappointed and indignant about the inefficient security measures. As a deterrent the Führer has ordered that more than half the escaped officers are to be shot. Therefore I order that Department V (controlling the KRIPO) hand over to Department IV (controlling the GESTAPO) more than half the recaptured officers. After interrogation it should be made to seem that the officers are being returned to their camp but they are to be shot en route. The shooting will be explained by the fact that the recaptured officers were shot trying to escape, or they offered resistance, so that nothing can be proved later. Amt IV will report the shootings to Amt V giving the reason. In the event of future escapes my decision will be awaited as to the procedure to be adopted. Prominent personalities will be excepted; their names will be reported to me and a decision awaited.

General Nebe, the Head of Amt V, was ordered to choose the names of the officers to be shot. He was in a state of considerable agitation as he examined the records and photographs of the 76 officers who had escaped through the tunnel. He sifted nervously through the documents exclaiming now and again, 'Ach, he is too young,' sometimes 'He is married with children' or 'He is for it'.

The urns containing the ashes of those shot were sent back to the camp, and a memorial was erected by their fellow officers at Sagan.

Of the 26 survivors, 15 were sent back to Sagan. Plunkett, the Mapping Chief, and two Czechs, Tonder and Dvořak, were kept in Gestapo prisons and concentration camps in Czechoslovakia; van Wymeersch, a French officer, went to Buchenwald (fortuitously) then to Sachsenhausen. The names of the remaining four were contained in the postscript to Himmler's Sagan Order which ran as follows:

Order for the transfer of Prominent Prisoners to Camp 'A' Sachsenhausen Concentration Camp.

The following officers – Wing Commander Day, Major Dodge, Flight Lieutenant Dowse and Flight Lieutenant James[1] are to be transferred to Camp 'A' Sachsenhausen.

To the outside world they are to be considered as escaped and not recaptured. The Commandant and his representatives are responsible with their heads for their secure housing and treatment.

[1] To this day I have no idea why Dowse and I were considered to be in this category. Perhaps Dowse was included because he was descended from a distinguished German family.

APPENDIX B

Courts Martial of Members of German Prison Shaft –
Colonel von Lindeiner, Captain Broili and nine others
after the Mass Escape at Stalag Luft III.

Field Court, Berlin 16 September 1944

The commandant, Colonel von Lindeiner, was censured heavily for a negligent attitude towards the microphones used for recording tunnelling noises on the wire perimeter. The microphones placed outside Barrack 104 (from which 'Harry' was dug) had registered consistently loud noises from May 1943. The consequent searches revealed no evidence of a tunnel, and the noises were attributed to the workers in coal dumps in the vicinity of the microphones.

This was deemed inexcusable since the microphones had led to the discovery of 'Tom' in September 1943. It was considered even worse that all listening apparatus had been put out of action for renovation and reorganisation during the winter months of 1943/44.

The extract from the summary of evidence continues:

On arrival at the camp every prisoner received, in addition to a bed and palliasse, knife, fork, spoon, dish, one coffee cup, two blankets, three articles of bed linen and one towel. In the period 15th. January 1943 to 19 April 1944, Group Administration advised the loss of the following public property;

1,699	blankets
192	bed covers
161	pillow cases
165	sheets
3,424	towels
655	palliasses
1,212	bolsters
34	single chairs
10	single tables
52	tables for two men
76	benches
90	double tier bunks
246	water cans
1,219	knives
582	forks
478	spoons
69	lamps
30	shovels

In spite of payment for damages in money by the prisoners, the fact remains that the overtaxed state of the German linen industry could not cope with such a strain. While German families who had lost all could only receive replacement for their lost possessions in the most needy circumstances, owing to the shortage of linen articles and household goods, the imprisoned 'Terror Airmen' lived among the things entrusted to them in the most devilish ways, and with them constantly continued the war against the Reich behind the barbed wire, and with success. There is no doubt that the prisoners purposely destroyed part of the things merely with the idea of causing damage to the Reich. . . .

All the accused were sentenced to terms of imprisonment. The sentences were cut short by the end of the war, and the Commandant and other members of his staff were then brought to England for interrogation.

APPENDIX 'C' TOM, DICK AND HARRY
North Compound, Stalag Luft III – April 1943 to March 1944

TUNNEL CONSTRUCTION

	Date Commenced	Trap	Depth	Length	Chambers at base of shaft	'Half Way Houses'	Railways & Trolleys	Fate	Items used in construction – approximate figures						
									Bed and Floor Boards	Double Bunks	Electric Wiring	Beading Battens	Klim Milk biscuit tins for Air Lines	Total Rope	Employed
Tom	11/4/43	Block 123 Passage in Concrete	25'	220'	1 Air Pump 1 Disposal 1 Workshop	2	1 Rly 3 Trolleys	Discovered 8 Sept. 1943	1500	35	400'	500'	500	230' Maximum	3 teams of 12 diggers = 36
Dick	11/4/43	Block 122 Wash Room in Sump	25'	60'	As above	–	1 Rly 1 Trolley	Used for Dispersal	500	10	100'	120'	150	60'	
Harry	11/4/43	Block 104 In Room under tiled base for stove	28'	365'	As above	2	1 Rly 3 Trolleys	Operated 24/25 March 1944	2000	45	500'	750'	750	370'	Carpenters and Technicians about 30+
									4000	90	1000'	1370'	1400	660'	

Cross Section 2' sq.ft. Average day in 1 day, 3ft – Maximum 14ft.

DISPOSAL OF SAND

April 1943 to September 1943

	Tons of Sand	Method	Capacity	No. of trips	Total Employed
Tom	70	Mainly trouser sacks, suspended by sling around back of neck, one down each leg with opening at bottom operated by pin attached to string leading to each trouser pocket. Carried by Penguins. 130 tons. Also carried in blankets and boxes. Spread over compound.	Trouser Sacks 8×8 = 16lbs	18,000 by 5 teams of 25 each (trouser sacks)	200+
Dick	30				
Harry	40				

January 1944 to March 1944

	Tons of Sand	Method	No. of trips	Dispersal Area	Total Dispersal Area Employed
Harry	90	Kit Bags – Capacity 80lbs – carried by Penguins routed through blocks in the dark to disposal point	Tunnel to dispersal area	Under Theatre with 12 Tons in "Dick"	80 of whom 12 worked under Theatre

Maximum dispersed in one day 4½ tons
Maximum in one evening 4 tons = 98 kit bags = 14' of tunnel
About 1 ton of sand = 3½ft of tunnel

Escape From the SS

Aftermath

When the escape of the five British officers from Sonderlager 'A'
Sachenhausen, on 23rd September 1944, was discovered a *Grossfahndung*
(National Alert) was ordered immediately, and the following notice was
posted all over Germany and the occupied countries:

The following five English officers are wanted by the police in Germany:
1. *DAY* Harry Melville. Born 3.8.1898 in Sarawak, Borneo. Height,
   183 cms. Brown hair, thin face, grey eyes, curved nose, slim figure,
   healthy complexion, coloured cheeks. Dress: Possibly only trousers
   and a shirt.
2. *DODGE* John Bigelow. Born 15.5.1894 USA. Height, 185 cms.
   Brown hair, broad face, egg shaped head, hooked nose, healthy
   complexion, dirty slightly coloured teeth. Dress: blue grey uniform.
3. *JAMES* Bertram Arthur. Born 17.4.1915 in Assam, India. Height:
   170 cms. Dark brown hair, oval face, blue grey eyes, small narrow
   nose. Has all his teeth. Small figure. Healthy complexion. Dress:
   blue grey uniform with double row of gold buttons (sic!)*
4. *DOWSE* Sydney Hastings. Born 21.11.1918 in London. Height: 170
   cms. Fair hair, small figure, pointed face, blue eyes, round cranium,
   sound teeth, small nose. Dress: blue grey uniform.
5. *CHURCHILL* John Torte Fleming Malcolm. Born 16.9.06 in
   Colombo. Height: 170 cms. Sturdy figure, fair hair, beard. Dress:
   olive green uniform.

These five escapees were last seen on 24.9.44 in the vicinity of Berlin. The
apprehension of these escapees is of the greatest importance. In the event
of the escapees resisting apprehension, use of weapons is to be resorted
to. If any of these escapees is apprehended the matter is to be referred to
Berlin and the five escapees shall be kept under strict guard. Search for
the escapees is to be made in the whole of the Reich and all countries
occupied by Germany. A sharp watch is to be kept at all frontier controls.

Reichskriminalpolizeiamt, Berlin
(Sgd.) Panziger, SS Oberführer

*My eyes are brown, and I was not wearing gold buttons!

This notice was broadcast over the German Radio at the end of September
1944 and again a week later for Churchill, James and Dodge only. On both

occasions it was monitored by British Intelligence.

Himmler ordered not only the shooting of the five British officers after *Verschaefte Vernehmung* (Interrogation under torture) but also the execution of the Commandant, his Deputy, the officer on duty, and the Architect who designed the camp. The order to execute the Germans was rescinded on reflection, perhaps, that trained killers were hard to replace. But two Gestapo men came to Sachsenhausen to carry out the instructions regarding the British officers. Inspector Peter Mohr and the other Kripo officers were determined to save the officers, if possible, and they made their own report which was accepted by their chiefs at Kripo HQ.

It may be of interest to quote, in his own words, a paragraph from Peter Mohr's letter to me of 20th December 1946 from the London Cage where he was held:

The mass escape out of Stalag Luft III, Sagan, was, as to its volume, *the greatest* and, according to Himmler's disastrous shooting order, in its consequence *the most tragical* escape of this war. The escape of the five British officers from Oranienburg, Camp 'A', which was passed for perfectly safely locked, has outdone the importance of the Sagan escape in a certain manner. It was the *most surprising* and for Himmler *most disagreeable* escape of prisoners that caused great confusion and almost severe consequences from both the British and German sides.

I thank the fortune that it was possible with my direct co-operation to save the lives of the British officers.

I am very happy that I was able, through Colonel Scotland, to get Peter Mohr released from the London Cage shortly after this. I met him in July 1947 in Hamburg where he was a witness for the prosecution in the trial of the SS men who shot the fifty officers after the Sagan escape.

Sachsenhausen Concentration Camp

Sachsenhausen, together with Dachau and Buchenwald, was one of the first big concentration camps to be built by the Nazis. Construction was begun in the summer of 1936 by an advance party of fifty prisoners from the concentration camp of Moorlager Esterwegen, and they were temporarily housed in a disused brewery in the nearby town of Oranienburg, about 20 kilometres north of Berlin. These were soon followed by hundreds more prisoners from the concentration camps at Lichterburg and Sachsenburg.

The SS drove the prisoners unmercifully and there were many deaths. A report from one of the prisoners follows:

> While the camp was being built there was no regular programme laid down for the prisoners. Working time was unlimited with only short breaks for food at midday and evening. Many times the prisoners were allowed only four hours' sleep. The work was carried on at an insane tempo. Prisoners had to do everything at the double. Movement at a normal human pace meant immediate transfer to the punishment company. There was no free time. . . .

A few miles away at the Olympic Stadium in Berlin. Hitler was staging the 1936 Olympics designed to show the world the 'glories of the new Nazi Empire!'

By 1941 the camp was completed and contained 50 barrack blocks set in a triangular area bounded by a ten foot wall surmounted by electrified wire, watch towers at regular intervals each with two guards and a heavy machine gun mounted, inside the wall rolled dannert wire carrying an electric current of 1,000 volts. Attached to the main compound was the *Kommandantur* with administrative offices, barracks for the SS guards and so on. Nearby were also the 'Industrie hof' and building yard which contained the blacksmith, carpenter, tin-smith, shoe factory, glasiers and chicken farms. Outside in the neighbourhood of Oranienburg were various satellite work Kommandos, brickworks, stoneworks, etc.

In the early days prisoners were mostly German Social Democrats, Communists, Trade Unionists, Jehovah's Witnesses, Priests, Pastors and any who opposed the Nazi regime. Criminals were indiscriminately mixed with the political prisoners. In November 1938, after the *Kristallnacht* following the assassination of a German diplomat in Paris by a Jew, about 1,800 Jewish prisoners arrived and were left out in the cold without food or shelter for some days, the survivors were mostly liquidated.

On 20th August 1939 a few prisoners from the *Zellenbau* were heavily manacled to the Gestapo and taken to Oppeln and Gleiwitz where they were later murdered by poisoned injections. The bodies were put into Polish uniforms and, during the German attack on the Gleiwitz transmitting station on 31st August, were left behind as 'proof' of Polish provocation, leading directly to the outbreak of the Second World War. This had been engineered by Heydrich.

After the war started prisoners from all the occupied countries of Europe began to arrive; barracks built to hold 140 were crowded to overflowing by 1941 when there was an average of over 200 per block, with a total of about 12,000 in a camp designed to hold half that number.

The concentration camps were not known pre-war because of fear – in one word 'Gestapo', the all pervading repressive weapon of a totalitarian State. Inmates who were lucky enough to be released were made to sign a statement that they would not make public things that they had witnessed.

The moment of arrival was a traumatic experience. After a terrible journey the new arrivals were kicked and beaten into the camp, dragging those unable to walk from injuries, they staggered through the main gate above which was the cynical inscription *Schutzhaftlager* (Protective Custody Camp) One of the survivors (Heinrich Lienau) of such an intake describes the scene.

Lined up in rows of five they were made to stand for hours in driving snow, bareheaded, forbidden to move or stamp their feet to keep warm. Then they were approached by three of the most brutal SS NCOs in the camp who 'inspected' them.

'Why are you here?' asked one of the first man in the front row.

'Because I was considered politically unreliable.' A blow in the face indicated that this was not the answer required.

'What have you done wrong? I want the right answer.'

'I was denounced, why and by whom, I don't know.'

'Yes, yes, you innocent angel,' sneered the NCO. 'And what party did you belong to?'

On receiving the answer, 'Social Democrat,' he gave him a hard right to the chin which knocked him back against the man behind who staggered back.

'Stand still, you scum,' shouted the NCO, and when he learnt that this man had been arrested because he was a communist he kicked him in the groin which doubled him up with pain.

In the meantime a Catholic Priest was receiving attention from the second NCO who hit him a blow below the belt. A young evangelical Pastor admitted to the first that he had spoken against the Führer. Raging, he turned on him. 'And did not the congregation drag you down from the pulpit and beat you to death?'

'No,' was the quiet and direct answer. 'The congregation agreed with me.'

The NCO was at first speechless. Then he discussed with the other two how the Pastor was to be liquidated, he should be stoned to death or made to lie buried under a pile of ice. In the end the Pastor received a resounding box on the ear.

Finally the prisoners were told to lie down, then they were made to roll through the ice and snow to the reception block. Some lay still, unable to complete the journey, and one died.

Sachsenhausen was not only the training school for all concentration camp personnel for the whole of Germany and the occupied countries, but was also the seat of the Central Command for all the concentration camps and kommandos which spread out like a spider's web over the whole of occupied Europe. This intensified the atmosphere of terror in the camp.

In 1938 an early Commandant Baranovsky remarked, 'Here no one laughs! The only one who laughs here is the Devil – and I am the Devil.' His successor, Hermann Lohritz, was no better, and had the reputation of being a mass murderer, in addition he was a racketeer on a huge scale and during his time at Sachsenhausen acquired a country mansion, vast possessions, and a yacht built in the camp by the prisoners. This may have led to his sudden disappearance in 1942. He was succeeded by Anton Kaindl, an Austrian, who, in fact, made a number of improvements in the living conditions of the prisoners, movement at the double, for instance, being abolished. This enabled prisoners to stay on their feet longer to slave for the Fatherland. A great many prisoners continued to die in various ways while Kaindl was Kommandant.

'*Arbeit macht Frei*' (Work makes you free) written large above the entrance to every concentration camp greeted the newcomer. The only freedom from work in Sachsenhausen was usually death. The prisoners were daily made to work ten to twelve hours a day on about 350 grammes of bread and some watery soup. Their bodies wasted and they became weaker and weaker; if they stopped or faltered in their toil they were immediately kicked, beaten or even killed by the guards.

Mostly they worked in the *Industriehof* making all kinds of things for the SS, but useless and soul-destroying tasks were often performed, as the continual moving from one place to the other of 400 heaps of sand for up to fourteen hours a day in the summer. Conditions in the *Klinkerwerke* were particularly grim. Here beside a large canal were being built a new brick works and the adjoining docking installation for ships and barges. The equipment used was primitive. In work requiring the removal of tons of earth and heavy bags of cement, prisoners were literally driven to death, in particular hundreds of gypsies, Jehovah's Witnesses, Jews and Poles were murdered. Every evening when they returned to barracks about thirty had died during the day. There were a number of suicides and many ran onto the electrified wire where their twitching bodies gradually turned black from the 1,000 volt current.

Others worked on outside kommandos, mainly in the armament industry where they were used as slave labour in many well-known German firms. Sometimes they were employed on secret work and could be liquidated on completion of the task.

One of the most notorious secret operations on which prisoners were employed was carried out in the camp. A Nazi directed counterfeiting operation was set up in an isolation block by an SS man Bernhard Krueger who employed 140 Jews, all engravers, to manufacture forged British currency in denominations of five, ten, twenty and fifty pound notes – the paper came from a factory in Brunswick. The notes, examined and passed by the director of a big Berlin Bank, were to be used for espionage purposes and to create inflation in Britain. Passports, identity documents, false code books etc. were also produced. Most of those involved were shot at the end of the war.

It must be said here that there were varying degrees of treatment depending on the prisoner's nationality and status. Russians, Poles, Czechs, Jews, German liberals and communists received exceptionally harsh treatment. Those from the occupied countries of Western Europe generally not quite so severe, while the Norwegians were the best treated of all and were allowed to receive private food and clothing parcels from home, these, of course, they shared with their comrades and often gave away more than they kept for themselves. Any British nationals brought to Sachsenhausen were normally executed as they were usually agents or Commandos, of the two who survived in the main compound, Sergeant Kemp of the Gordon Highlanders, escaped from a POW Camp and brought to Sachsenhausen on recapture, spent much of his time in the *Strafkompanie* testing boots for the Russian Front, the other, Captain Starr, had an easier time – after about ten days in the *Strafkompanie* it was discovered that he was a good artist and he then spent his time painting and decorating huts.

However the majority of prisoners were starved, ill-treated and lived in appalling conditions. As the numbers increased the conditions got worse with gross overcrowding in the blocks. Of 52 Austrians brought into the camp on one transport only two arrived alive. In spite of severe frost, no winter clothing was issued and there were many deaths from cold and exposure; there were outbreaks of dysentery and typhus due to overcrowding, starvation and unhygienic conditions. In January 1940, 800 prisoners incapable of work were made to stand for hours in fifty degrees of frost. Next day 430 were dead. Towards the end of the war numbers were swelled by the arrival of many prisoners from camps in the eastern territories overrun by the Russians, and by April 1945 camp strength had risen to 48,000.

Between 1936 and 1945 over 45,000 prisoners died from starvation ill treatment, overwork and disease.

Many more human lives were extinguished in a deliberate and planned policy of murder and extermination. Two of the most heinous crimes in this category were the extermination of a large group of Poles in 1940 and the shooting of thousands of Soviet prisoners of war in 1941.

In March 1940 a mass intake of 17,000 prisoners, mainly Poles, arrived in the camp. In the period to September the SS and specially chosen criminal elements among the prisoners decimated the entire group by terror and murder. Some of the few survivors were sent to Flossenburg, Neuengamme, Dachau and Gross-Rosen, the remainder, 320, were shot as hostages in November.

The cold blooded liquidation of 18,000 Soviet prisoners of war, both officers and men, was carried out during September, October and November 1941. In Hitler's Commissar Order of 6th June 1941, it was laid down, ' . . . in the fight against Bolshevism consideration and regard for International Law are wrong, and it is therefore ordered that Political Commissars of the Soviet Army are to be killed at once.' This order contained clauses which allowed, among other things, the murder of prisoners of war who were to be executed unobtrusively in the nearest concentration camp. In Sachsenhausen preparations for the killings were started in the middle of 1941 in the *Industriehof* where special barracks were built for their reception. The first transports began to arrive in September. The Russians were crammed into the barracks and treated worse than animals. *Auswurf der Steppe* (Refuse from the Steppes) the Nazi Hierarchy had decreed. Their clothes were taken away, they received only bread and soup every two days, and they died of TB, starvation, typhus and dysentery; their bodies were piled up and carried in carts across the *Appellplatz* to the crematorium. The transports of Russians continued to arrive. By then the *Genickschuss Anlage* (Neck shot installation) was ready. They were told they were going to an isolation block and were led to a special barrack. In turn they were told to undress and were then led into a 'medical inspection' room where stood a 'doctor' in a white coat who instructed the prisoner to stand against a wall to have his height measured, when the measuring bar touched the top of his head an SS man fired through a slit in the wall behind. Loud music piped through a loud speaker deadened the noise of the shot. The body was dragged out to the crematorium, the blood was wiped up, and the next victim was brought in. In this manner about 250 men a day were systematically murdered. The smoke from the burning bodies lay like a pall over Oranienburg. The SS men were nearly always dead drunk after a day of murder and their drunken laughter could be heard over the address system of the camp. They were decorated with the Iron Cross, Second Class, and rewarded with a holiday in Capri.

Murder in Sachsenhausen was routine and continued week in, week out, year after year. As time went on the murder machine was stepped up, and accelerated towards the end of the war. The main agencies of destruction we₹e the *Strafkompanie, Krankenbau, Zellenbau,* and Station Z (These are described below).

Besides Slavs and Jews (most of whom, as is well known, were exterminated at Auschwitz) German political prisoners were high on the list for liquidation and wore a red triangle, apex down, on the sleeve. Markings denoting various categories of prisoners follow:

Colour	Denoting
Red	Political
Yellow star	Jewish
Lilac	Bible student (Usually Jehovah's Witness)
Blue	Educational (Those arrested after being abroad – now being acclimatised in the wonderful new Germany)
Green	Criminal
Black	Asocial (Work shy, gypsies, etc.)
Rose	Homosexual
2 cross bars on coat collar unshaven head (otherwise all had shaven heads)	'Prisoner of Honour' – mostly SA and SS accused of murder (in private life) and similar crimes.

To assist the SS in the administration of the camp certain prisoners were placed in key positions, as the *Lagerälteste* (Camp Senior) and the *Blockälteste* (Block Senior) Depending on the character of these men life could be made either tolerable or a hell on earth for the people in the block. While a good *Blockälteste* could not stop the worst excesses of the SS, by clever manipulation he could deflect some of the terror and in some cases even save the lives of prisoners. It was different if a criminal was appointed *Blockälteste* (see *Strafkompanie* below)

Strafkompanie (Punishment Company)

The *Strafkompanie* was one of the most barbaric institutions of the concentration camp. It was said in Sachsenhausen that the only way out of the SK was 'up the chimney' (of the incinerator). It was a punishment measure decreed by the camp administration; a considerable number of prisoners in the SK were, however, sent straight from outside by order of the Gestapo or Kripo, usually with the notation on their documents 'R.u.' (*Ruckkehr unerwünscht* – Return not desired) Very often they were prisoners who had been released from a concentration camp in the early years of Hitler's dictatorship and had then resumed their previous political activity. They were known as 'backsliders' and had to wear a special marking so that the SS men would recognize them as particularly dangerous anti-Nazis.

The SK was housed in the isolation block, and the *Blockälteste* was always a criminal and he was assisted by other criminals. New arrivals had to squat for hours with outstretched hands, then they were 'officially received' being driven into the washroom of the isolation block and hosed down with cold water fully clothed, after which they were driven, without food, to their sleeping quarters where they had to sleep underneath the beds. When they awoke in the morning, two criminals stood at the door with hatchets and aimed blows at the prisoners going out; new arrivals often suffered injuries and soon died. Corpses hung in the lavatory every morning as a result of the nightly orgies of cruelty by the criminals.

They were made to work from morning until late evening, always at the double, inhumanly beaten with clubs. They would be made to load and unload lorries with the same load, over and over again, at a senseless pace, or to work for hours knee deep in water in the clay pits of the *Klinkerwerke* in all seasons of the year. Sometimes they were tied by wire to lorries and dragged along the track or had heavy cement bags tied around them as punishments. They were made to lie, jump up, roll, leap about or crawl, totally exhausting them.

Oberscharführer Ficker, the SS Blockführer of the SK, at his trial after the war, said that in the summer of 1942, of an average strength in the SK of 70 to 80 there were seven to ten murdered daily and a further four or five who died from illness or exhaustion. – a 17% daily loss which was quickly made up again with fresh victims. From 1943 many of the SK prisoners were put on the boot-testing Kommando which entailed marching and sometimes doubling around a track testing German Service footwear. The track was about one kilometre in circumference and was made up in two hundred yard sections of sand, wet clay, concrete, water, stone chips, tarmac etc. They had to complete at least forty circuits (about 25 miles) on starvation rations often carrying in addition a 30lbs. pack filled with sand. Those who collapsed were set on by dogs. In the evening they were paraded to witness floggings and sometimes a public execution.

All this was quite in accordance with the principle 'Destruction through work' as agreed between the Nazi Minister of Justice Dr Thierack and Himmler.

Krankenbau (Sick Quarters)

Here, where the sick should have been healed, thousands of prisoners were murdered in the name of 'medical science'.

It consisted of two sections: a show place with operating theatres surgeries, X Ray room, and all the latest medical equipment, and two barracks with nice beds, clean bed linen etc. around which were shown foreign journalists, delegations from Italy and Spain, and senior officers of the Wehrmacht. The other four barracks were not shown. Here lay hundreds of emaciated prisoners crammed into three tier bunks. They were suffering from TB, dysentery, typhus, scarlet fever and every imaginable disease, and only the worst cases were allowed in. They received little attention, except from their own comrades acting as medical orderlies who were given the minimum of medicaments. In three months at the end of December 1942 about 1,230 died in the sick quarters.

The sick were used for all kinds of medical experiments – the testing of vaccines against TB, sepsis, typhus, jaundice and other diseases with which they were deliberately infected. The method for experimenting on sepsis was to incise the leg causing a large wound, fill it with dust and straw and then sature it. A newly discovered drug was then tried out to ascutais the effect. Mostly the patients died. Other experiments were made with gases, phosphorus burns (artificially created), the effects of various poisons, and a preparation for slowing down the heart or creating sleeplessness. The victims were used for testing the effects of poisoned bullets and new types of hand grenades.

Adjoining the sick quarters was a large mortuary filled with hundreds of corpses with SS doctors dissected looking for interesting specimens. Universities and anatomical institutes were supplied with skulls, skeletons and organs of anatomical interest.

Zellenbau (Cell Book)

The worst tortures and humiliations were reserved for those consigned to the cell block. The full extent of the atrocities committed during the years Oberscharführer Eccarius was in charge will never be known, because few prisoners incarcerated therein ever lived to tell the tale.

There were 80 cells contained in a 'T' shaped block isolated from the main compound by a high wall. In the cells prisoners were beaten, trussed up on the floor *krummgeschlagen* so that the slightest movement caused them unspeakable agony, left in darkened cells and fed only every two days on bread and water, hosed down with cold water and left to freeze in winter, with the heating turned off. A particularly painful torture was the *Pfahl* or Post. The prisoner's hands were tied behind his back at the wrists, he was made to stand on a stool below the post from which a chain was suspended, this was attached to the binding at the wrists, the stool was kicked away and the prisoner was suspended by his arms which were forced backwards and upwards causing excruciating pain; he was left thus for several hours.

Prisoners were despatched by being beaten to death, shot, hanged or painfully throttled. Many were sent to Station Z for liquidation by shooting, hanging or gassing. Two British officers lay chained up to a cement block in a darkened cell before they were shot. In a corner of the exercise yard was an underground bunker, the entrance to which was closed by an iron door; Eccarius used to leave prisoners here to starve. Communists, Social Democrats, Anti-Fascists, priests, pastors, and resistance fighters from all over Europe were confined here in great numbers, tortured, starved and murdered.

All prisoners were kept in solitary confinement, but there were degrees of arrest. Normal arrest was in a lighted cell with rations, middle arrest was the same but with rations cutailed, and full arrest was in a darkened cell. All categories, however, had an equal chance of execution.

As the Soviet Army closed in on Berlin, Eccarius pushed his victims off to Station Z for liquidation. On the day the camp was liberated there were only thirteen surviving in the cells out of a total of about 100. Thus closed one of the most horrifying chapters in the dark story of Sachsenhausen, the most gruesome secrets of which are hidden to this day.

Station Z

An innocent looking installation adjoining the main camp housed the ultimate death factory at Sachsenhausen. The letter 'Z' signified that this was the last lap for tens of thousands of victims who were slaughtered here.

Most of the executions were carried out in the *Genickschuss* installation built on the lines of that used to murder the Russians in 1941 and used as a model for Dachau, Mauthausen, Buchenwald, Neuengamme, Gross-Rosen and other concentration camps. In 1943 on the initiative of the Camp Commandant Kaindl, as advised by the SS Camp Doctor, a gaschamber was built, disguised as a shower room. Zyklon B gas ampoules were used and when operated were blown through a vent in the wall by a fan. When the SS man watching through a window saw that all the victims were dead, the gas was extracted and the bodies were dragged out to the crematorium. Besides many other nationalities, about 3,000 Jews were gassed here.

Adjacent to Station Z and really part of it was an *Erschiessungsgraben* (lit. trench for shooting dead) containing the rifle range and butts where the shooting took place, and also a particularly beastly and sadistic form of mechanical gallows for four victims at a time; their feet were secured in clamps and, with their heads in slings, their bodies were literally torn apart by means of a pulley.

There was a mortuary for the bodies; this was always full although the four ovens in the crematorium belched smoke day and night, weekdays and Sundays. Another large room, disguised as a garage, was used as a place for ashes and urns. In rare cases relatives would be sent the ashes of somebody who had been liquidated – on payment of the fee and transport costs but they would not be the right ashes.

Besides prisoners from Sachsenhausen, the Gestapo consigned whole transports full of condemned prisoners direct to Station Z for execution.

Some idea of the extent of the murders in Sachsenhausen can be gleaned from the statistics compiled from the statements of condemned SS men, surviving prisoners and discoveries in the region of Station Z. Two pits near the crematorium contained 27 cubic metres of human bones and ash. The SS Lagerführer (Camp Leader) of the *Klinkerwerke* said at his trial that he had, in January 1945, thrown 8 to 9 tons of human ash into the canal at the Hohenzollerndamm. In a large wooden shed near Station Z were found, after liberation, wagon loads full of men's, women's and children's clothing, eight cases with over half a ton of human hair, 504 cubic metres=904,600 pairs of shoes. In the cellar area below sick quarters were found several cases packed with 300,000 metal and porcelain teeth, crowns and false teeth.

In the opinion of the experts these remains indicated that 77,000 to 80,000 people had been liquidated.

Slave Labour in Industry

The SS and the armament concerns, by whom the prisoners were employed, made vast profits from slave labour. By hiring out prisoners the SS made about 50 million marks a month.

Book keeping for Mass Murder

	RM	RM
Daily hire of a prisoner	6.00	
Deduct food	0.60	
Deduct clothing and amort.	0.10	
Average life expectancy 9 months=270×5.30 RM		1,431.00
Proceeds from rational utilization of the corpse		
1. Gold for teeth		
2. Clothing		
3. Valuables		
4. Money		
Deduct cost of burning	2.00	
Average net profit		200.00
Total profits for nine months		1,631.00 RM

Statement of the former Kommandant Kaindl
at his trial in 1947

'In this way Himmler's representative Pohl made a huge fortune. In the year 1942/43 he paid out over a million marks for the improvement and furnishing of his property . . .'

Total Death Toll in Sachsenhausen

Between the years 1936 and 1945, of the 200,000 who passed through Sachsenhausen over 100,000 died.

*Trial of former SS Standartenführer Anton Kaindl and
fifteen others – Berlin 1947.*

A Soviet Military Court tried Kaindl and fifteen of his subordinates in
Pankow Town Hall, Berlin at the end of 1947.

Kaindl admitted that he had installed new machinery for liquidation; a
gallows, shooting place and gas chamber and that altogether 42,000
prisoners had perished while he was Commandant, most of them executed.

Kaindl and most of the others received life sentences. There was no death
sentence in the Soviet Union!

Postscript.

After the war the Russians used Sachsenhausen as a detention camp for
Germans. In 1945/46 the prisoners were predominantly former leading
Nazis, judges, officials and teachers etc.

In the following years 'Imperialist agents' and 'spies' were arrested on
false charges and imprisoned in Sachsenhausen. 'Enemies of the working
class' were also arrested and detained in the camp. These were mainly
members of democratic parties, notably Social Democrats, who objected to
the merger with the Communists.

Sachsenhausen, in East Germany, is now a Memorial to the victims of
Nazi terror. All the huts have been taken down with the exception of a few.
Station Z and one wing of the *Zellenbau* have been left standing. At the apex
of the triangle formed by the walls stands a tall monument.

Flossenburg Concentration Camp

International Military Tribunal Nuremburg

Report of Investigation of War Crimes – 3rd. U.S. Army 21/6/45

Flossenburg Concentration Camp was founded in 1938 as a Camp for Political prisoners. It had 47 satellite camps and kommandos for male prisoners and 27 for female. Some outer kommandos were particularly bad, like Oberstaubling on the Danube where work was mainly underground labour and many died. Of 700 prisoners who were transported there in February 1945 only 405 were alive on 15 April 1945.

Flossenburg Concentration Camp can best be described as a factory dealing in death. Death by hunger and starvation rations, sadism, inadequate housing and clothing, medical neglect resulting in disease, beatings, hand-hanging, hanging by the neck, freezing, shooting etc. poison injections, shooting in back of neck.

The general objective was the mass elimination of prisoners by every known method, mainly by starvation and overwork. There were innumerable executions, including mass hangings; the prisoners were often beaten before being hanged so that they cried out to be hanged. Hanging by wrists with heavy barrel suspended from ankles was another method, this tore the insides apart. At first the SS men were given extra rations for executions, but later there were so many that this practice was stopped.

At Christmas 1944 there was a mass hanging of prisoners in front of a decorated Christmas Tree. . . 'It was a terrible sight that combination of prisoners hanging in the air and the glistening Christmas Tree'[1]

On 20th April 1945 the camp was evacuated. 15,000 started on a forced march to Dachau. No provision was made for feeding or sleeping on this trip. Any who fell out were shot in the back of the head. Thousands were killed on the way; prisoners were taken out in groups of five to fifty forced to dig pits and then shot.

The victims included Russians and Poles, who were in the majority, Germans, Austrians, Italians, Belgians, French, Czechs, Hungarians, British and American prisoners of war.

[1] The prisoners hanged were mostly Russian officers, while the SS drank schnapps and wine, forcing the other prisoners to watch and to sing – refusal meant a lashing with a whip usually on the face.

GLOSSARY

SS Ranks and their Army Equivalents

Oberstgruppenführer	general
Obergruppenführer	lieutenant-general
Gruppenführer	major-general
Brigadierführer	brigadier
Oberführer	no equivalent rank
Standartenführer	colonel
Obersturmbannführer	lieutenant-colonel
Sturmbannführer	major
Hauptsturmführer	captain
Obersturmführer	lieutenant
Untersturmführer	second lieutenant
Oberscharführer	warrant officer
Scharführer	sergeant
Unterscharführer	corporal

Index

* 'Tom' and 'Dick' not operated but were of great significance in Escape Org.